CORE-SATELLITE PORTFOLIO MANAGEMENT

CORE-SATELLITE PORTFOLIO MANAGEMENT

A Modern Approach for Professionally Managed Funds

J. CLAY SINGLETON

McGraw-Hill

New York Chicago San Francisco Lisbon London Madrid
Mexico City Milan New Delhi San Juan Seoul
Singapore Sydney Toronto

The McGraw·Hill Companies

Copyright © 2005 by J. Clay Singleton. All rights reserved. Printed in the United States of America. Except as permitted under the United States Copyright Act of 1976, no part of this publication may be reproduced or distributed in any form or by any means, or stored in a data base or retrieval system, without prior written permission of the publisher.

1 2 3 4 5 6 7 8 9 0   DOC/DOC   0 9 8 7 6 5 4

ISBN 0-07-141337-5

McGraw-Hill books are available at special discounts to use as premiums and sales promotions, or for use in corporate training programs. For more information, please write to the Director of Special Sales, Professional Publishing, McGraw-Hill, Two Penn Plaza, New York, NY 10121–2298. Or contact your local bookstore.

MW

This book is printed on recycled, acid-free paper containing a minimum of 50% recycled de-inked paper.

To my wife and best friend, Kathy,
and to our family,
Robert, Kerri, Caitlyn, and Chelsea

ABOUT THE CONTRIBUTORS

Jeffrey M. Antonacci, CFA
Senior Consultant, Ibbotson Associates

Jeffrey Antonacci serves as manager of Ibbotson's fund-of-funds team, where he is responsible for managing a team of consultants that develops and manages asset allocation and fund-of-funds programs for institutional and retail clients. A frequent speaker at financial services client conferences, Mr. Antonacci lectures on asset allocation, manager selection, investment style diversification, market forecasting, and alternative asset classes.

Prior to joining Ibbotson Associates, Mr. Antonacci was an institutional investments product manager for Northern Trust Global Investments, where he was responsible for developing competitive intelligence and monitoring, analyzing, and evaluating investment managers. Prior to joining Northern Trust Global Investments, he held supervisory positions in Northern Trust's Daily Valuation Division, where he was responsible for the valuation and financial statement analysis of institutional employee benefit plans.

Mr. Antonacci received an M.B.A. from the Kellogg Graduate School of Management at Northwestern University and a B.S. in Finance from Indiana University. He is also a CFA charterholder, a member of the CFA Institute, and a member of the Investment Analysts Society of Chicago.

Peng Chen, Ph.D., CFA
Director of Research, Ibbotson Associates

Peng Chen is Managing Director at Ibbotson Associates. He is responsible for Ibbotson Associates' overall research activities. Ibbotson Associates is an independent asset allocation consulting firm that provides data, software, consulting, research, training, and presentation materials to the investment profession.

Dr. Chen conducts research projects on asset allocation, portfolio risk measurement, nontraditional assets, and global financial markets. He has also contributed to the development of various Ibbotson products and services, including software, consulting services, educational services, and presentation materials. His writings have appeared in the *Financial Analyst Journal, Journal of Portfolio Management, Journal of Investing, Journal of Financial Planning, Bank Securities Journal, Journal of the Association of American Individual Investors,*

Consumer Interest Annual, and the *Journal of Financial Counseling and Planning*. He received the Articles of Excellence Award from the Certified Financial Planner Board in 1996 and the 2003 Graham and Dodd Scroll Award from the *Financial Analysis Journal*.

Dr. Chen received his bachelor's degree in Industrial Management Engineering from the Harbin Institute of Technology and his master's and doctorate in Consumer Economics from the Ohio State University. He is a CFA charterholder.

Bradley S. Daniels, CFA
Schlarbaum Capital Management, LP

Brad Daniels was a portfolio manager at Schlarbaum Capital Management, LP, when he coauthored a chapter for this book. He has worked in the investment industry since 1983. Prior to joining Schlarbaum Capital Management, LP, he was a member for eighteen years of the equity team at Miller Anderson & Sherrerd, which merged with Morgan Stanley Investment Management in 1996. He worked directly with Gary Schlarbaum for fifteen years on the small-cap core and small-cap value strategies and then oversaw the strategies upon Mr. Schlarbaum's departure from Morgan Stanley.

Prior to joining Miller Anderson & Sherrerd, Mr. Daniels was an associate at Kidder, Peabody & Co., Inc., from 1983 to 1985. He received his B.S. from the University of Pennsylvania in 1983 and his M.B.A. from the Wharton School at the University of Pennsylvania in 1989, and is a CFA charterholder.

Samuel W. Halpern
Executive Vice President and Board Member, Independent Fiduciary Services, Inc.

Samuel W. Halpern is associated with Independent Fiduciary Services, Inc., a pension investment consulting firm based in Washington, D.C. His expertise includes advising public and private investment funds and fiduciaries on controls over investment risk and expense, alternative investments, governance, prudent investment practices, and related matters. He has been integrally involved in every operational review/best practices study IFS has performed, collectively concerning over $550 billion in assets, and all "independent fiduciary transactions," where the firm acts as an independent decisionmaker, replacing the regular plan fiduciaries when they suffer a conflict of interest. He also is centrally involved in the firm's ongoing, broad-based investment consulting to ERISA-covered defined benefit, defined contribution, and welfare plans, including advising clients on investment policy, asset allocation, manager selection and monitoring, custody, brokerage, and related matters.

Previously a partner in a Washington, DC labor law firm, Mr. Halpern specialized in the field of fiduciary responsibility regarding ERISA-covered investments. Before entering private practice, he litigated fiduciary responsibility cases under ERISA at the U.S. Department of Labor, where he helped develop standards governing pension fund investments. He graduated Phi Beta Kappa from Brown University, attended the London School of Economics, and received his law degree with honors from the George Washington National Law Center in Washington, DC.

Andrew Irving, J.D.
Senior Vice President and General Counsel, Independent Fiduciary Services, Inc.

Andrew Irving is Mr. Halpern's colleague at Independent Fiduciary Services, Inc. Mr. Irving joined IFS in 2003 after 25 years of private law practice in the New York City office of the international law firm Bryan Cave LLP and its predecessor in New York, Robinson Silverman Pearce Aronsohn & Berman.

Mr. Irving's work for IFS focuses on operational reviews and fiduciary transactions, as well as oversight of IFS's internal legal affairs and ongoing consulting services. His law practice before joining IFS focused on the representation of public, Taft-Hartley and corporate pension and welfare plans, labor unions, corporate plan sponsors, and financial institutions serving the benefit plan community. He has devoted much of his time to advising clients on issues of fiduciary responsibility in investment decision making, and has also litigated cases in state and federal courts that raised those issues. He also worked with plan fiduciaries and the investment community designing sophisticated investment products and strategies to comply with statutory requirements such as synthetic guaranteed investment contracts, direct real estate investments, and hedge "fund of fund" vehicles. Having worked with leading investment and actuarial firms, as well as with some of the largest public and private sector pension plans, he has in-depth knowledge of the complex environment in which institutional investment decision makers carry out their fiduciary responsibilities.

Mr. Irving received his B.A. cum laude from Yale University and his law Juris Doctor from Columbia Law School, where he was a member of the Law Review. He has published articles in various professional journals published by the American Bar Association, the International Foundation of Employee Benefit Plans, and the Research Institute of America, and has edited official reports of the Committee on Labor and Employment Law of the Association of the Bar of the City of New York.

Ranga Nathan, CFA
Principal, InvestMatrix Inc.

Ranga Nathan is a principal at InvestMatrix Inc., a consulting firm specializing in risk management and the structuring of investment products, including exchange-traded funds and hedge funds.

Mr. Nathan started his career at Citibank (Asia) and Chase (Europe). He then spent over ten years at Waldner & Co., which pioneered foreign exchange and interest rate risk management research, and he eventually became the firm's president. At Waldner, he (a) developed models to identify directional changes in the foreign exchange, interest rate, equity, and energy markets; (b) was the project leader of all risk management consulting assignments for multinational firms and institutional investors in North America, Europe, and Asia; (c) developed structured investment products for an international base of institutional and individual investors; and (d) supervised research, trading, back office, middle office, and compliance functions relating to overlay management and alternative investments.

After leaving Waldner, Mr. Nathan assumed the position of Senior Vice President, Global Risk Management, at a division of Sakura Bank (currently part of the Mitsui Banking Corporation), where he developed risk management products and managed hedge funds-of-funds. After that, at Nuveen, he was involved in developing equity and fixed-income exchange-traded funds. After buying the equity ETF business from Nuveen, he assisted in the launch of the first ETFs based on enhanced indexes.

Mr. Nathan has written articles on risk management, index products, and alternative investments in *Euromoney, Derivatives Quarterly, Global Pensions*, the *Journal of Indexes*, and other publications. He was on the editorial board of *Derivatives Quarterly* and is a review board member of the *Journal of Indexes*. He has also contributed chapters in books such as *Global Investment Risk Management* and *ETF's: New Approaches and Global Reach*. He is a member of PRMIA, the professional risk managers' association, and of the Investment Analysts Society of Chicago. He is also President of the Chicago chapter of QWAFAFEW, a contrived name for an association of quantitative professionals in investment management and related fields. He has a Masters in Business from a school previously affiliated with MIT and is a CFA charterholder.

Joseph P. Pinsky, CFA
Senior Consultant, Ibbotson Associates

Joe Pinsky has 5 years of experience in the financial services industry and has developed strategic asset allocation programs for more than 20 of the major U.S. insurance companies, broker-dealers, mutual fund firms, and retail banks. He assists clients with questionnaire development, asset allocation modeling, manager selection, and due diligence. He also assists in conducting research and has been published in the *Journal of Investing* for his work on direct energy investments. Mr. Pinsky is a CFA charterholder.

James A. Pupillo, CIMA, CIMC

Jim Pupillo graduated with a B.S. degree in Management-Administration and Marketing from Indiana University, Bloomington. He has been involved in the investment management consulting business since 1987.

As a senior institutional consultant for a major brokerage firm, Mr. Pupillo has been recognized for providing extraordinary investment consulting services and has qualified to serve institutional and private clients. In honor of the late John Coggins, Mr. Pupillo was the first recipient of the John Coggins Award exemplifying leadership through creative contributions and integrity. Mr. Pupillo is also the recipient of the Harry Irvine Award, given to the consultant who demonstrates the highest ethics and greatest commitment to assuring that his/her clients continue to achieve their long-term goals. Mr. Pupillo was chosen as one of "America's Top 100" investment management consultants by *On Wall Street* magazine and was selected by the Society of Senior Consultants to participate on the advisory workgroup for the High Net Worth Client Standards Initiative Project.

Mr. Pupillo is 2003–2004 President of the Association of Professional Investment Management and a past Advisory Board Chairman and President for the Institute for Certified Investment Management Consultants (ICIMC), a nonprofit professional society that certifies investment management consultants internationally. He has been an instructor for the Arizona State University (ASU) Nonprofit Management Institute's certification program. He also organized the first conference on university-based certification programs in nonprofit management, sponsored in conjunction with the ASU Nonprofit Management Institute and Consulting Group.

Mr. Pupillo cohosted the Financial Satellite Network's program *Managed Money*, an educational television series as well as the radio program *Money Managers Insight* on KFNN (1510 AM radio). He has also written several articles published by the financial media on the topic of investment management consulting and fiduciary responsibility. He has earned the Certified Investment Management Consultant (CIMC) designation from the Institute for Certified Investment Management Consultants. He has also obtained the Certified Investment Management Analyst (CIMA) designation offered by the Investment Management Consultants Association through the Wharton Business School, University of Pennsylvania. He works with his associates in Scottsdale, Arizona.

Gary G. Schlarbaum, Ph.D., CFA
Schlarbaum Capital Management, LP

Gary Schlarbaum is Principal and Portfolio Manager at Schlarbaum Capital Management, LP, a firm that he cofounded with his son in 2002. Dr. Schlarbaum has worked in the investment industry since 1980.

Prior to cofounding Schlarbaum Capital Management, LP, Dr. Schlarbaum was the head of the domestic equity team at Miller Anderson & Sherrerd, which merged with Morgan Stanley Asset Management in 1996. Dr. Schlarbaum was directly responsible for managing the Morgan Stanley Institutional Fund Trust U.S. Small Cap Value Portfolio from 1988 until March 2002. Prior to joining Miller Anderson & Sherrerd in 1987, Dr. Schlarbaum was Head of Asset Allocation at First Chicago Investment Advisors (now Brinson Partners), where he was employed from 1984 to 1987. He was Professor of Finance at Purdue University from 1969 to 1984.

Dr. Schlarbaum is on the board of trustees of Coe College and Bryn Mawr Presbyterian Church. He is currently a member of the Philadelphia Society of Security Analysts, CFAI, the American Finance Association, and the Shakespeare Society. He also served as the past Chairman of the Candidate Curriculum Committee of the Institute of Chartered Financial Analysts. He is a frequent writer and lecturer on many investment-related topics; his most recent document, "Value-Based Equity Strategies," has been reprinted in *Selected Topics in Equity Portfolio Management*, in English and in various other languages.

Dr. Schlarbaum graduated from Coe College (B.A.) in 1965 and the University of Pennsylvania (Ph.D. in Finance) in 1971. He is a CFA charterholder.

Clifford A. Sheets, CFA

Cliff Sheets is a seasoned investment professional with over 24 years of direct capital market experience in various institutional settings. His experience includes individual company analysis, market analysis, investment strategy and investment policy formulation, portfolio management, investment performance review, and the development and management of professional investment staff.

He currently serves on the board of trustees of the American Red Cross Retirement System and chairs the finance committee, which oversees the management of the investments of the pension plan. Mr. Sheets was Director of Securities at AEGON USA, where he was the senior executive responsible for fixed-income securities assets totaling approximately $70 billion. In this capacity he served on various group decision-making committees that oversaw the portfolio strategy for the general account and approved investments in nonpublic assets, including private placements, alternative investments, and commercial mortgage loans. During his eleven years as a manager at AEGON USA, he was also responsible for public corporate portfolio management and credit analysis.

Prior to joining AEGON USA, Mr. Sheets headed the fixed income management department at Bank One, Indianapolis. In addition to his supervisory duties there, he managed taxable fixed income portfolios with an emphasis on employee benefit accounts of both government and corporate sponsors. He also managed a closed-end bond mutual fund portfolio and supervised the management of open-end bond and money market portfolios. Mr. Sheets began his career as a securities analyst at American United Life Insurance Co. in Indianapolis, where he analyzed credits of both public and private placement borrowers across multiple industries.

Mr. Sheets received an M.B.A. in Finance from Indiana University in 1982, and a B.A. in Business Management from the University of Northern Iowa in 1977. He is a CFA charterholder.

Hilary Till
Premia Capital Management, LLC

Hilary Till cofounded the Chicago-based Premia Capital Management, LLC, of which she is a Portfolio Manager, with Joseph Eagleeye. Premia Capital specializes in detecting pockets of predictability in derivatives markets using statistical techniques. She is also a principal of Premia Risk Consultancy, Inc., which advises investment firms on derivatives strategies and risk management policy.

Prior to coming to Premia, Ms. Till was Chief of Derivatives Strategies at Boston-based Putnam Investments. Her group was responsible for the management of all derivatives investments in domestic and international fixed income, tax-exempt fixed income, foreign exchange, and global asset allocation. In 1997, for example, the total notional value of derivatives structured and executed by her group amounted to $93.2 billion. Prior to coming to Putnam Investments, Ms. Till was a quantitative analyst at Harvard Management Company (HMC) in Boston. HMC is the investment management company for Harvard University's endowment.

Ms. Till has a B.A. in Statistics with General Honors from the University of Chicago and a M.Sc. in Statistics from the London School of Economics (LSE.) She studied at LSE under a private fellowship administered by the Fulbright Commission. Her articles on derivatives, risk management, and alternative investments have been published in the *Journal of Alternative Investments, Derivatives Quarterly, Quantitative Finance, Risk* magazine, and the *Singapore Economic Review*.

Kenneth E. Volpert, CFA
Principal and Senior Portfolio Manager, The Vanguard Group

Ken Volpert oversees the Valley Forge, PA–based Vanguard's Bond Indexing Group, which manages over $42 billion in mutual fund assets. He also comanages Vanguard's $6.5 billion Inflation-Protected Securities Fund.

Mr. Volpert currently manages over $32 billion in three bond index mutual fund portfolios and EUR 1 billion in five offshore nondollar bond index funds. He comanages the $6.5 billion Vanguard Inflation-Protected Securities Fund. The investments in his portfolios cover the full range of domestic markets (Treasury, mortgage-backed, and corporate securities with maturities of up to 100 years) as well as the world government and corporate markets. Prior to joining Vanguard in 1992, Mr. Volpert was vice president and senior portfolio manager with Mellon Bond Associates, where he was responsible for managing over $5 billion in bond index portfolios.

Mr. Volpert wrote a chapter on "Managing Indexed and Enhanced Indexed Bond Portfolios" published in numerous Fabozzi publications. He is also a member of the Lehman Index Advisory Council, the Association for Investment Management and Research, and the Philadelphia Analysts' Society. He has over 20 years of fixed income management experience (more than 15 years of bond indexing experience), is a CFA charterholder, and holds a B.S. in Finance from the University of Illinois-Urbana and an M.B.A. from the University of Chicago.

CONTENTS

FOREWORD   xvii

PART ONE   OVERVIEW   1

Chapter 1   A Core-Satellite Approach to Portfolio Management   3

Chapter 2   Quantitative Finance   23

Chapter 3   Core Equity

James A. Pupillo, CIMA, CIMC   51

Chapter 4   Core Fixed-Income Management

Kenneth E. Volpert, CFA   87

PART TWO   SATELLITE ASSET CLASSES   113

Chapter 5   Satellite Bonds—High Yield and Distressed Debt

Clifford A. Sheets, CFA   115

Chapter 6   Management of Currency Fluctuations Associated with
International Investments

Ranga Nathan, CFA   145

Chapter 7   Treasury Inflation-Protected Securities

Peng Chen, PhD, CFA   169

Chapter 8   Hard Assets

*Peng Chen, PhD, CFA; Jeffrey M. Antonacci, CFA;
Joseph P. Pinsky, CFA   199*

Chapter 9   Finding Value in Small Stocks

       Gary G. Schlarbaum, PhD, CFA, Bradley S. Daniels, CFA   223

PART THREE   PRACTICAL ADVICE   251

Chapter 10   Risk Measurement of Investments in the Satellite Ring
              of a Core-Satellite Portfolio

       Hilary Till   253

Chapter 11   Identifying and Adopting Best Practices for
              Institutional Investors

       Samuel W. Halpern; Andrew Irving, JD   297

INDEX   339

Fiduciaries of pension, endowment, and eleemosynary funds gener-
ously accept substantial responsibilities, face complex challenges, and
assume significant personal liability in order to serve their beneficiaries. The primary compensation they receive is the deep personal satis-
faction of helping many faceless people, some yet unborn, finance their
future needs.

The training many fiduciaries receive to prepare for their substantial duties and decide difficult issues, however, is often limited and
unrelated to their primary professional activities. This book, *Core-
Satellite Portfolio Management*, is designed for and directed to such
fiduciaries. Therefore, the perspective is deliberately high-level and
broad-ranging, intending more to familiarize fiduciaries with the
"big picture" issues and to help them mentally organize the process,
rather than to convert them into technical experts in any particular discipline.

The "core-satellite" approach advocated by this book is, in my
view, less a new portfolio management approach than a useful way to
organize, think about, analyze, and describe portfolio management
approaches that have been used and tested for many years, but using
different words and rubrics. The core-satellite approach merely for-
malizes and better articulates portfolio management practices that
existed even prior to the formal recognition of passive and active/pas-
sive management styles, which can be traced back to the 1970s. In
some sense, passive management, which has come to be formally recognized and accepted during the last quarter century or so, was prac-
ticed in less formal ways during prior years, as many "core" holdings
were held more for core diversification purposes than for extraordinary
expected returns. (Think about how virtually all pension funds held
IBM in earlier years as a core holding, more as a diversifying anchor

vs. the S&P 500 index instead of a truly judgment-based active hold-ing.) Such holdings were not in any sense actively managed (consid-ered continuously for sale or purchase depending upon changing judgments regarding expected returns or risks).

With increasing volumes of portfolio data and the growing preci-sion and uniformity of performance measurements, it has become con-vincingly clear that certain parts of the capital markets are quite competitively priced by thousands of investors vying for returns in an increasingly transparent marketplace. Investing is perhaps the only competitive arena where the "average" result is mechanically obtain-able using computers, or nearly so. Very few professional investment managers demonstrate any persistent ability to outperform the average result for large capitalization equity portfolios after transaction costs and management expenses, and the few that claim to do so are bal-anced by the few who persistently underperform. (These persistent underperformers tend neither to advertise their records nor to win new clients; eventually they fall by the wayside.) Other market sectors, such as high-quality fixed income, demonstrate similar characteristics wherein the "passive average" (after costs) result ranks toward the upper portions of the competitive performance rankings. Academic logic and quantitative risk analyses demonstrate very plausible reasons for these results and indicate that we should not be surprised by these findings, which have obtained for many years through various market cycles. Therefore, it makes sense to implement "core" portfolio hold-ings in efficiently priced sectors in the lowest-cost form possible, which means some portion is invested using passive management tech-niques. This approach is developed further in Chapter 1.

Chapter 1 also emphasizes the easy-to-accept importance of *asset allocation* as the key driver of portfolio investment results over time. Fiduciaries must decide on the definition of the asset classes they wish to include in the portfolio and must decide whether each asset class should be viewed as core or satellite. (The considerations impor-tantly include the investment expertise and experience set of the fidu-ciaries.) How the respective asset class weighting targets are established by the fiduciaries and how they are maintained through time (reweighted with differential market performance) will probably be the most important determinants of portfolio results. The fiduciaries' choice of benchmark for each asset class is also mentioned as very important in Chapter 1 and further explored with helpful details in Chapters 3 and 4. While no prescription is offered—or can be offered—to make benchmark selection easy, considering the nature and timing of the portfolio liabilities is correctly identified as the key input to this process.

To provide important explanatory background that fiduciaries should become familiar with, Chapter 2 provides a review of the *quantitative investment concepts*, but does so without excessive technical detail or requirement for mathematical expertise to understand. It explores the important concept of correlation and explains why diversification works to reduce risk. It reviews the concept of the "efficient frontier" and identifies the important assumptions behind much quantitative research and indicates how those assumptions are not perfect reflections of reality, but are still relevant enough to be useful. Finally, it reviews the concept of risk factors and stresses the importance of risk measures and risk monitoring.

Chapters 3 and 4 focus on management of the *core portion* for equities (Chapter 3) and fixed income (Chapter 4) assets.

Chapter 3 gets more into the "how to" of constructing the core portion of a core-satellite portfolio for *equity* holdings. It stresses the importance of benchmark construction and reviews the factors fiduciaries should consider in choosing indices. It provides a very useful table summarizing the key features of the popular equity indices from which benchmarks can be selected or constructed on a customized weighted basis. It reviews the differences between market risk and residual or "active" risks, measured as tracking error. Chapter 3 advocates the development of a "risk budget" for use in allocating tolerable risk between core and satellite positions. It makes clear that the risks that are important for investing are forecasts of future risks, which are not to be confused with past measurements of historical risks. Finally, it reviews important factors for several vehicles that can be selected by fiduciaries to implement various core strategies.

Chapter 4 suggests how best to use the core-satellite approach to exploit the efficiencies and in efficiencies in the *fixed income* markets, by locating the higher quality liquid sectors in the core, managed passively at very low costs, with more specialized sectors located in satellites, with the goal of outperforming the relevant benchmark. It reviews the different kinds of fixed income risks (duration, credit quality, convexity/prepayment/callability, sector, currency, inflation linkage, etc.) and suggests the tracking error associated with each in various strategies. It also reviews some of the most popular fixed income indices and indicates how they are comprised of differing quality levels and sectors.

Chapters 5 through 9 focus on specialized asset classes that are good candidates for *satellite portfolios*, which are intended to provide opportunity for extraordinary return along with diversification benefits to the remainder of the portfolio.

Chapter 5 provides an excellent overview of *high yield debt*, including public "junk bonds," Rule 144a securities, private placements, bank loans, and collateralized debt obligations (CDOs). It includes a discussion of market history and indicates the historical correlations between various categories. It also discusses *distressed debt*, which are bonds that have fallen into bankruptcy, liquidation, or have a high risk of ending up in either position. It discusses the special skills that are necessary to manage these asset classes and the management fees that should be expected.

Because fiduciaries must consider and decide whether to hedge or not to hedge *foreign currency exposures*, Chapter 6 deals with the impact that currency fluctuations can have and how they can or should be managed. It implicitly assumes that the portfolio has foreign currency exposures by virtue of its existing investment strategies, such as a foreign equity satellite portfolio, and advocates a separate currency "overlay" program managed by one or more foreign currency management experts to eliminate or possibly even enhance the foreign currency impact of the existing foreign exposure. Chapter 6 reviews the arithmetic a fiduciary should understand about how foreign currency exposure arises and how it is influenced by economic factors.

For fiduciaries that have an obligation to protect the future *purchasing power* of beneficiaries, Chapter 7 is particularly relevant. It deals with a relatively new and interesting U.S. asset class called *Treasury inflation-protected securities* (TIPS). TIPS offer fiduciaries an opportunity for portfolio diversification that no other satellite instrument or asset class can replicate. This chapter explains how TIPS work, explores their return patterns and relationships with those of other asset classes, and reviews their brief history, which reveals a small but rapidly growing presence. It explains how the difference between nominal bond yields and TIPS yields provides a good indication of the market's aggregate forecast for future inflation. Chapter 7 explains and quantifies with good charts why fiduciaries with other financial assets (like stocks and bonds) should be strongly motivated to include TIPS as a satellite portfolio.

Chapter 8 focuses on additional inflation hedges—hard assets, including nonperishable real assets like energy, precious metals, real estate, and timber—and soft assets, including agricultural products and livestock. These assets are typically not traded on exchanges (like stocks and bonds) and frequently have lower liquidity and other specialized features that often require specialized management. The chapter then focuses on direct energy assets (*oil and gas*) as a representative sample. Because of the lack of readily available and reliable performance data, the chapter also stresses the importance of building a synthetic historical return series for analytical purposes, and presents a methodology for doing so for direct energy investments. It advocates that cyclical patterns, linkages to inflation, and correlations with other asset classes must be studied and understood, so that likely risk and return impacts on the remaining portfolio can be modeled and predicted. The chapter demonstrates how an energy satellite can increase the expected return and/or reduce the expected risk of the total portfolio.

Chapter 9 explains and advocates a valuation methodology to manage a satellite portfolio consisting of *small capitalization* stocks. It reviews the results of a study covering the period from 1990 through 2003. During this period, the proposed valuation methodology, based on a weighted combination of P/E ratios and earnings revisions (both ranked within 12 sectors), handily outperformed the "average" for small stocks, which were defined as the stocks ranked 1001 through 3000 at the beginning of each calendar quarter. This provides food for thought for any fiduciary.

Chapters 10 and 11 provide useful practical *advice and checklists* to aid fiduciaries in thinking about the important issues, developing a mindset of prudent consideration and compliance, and monitoring important measures on an ongoing basis.

Chapter 10 deals with *risk measurement* of many commonly used satellite investments. It points out the perils of using Sharpe ratios for judging the attractiveness of satellite investments, especially hedge funds, that pursue investment strategies with asymmetric return distributions or serial autocorrelation. Because of the implicit short put option position associated with negatively skewed payoff distributions (such as many hedge fund strategies including small-cap), illiquid positions, untraded holdings (where the prices may be stale or not appropriate), and assets with asymmetric correlations with strong and weak equity markets, the Sharpe ratio produces a misleading measure of the portfolio's reward/risk character. Fiduciaries need to be aware of the misleading nature of such measures and understand how any satellite strategy correlates with the larger portfolio.

Chapter 11 is somewhat different from all the other chapters and identifies what it calls "best practices" for institutional investors. While I do not usually like the implied arrogance of and lack of rigor in the term "best practices," I can offer no better name for the useful collection of *legal, professional, regulatory, operational review, audit, and other perspectives and references* provided in this chapter. "What Fiduciaries Should Think About" would be an equally apt title for this chapter. "What Fiduciaries Should Lose Sleep Over" is also descriptive. The checklist of issues to ponder and address and bases to touch are good ones for a fiduciary of any portfolio.

In sum, *Core-Satellite Portfolio Management* provides any fiduciary with a useful way to think about the portfolio management problem and to structure the process, a method to allocate the risks, a thoughtful way to coordinate the components, a rigorous way to measure the results and appraise and compensate the managers for value added, and a means to monitor and fine-tune the parts through time.

Tom Messmore, CFA
TE Messmore Associates, LLC
44 Central Street
Alton Bay, NH 03810

CORE-SATELLITE PORTFOLIO MANAGEMENT

PART I

Overview

A Core-Satellite Approach to Portfolio Management

INTRODUCTION

Fiduciaries are responsible for many important decisions that determine whether the funds entrusted to their care will meet the beneficiaries' goals and objectives. Most fiduciaries intuitively recognize that how their portfolio of assets is allocated among different possible investments is a key decision. Fifty years ago Harry Markowitz came up with a mathematically based asset allocation methodology that produces what are called *optimal portfolios*. This methodology swept the investment profession and came to dominate all discussions of asset allocation. Unfortunately, for reasons we will go into later, these portfolios are rarely optimal for most real-world situations.

A core-satellite approach is a more qualitative way of thinking about asset allocation strategies that help the portfolio accomplish its goals and meet its obligations. Simply put, a portfolio managed from a core-satellite perspective allocates some money to core asset classes and uses them to help the portfolio keep pace with the broad markets. Other funds are allocated to the satellite ring and give the portfolio a chance to grow faster than the broad market averages.

Most fiduciaries divide their portfolios into asset classes, and many fiduciaries have separate professional managers for each asset class. Dividing the portfolio among several managers is a prudent approach; it also places the responsibility for designing and managing the whole portfolio squarely where it should be—on the shoulders of the fiduciary.

This book has been written primarily to help fiduciaries manage their portfolios. Whether you serve on the investment board of a corporate pension plan, a university endowment fund, or a charitable trust, or on the finance committee of your church, mosque, or synagogue, you have an important responsibility to see that the funds entrusted to you meet both the donors' and the beneficiaries' goals and objectives. This book is designed to help you meet that responsibility with a core-satellite structure that will guide you to rational and prudent portfolio management decisions.

THE CORE-SATELLITE STRATEGY

Many professional money managers have adopted a core-satellite strategy for their portfolios. The popularity of the core-satellite approach comes from the observation that some asset classes are more competitively priced than others. Like other things in life, the more competitive the pricing, the less likely you are to find a bargain. A core-satellite approach puts the most competitively priced assets, like large U.S. companies, in the core. The core is managed to match the returns of a broad market index, like the Standard & Poor's 500 Index or the Dow Jones Industrials. The more funds invested in the core, the more the portfolio will behave like the broad market. Some of the money, however, could be invested in satellite asset classes, like private equity or high-yield bonds. Here the pricing is less competitive and professional managers stand a better chance of adding value by picking up bargains.

The core-satellite approach is a way of thinking about allocating money among asset classes. Research and common sense both suggest that a portfolio with 70% invested in stocks and 30% invested in bonds should offer a higher return—and more risk—than a portfolio with 70% in bonds and 30% in stocks. Similarly, a portfolio with 70% allocated to the core and 30% to the satellite ring will perform more like the broad market than a portfolio with the opposite allocation.

Even though asset allocation is a simple concept, its execution is complex. The fiduciary is almost always confronted with seemingly inconsistent choices among asset classes, strategies, and investment managers. Most fiduciaries seek professional advice. While this is a good idea, the advice itself can be contradictory. To get a handle on the decisions that go into portfolio management, many fiduciaries and portfolio managers have adopted a core-satellite approach. This approach, which is described in detail in this book, should help you sort through the alternatives to find the best approach for your portfolio.

The Role of Quantitative Finance in Asset Allocation

About fifty years ago the economist Harry Markowitz proposed an innovative quantitative solution to the problem of portfolio allocation. His methodology, which involved a number of simplifying assumptions and advanced mathematics, contributed much to our understanding of portfolio behavior.

Since that time many portfolio managers have employed the esoteric formulas of mathematical optimization to calculate an asset allocation. In 1990 Harry Markowitz shared the Nobel Prize in Economics for his contributions to portfolio theory.

While quantitative finance is important, it is an idealized model, and as such, it works best in an idealized world. Chapter 2 describes modern portfolio theory and mean-variance optimal portfolios. In that chapter we also explain the shortcomings of this theory and explain why it is typically not suitable for practical applications.

Why a Core-Satellite Approach Is Important for Fiduciaries

Most investment professionals know that modern portfolio theory does not provide real-world asset allocation solutions. Many fiduciaries rely on a core-satellite concept to help them achieve their goals. Professional money managers have the best chance of earning their fees and increasing the portfolio's return when they invest in the less competitive areas of the capital market. Fiduciaries can take advantage of these insights by following the core-satellite approach described in this book.

This book will explain the core-satellite approach in detail and give you examples of how it is used. In this chapter we discuss the asset classes that fit in the core and explain why they make sense there. Chapters 3 and 4 address the core asset classes in turn. In Chapters 5 through 9 we describe asset classes that can be used as the satellite(s) in great depth because it is important that you understand how each of these asset classes behaves individually and as part of your portfolio. One size does not fit all. Your portfolio will have characteristics and liabilities that make it unique. Furthermore, few fiduciaries start without the legacy of an existing portfolio, which probably has been managed with care and regard for the beneficiaries. While we cannot prescribe an asset allocation for every case, the core-satellite approach can help you select reasonable strategies that stand a good chance of meeting your portfolio's goals and obligations. Chapter 10 covers risk measurement to help you understand the difficulties in measuring this important concept. Finally, Chapter 11 summarizes things every fiduciary should know and relates best practices for the financial, legal, and organizational challenges you will face.

PUTTING THE CORE IN THE CORE-SATELLITE PLAN

The Power of Asset Allocation

Most people are familiar with the power of compound interest. The story usually starts with the Dutch paying the Algonquin Indians 60 guilders worth of beads and trinkets for the island of Manhattan. If, as the story goes, those beads that were worth $24 in 1626 had been invested at 5% per year, the Indians would have been worth about $2.6 billion by the end of 2003. Asset allocation can be equally powerful. We can use two asset classes—U.S. stocks and U.S. government bonds—to conduct a simple demonstration. From 1926 until the end of 2003 stocks, as measured by the Standard & Poors' 500 Index (S&P 500), produced an average annual return (including dividends) of 12.4%. During that same period the annual return of U.S. government bonds (as measured by Ibbotson Associates' long-term government bond index) averaged 5.8%.[1] This 6.6% difference in annual returns means that $1,000 invested in stocks in 1926 would have grown to $2,284,785 by the end of 2003 and that the same investment in bonds would have yielded only $60,564. Stocks performed much better than bonds on average over these 77 years. Consequently, a portfolio invested in stocks would have outperformed a portfolio invested in bonds.

Why have stocks experienced a higher average rate of return than bonds? Without clouding the issue with too much detail, most investment professionals believe stocks are inherently more risky than bonds. From 1926 through the end of 2003 annual stock returns ranged from 53% to −43%, while annual bond returns ranged from 40% to −9%. Hence, stock returns were much more volatile than bond returns. The old saying "Nothing ventured, nothing gained" captures the notion that to earn the higher average rate of return offered by stocks one has to be willing to take the risk that stocks will do poorly or even lose their entire value. In contrast, held to maturity, government bonds return their face value to their owners. Even if that bond had been sold and a new one purchased every year, bonds were still less risky than stocks.

Because stocks have earned, and probably will continue to earn, a higher rate of return than bonds over time it might appear to make sense to just invest in stocks, especially for a pension fund where most of the money will not be needed for some time. This reasoning is probably wrong. Another example serves to make the point. From 1973 through 1974 the U.S. stock market (again measured by the S&P 500 Index) experienced one of its most significant 2-year declines—almost 40%. The market eventually recovered, but it was not until 1978 that a dollar invested in December 1972 was once again worth more than a dollar. Even so, that 1972 stock market dollar had grown to $20.90 at the end of 2002. The 1973–1974 decline helps put the 2000–2002 bear market in perspective. In the latter period the S&P 500 suffered three successively larger back-to-back declines: −9.1%, −11.9%, and −22.1%. By the end of 2002 the market had fallen by about 40% from its year-end 1999 value. Even so, the market level at the end of 2002 was almost 20 times its value compared to 1978. The boom-and-bust cycle seems to be on a ratchet—even though the market has had some spectacular falls, new peaks are reached periodically. In that sense, allocating all the money to stocks would be reasonable. Unfortunately, beneficiaries who needed the money in the meantime—between the peaks—would be at a substantial disadvantage. Most fiduciaries operate in the real world where when the market falls at least some of their beneficiaries cannot afford to wait for the next recovery.

Since 1926 it has also often been the case that when stocks did well bonds did poorly. While this relationship was not always true, it worked often enough to suggest that fiduciaries might be better off putting some of their funds in bonds to balance the variability of stocks. While this portfolio would never return as much as stocks, it would do better than straight bonds. That sort of moderating behavior is attractive to many fiduciaries who believe prudence is consistent with a middle-of-the-road approach that provides a reasonable return for the beneficiaries without subjecting them to all the risks of stocks. An asset allocation strategy, therefore, that gives up some of the returns available in the high-flying equity asset classes for the stability of a more balanced approach makes sense for most fiduciaries. Another old saying, "Don't put all your eggs in one basket," expresses the benefits of diversification in asset allocation.

If asset allocation makes sense then it also makes sense to construct portfolios that capture the best of the potential returns available in stocks while offsetting some of the inherent risks. With so many asset classes to choose from it becomes a bewildering maze, especially because the offsetting nature of each pair of asset classes needs to be considered. In the next chapter we will review some of the quantitative tools financial economists use to help measure and combine all the important considerations. In our experience, however, seasoned fiduciaries do not use these elegant mathematical tools as substitutes for sound judgment. In fact, few fiduciaries or investment professionals rely on these tools to calculate their asset allocation. An increasing number are using a core-satellite approach to build portfolios.

Make no mistake—a core-satellite approach is not a cure-all. It can, however, provide a useful framework within which fiduciaries can construct an asset allocation policy and judge the suitability of various asset classes. Here is a broad overview of the core-satellite approach, which will be discussed in great depth in later chapters.

Asset Classes

Asset classes are more than just stocks and bonds. In fact, both stocks and bonds have several subclasses that most investment professionals consider when building portfolios. The basic criterion for something qualifying as an asset class is that its pattern of returns must be different enough from other asset classes to make it a worthwhile investment. A potential asset class that closely duplicates the returns and risks of an existing asset class would be pointless. Asset classes must also hang together in the sense that they share a pattern of returns. This pattern could come from contractual obligations, as in the case of bonds, or economic affinity, as in the stocks of small companies. A sample of some of the major asset classes typically considered by professional investors for U.S.-based portfolios is shown in Exhibit 1.1.

EXHIBIT 1.1

Sample asset classes

U.S. Stocks	U.S. Bonds
Large	Government
Small	Corporate
Non-U.S. Stocks	High-Yield
Real-Estate	Municipal
Commercial	Inflation-Protected
Residential	Non-U.S. Bonds
Venture Capital	Commodities
Hedge Funds	Timber

One important characteristic that distinguishes asset classes from each other is the attention they get from investors. The basic rule is that the more attention they get the less likely they are to trade at bargain prices. For example, the 500 large stocks that make up the S&P 500 Index are closely watched by investors around the world. These companies' earnings and sales are scrutinized, stock trades occur, and all the relevant information is quickly reflected in the companies' stock prices. Active managers who trade only the stocks in the index based on publicly available information alone probably have little chance of earning more than the average of the index itself, much less recouping their own expenses and trading commissions. If the same managers focused on small, undiscovered companies without much institutional ownership or public interest, it seems reasonable to assume insightful managers would be able to find undiscovered values and would earn a higher rate of return over time. Fiduciaries who combine investments from inside and outside the mainstream are practicing core-satellite portfolio management.

Core-Satellite Asset Allocation

A basic component of the core-satellite approach is separating asset classes into two groups: the core and a satellite ring. Large capitalization[2] U.S. stocks (e.g., the S&P 500) and U.S. government bonds are very competitively priced. These asset classes become the core. We recommend that fiduciaries not waste time or money asking active managers to manage these asset classes. Instead we recommend these asset classes be indexed so that they earn the market average. Indexing means the investment replicates an index as closely as possible. For example, one approach to indexing would be to hold all the stocks in the S&P 500 Index in proportion to their weight in the index.

Indexing an asset class is not exactly like flying on autopilot. Managing funds so that their returns follow an index like the S&P 500 takes expertise, but it is almost always less expensive than active management in terms of fees. Administrative mechanisms like automated order systems, index futures and options, and exchange-traded funds help managers mimic the index by facilitating trades in all the stocks in an index simultaneously. The benefit is that the money dedicated to the core of the portfolio—both stocks and bonds—matches the returns of the broad capital markets. These funds exhibit the widest diversification available.

Once the core is established, a satellite ring can be constructed with less competitively priced asset classes. Here is where active professional management has the best opportunity to add value by picking undervalued stocks, bonds, and specialized investment vehicles. The key is to assemble the satellite asset classes in such a way that they complement each other and the asset classes in the core. All of the asset classes we will be discussing in Chapters 5 through 9 have unique characteristics that make them attractive additions to most core portfolios. You should be familiar with these characteristics and alert for any tendency that might be incompatible with the special needs of your specific portfolio. Whatever the current configuration of the portfolio, carefully adding satellite asset classes can usually improve diversification and help the portfolio weather difficulties in any of its asset classes.

Market Weights in the Core

A typical core portfolio would hold both large-cap U.S. stocks and government bonds. These asset classes are highly competitive and active management will have difficulty adding value. Together they dominate the market in terms of capitalization. To match the returns in the overall market, the allocation between these broad asset classes should be the same as their weighting relative to the total market. In Exhibit 1.2 the market weight of bonds (government and corporate) ranged from as high as 77% in 1953 to as low as 48% in 1999, averaging 62% bonds since 1952. At the end of 2003 the percentages stood at 53% debt and 47% equity. These percentages change gradually. The funds could be committed in proportion to their market weights to index managers using benchmarks like the S&P 500 for the stocks and the Lehman Brothers Aggregate Index for the bonds. These indexes are designed to represent the broad markets they track. Although many different broad market indexes are available, they all closely parallel one another so the differences will probably be insignificant.

U.S. stock and bond market value weights, 1952–2003

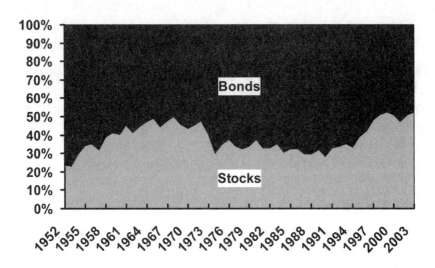

Core versus Satellite

A major question is how much of the money should be allocated to the core and how much to the satellite. Unfortunately we do not have a formula that will answer this question. If you omit the satellite ring the portfolio will experience about the same returns as the broad markets. As funds are allocated to satellite asset classes the portfolio typically will have higher returns and risk. The allocation then becomes one of comparing costs and benefits. Chapter 3 addresses this question in the form of a risk budget.

Although there probably is no such a thing as a free lunch, you can find portfolios where returns increase and risks decrease by judicious allocations to the satellite ring. For example, micro-cap stocks (stocks with very low market capitalization) have had a history of higher returns and more risk than large-cap stocks, with a tendency to act as a counterbalance—doing well when large-cap stocks do poorly and poorly when they do well. If we added a small allocation of small-cap stocks (Chapter 9) to a portfolio that was market weighted in large-cap U.S. stocks and government bonds, we would expect returns to go up with a very modest increase in portfolio risk. A cost-benefit analysis (added return per unit risk) would suggest that a small-cap allocation was a worthwhile investment. (You can read more about measuring the return per unit of risk in Chapter 10). Private equity investments also have a history of counterbalancing large-cap stocks. While similar to small-cap stocks, private equity differs in important ways that qualifies this investment as a separate asset class. We would expect that adding private equity to a market-weighted large-cap stock and government bond portfolio would have a similar favorable cost (risk) and benefit (return) result. Adding both private equity and small-cap stocks would provide some of the same benefits but probably would not diversify the portfolio as much because these two asset classes tend to follow similar return patterns.

The experience of the fiduciaries is another factor to consider in adding satellite asset classes. The fiduciaries should be familiar with the asset class. While most people have probably seen tree farms, few understand the history of timber as an investment. The opportunity to invest in timber comes in different forms, each of which has advantages and disadvantages. Fiduciaries should understand the legal structures and learn all they can about the investment characteristics of each asset class. Experience investing in the asset class is invaluable. If none of the fiduciaries have that experience, sound advice would be to start with a modest allocation to gain familiarity with that asset class. Once the investment

has been made, the fiduciaries will have access to professional managers who can answer questions and guide the fiduciaries' education, research, and discussion. In our experience whatever returns might be forgone by delay are more than
made up when the fiduciaries better understand the asset class.
Prudence alone suggests fiduciaries should walk before
they run.

A Question of Style

Many investment professionals subdivide the equity asset class
into growth and value styles. Although experts disagree on
exactly how these styles should be defined, the general idea is
that growth style stocks have displayed strong earnings growth
and are likely to continue rewarding their shareholders through
growth. Value style stocks are characterized as bargains. They
have shown little growth and sell at prices that are cheap
relative to their earnings, sales, and cash on hand. Because
research has suggested that these two styles tend to follow different return patterns and can counterbalance each other, they
are often considered separate asset classes. Many index providers have developed growth and value indexes. Investment
professionals generally consider the market as being roughly
equally divided between growth and value stocks. That is, a
market index like the S&P 500 is dominated by neither growth
nor value. Small-cap stocks are also differentiated as either
growth or value, and again the common assumption is that the
market is divided equally between the two styles.

Some fiduciaries consider both large-cap growth and
value styles as part of the satellite ring. Another possibility is
to place these styles in the core. A portion of the large-cap
stock index allocation could be diverted to active growth and
value managers. If the growth and value dollar allocations

were equal and the market split between growth and value stocks was also equal (in a cap-weighted sense), the core portfolio should still mimic the market. If the managers can add value, the portfolio will be better off. It would be difficult, however, for large-cap growth and value managers to consistently add value over time in excess of their incremental fees and incremental risks. Just because the manager focuses on either growth or value does not change the underlying competitive nature of the market for these large-capitalization stocks. We will return to the question of value and growth styles in Chapter 2. On the other hand, small-cap stocks belong in the satellite ring because managers probably have more potential to add value in small stocks. In this context differentiating between small-cap growth and value may make sense as a satellite strategy. Small-cap stock value investing is covered in Chapter 9.

Which Asset Classes?

This book cannot cover all the potential asset classes much less all the possible combinations of asset classes. By necessity we will not mention some asset classes that could be valuable. What we have done is to exercise our judgment, based on our experience and the experience we have collected from others, to make reasonable recommendations about what fiduciaries should do. We have done our best to label these judgments and explain why we think they are reasonable. If we have provided a framework within which the questions of asset allocation make sense, we will have succeeded. We will provide our recommendations to the questions that arise wherever we have something to add. In the final analysis, however, each portfolio is different and each asset allocation policy should reflect those differences. In truth no one knows the answers with certainty. There is no substitute for fiduciaries taking responsibility for their own education to produce prudent and sound judgments.

Which Index Makes the Best Core Benchmark?

Choosing a set of indexes for the core portfolio is a key part of the core-satellite approach. Each index should represent its market fairly, be investable so that the manager can hold as many of the assets in the index as necessary, and be published by a third party to ensure independence. Fortunately, most indexed investment products are based on widely recognized indexes that do nicely in a core-satellite approach. Some of the best-known equity indexes like the S&P 500 are not averages of all stocks or even a random sample of all stocks. The S&P 500 is a managed portfolio assembled by a committee. This committee's charge is to make the index as representative of the stock market as possible. Over time they have done a good job as the S&P 500 has closely tracked the equity market. Alternatives like the Russell 1000 or the Wilshire 5000 follow the market equally well. Chapter 3 considers these and other benchmarks in more detail.

The U.S. equity market is made up of over 10,000 publicly traded stocks. Exhibit 1.3 shows the distribution of the 4,309 NYSE-, AMEX-, and NASDAQ-listed companies by their market capitalization.[3] By far the majority of these are small in terms of market cap. When NYSE-traded stocks are ranked and divided into deciles by market cap and then used to classify all of the exchange-listed companies by size, only 4% of these companies appear in the largest decile although they constitute 70% of total market capitalization. These companies dominate any capitalization-weighted index in which they appear. This is one reason why most market indexes focus on these companies. Another reason that large companies are important is their liquidity. It is easier—and less expensive—to buy $1 million of a large company like General Electric (market cap of $311 billion and 3.2% of the S&P 500's value at the end of 2003) than it is to invest the same amount of money in a small company with a market cap of $25 million. That is not to say that small-company stocks are not a suitable investment—they are. In fact, their differences, lack of publicity and lower liquidity, qualify them as a separate asset class that works well in the satellite ring. Exhibit 1.3 also shows the other attraction of small companies: Over time they have averaged higher rates of return than large companies.

EXHIBIT 1.3

Equity market capitalization and market sizes, NYSE, AMEX, and NASDAQ markets

NYSE Size Decile	Decile Market Cap (in thousands)	Number of Companies	Percent of Total Cap	Average Return*
1 (largest)	$7,419,638,030	168	64.91%	11.4%
2	1,471,629,952	186	12.87	13.2
3	746,716,927	198	6.53	13.8
4	451,145,013	200	3.95	14.4
5	337,041,577	221	2.95	14.9
6	290,452,647	277	2.54	15.3
7	238,327,258	343	2.08	15.7
8	171,437,318	379	1.50	16.6
9	168,889,652	613	1.48	17.7
10 (smallest)	136,028,242	1,724	1.19	21.7

* Average returns from reranking the NYSE deciles quarterly, from 1926 through 2003. All daata as of December 31, 2003.

(Source: Ibbotson Associates.)

We suggest that large company stocks be assigned to the core. The core is then tied to the equity market return because large caps dominate the equity market. U.S. bonds make up the other component of the core. Government bonds are various obligations of the U.S. government and have always made their interest payments and repaid their principal on time. Held to maturity, government bonds offer almost no risk of loss of principal. If these bonds are sold before maturity— to meet cash needs, for example—their value will depend on prevailing interest rates. As we saw above, however, even someone who bought and sold government bonds every year would still have faced less risk than an equity investor. High-grade corporate bonds are similar. Investing in bonds rated highly by Moody's, Standard & Poor's, or Fitch predict a minimal risk of default. With both stocks and bonds the core will follow both markets while taking advantage of diversification to approximate the (cap-weighted) market over time.

The Performance of the Core

Exhibit 1.2 showed the market weights of bonds and stocks from 1952 through 2003. Over this period bonds averaged 62% and stocks 38% of the capital markets. A portfolio that sought to replicate the total market return, therefore, would have been invested similarly.

If this portfolio had been rebalanced to market weights every year from 1952 through the end of 2003, it would have averaged 9.0% per year compared to 12.9% for stocks and 6.8% for bonds. Because of the countervailing effects of mixing stocks and bonds, the core portfolio would have had a smaller range of annual returns, 35.5% to −10.4%, than either pure stocks (52.6% to −26.5%) or pure bonds (42.5% to −8.1%).[4] Once again we see the power of asset allocation. The core, divided between large stocks and bonds, produced a higher rate of return than bonds alone. Although the core portfolio did not earn as much as stocks alone, its return-to-risk ratio[5] was 0.92, better than either stocks alone, 0.77, or bonds alone, 0.68. Adding satellite asset classes to this core portfolio offers the potential to further build returns on a solid market-oriented base.

WHAT'S NEXT?

Chapters 3 and 4 discuss the core asset classes in more depth. Chapters 5 through 9 discuss several potential satellite asset classes. Once you understand how each of these asset classes behaves we will provide some practical advice, concluding with a discussion of best practices (Chapter 11). Along the way we will review risk measurement (Chapter 10) and exchange rates (Chapter 6). A core-satellite approach brings you the best of both worlds; the core mimicking, for the most part, the broad markets, with the satellite providing the potential for growth. Chapter 2 looks at quantitative portfolio management. We believe these quantitative tools are valuable for three reasons. First, they help us understand why the interaction between satellite asset classes is important. Second, they are a good check on whether we can improve the risk-return relationship of the portfolio. Finally, the language of professional portfolio managers is imbued with the terminology of quantitative portfolio management. All fiduciaries need to understand this language as they work with these investment professionals.

N O T E S

1. This calculation assumes these bonds were held for only 1 year to maintain a 20-year maturity. This assumption may be unrealistic, as many investors hold bonds until maturity, but it does give us a basis for comparison.

2. Market capitalization (cap for short) is computed as shares outstanding times market price per share.

3. The deciles are formed by ranking all companies on the NYSE (less closed-end mutual funds, REITs, and the like) in order of market capitalization. This list is split into 10 groups, each with the same number of companies. Companies from the AMEX and NASDAQ are then added to the appropriate decile, depending on their market capitalization. The number of companies in each decile, therefore, varies from its initial equal population based on the NYSE only. The market cap and number of companies are as of September 30, 2003.

4. These performance numbers are slightly different from those presented earlier because they are from a different time period.

5. Annual average return from 1952 through 2003 divided by the standard deviation of those returns.

CHAPTER 2

Quantitative Investments

Quantitative techniques have revolutionized the way academics and practitioners think about investments. From its beginnings with Harry Markowitz's (Markowitz 1952, 1959) mathematical solution to the problem of allocating a portfolio, the quantitative approach has inspired thousands of scholarly research papers and minted any number of PhDs. The quants have also taken much of this academic work into practice—sometimes as former professors, more often as bright PhDs and MBAs from prestigious business schools inspired by the rigor and precision of quantitative investments.

After many retellings and refinements in exposition, the story is essentially the same today as it was in 1952 when Markowitz first published his work. The key assumption is that all investors either: (a) believe that the returns to all assets can be characterized as following a bell-shaped curve (normal probability distribution) or (b) evaluate assets based only on their expected return and expected volatility (variance).

Hence all assets can be characterized by their expected return and variance. In fact, as Exhibit 2.1 shows, the assumption of a bell-shaped curve is not too far off—for some asset classes.

One of the more useful and civilized rules of academic discourse is that professors usually grant the opening gambit—in this case the parallel assumptions about returns—to see where the argument leads. We will do the same while retaining the right to come back to these assumptions. We will see later that these assumptions enable elegant mathematics but produce troubling implications for practical applications. Along the way we will see how these assumptions (and some others) can be used to produce very precise portfolio asset allocations

EXHIBIT 2.1

Histogram of U.S. large-cap stock market returns, 1926–2003

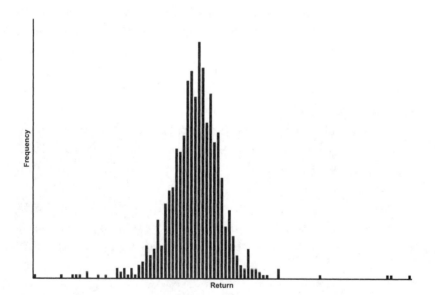

and risk measurements that are the fundamental tools of quantitative investments.

If all assets can be characterized by their expected return and variance, the portfolio allocation problem becomes one of maximizing the expected return while minimizing the expected variance. We assume that people prefer more to less (and hence want to maximize their expected returns) and dislike risk (represented by the variability of those expected returns). A portfolio that produces the highest expected return with the minimum variance would then be universally desired by everyone. In practice, because the maximum return and minimum variance portfolios are mutually exclusive, the problem is usually recast to maximize return for an acceptable level of risk or, conversely, to minimize risk for an acceptable level of return.

Once we have forecasted the expected returns for a set of potential investments, the expected return on any portfolio of those assets is the weighted average of the individual investments expected returns. The weights are the percentage invested in each asset. For example, if we have a portfolio of three assets with one-third of our funds invested in each, we can find the expected return on the portfolio by adding one-third times the expected return on the first asset, one-third times the expected return on the second asset, and one-third times the expected return on the third asset. Exhibit 2.2 illustrates the point.

In Exhibit 2.2 we have forecasted expected returns on three securities as 21%, 15%, and 9%. We have allocated an equal amount to these securities so each constitutes one-third of the portfolio. Each, in turn, contributes to the expected portfolio return in proportion to its weight. The expected return on the portfolio, therefore, is 15%, the weighted sum of the contributions from each security.

EXHIBIT 2.2

Example of portfolio expected return as a weighted average of three constituent assets

Security	Expected Return	% of Portfolio	Contribution to Portfolio
ABC	21%	33.33%	7%
DEF	15%	33.33%	5%
GHI	9%	33.33%	3%
Expected Portfolio Return			15%

One of the key investment insights Markowitz's work offers is that the expected variance of a portfolio is *not* the weighted sum of the constituent variances. Because assets tend to move together to some extent, that comovement must be taken into account. To see the point consider two assets that are mirror images of one another—they move together exactly. The variance of a portfolio of these assets would be the variance of either asset as their variances are identical. If the two assets move together exactly but in opposite directions, however, the gains of one will offset the losses of the other. As one goes up the other goes down. The variance of the portfolio then *is less than* the weighted sum of the variances of the constituent assets. We know this from the phrase: "Don't put all your eggs in one basket." Exhibit 2.3 shows how this relationship works. Here we have used just two assets to make the point clearer.

In the left panel of Exhibit 2.3 we see the returns for two assets (measured on the vertical axis) and the pattern on their return over time (measured along the horizontal axis). These two assets parallel one another exactly. Asset A has the same

EXHIBIT 2.3

Correlations:

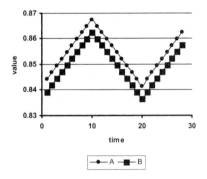 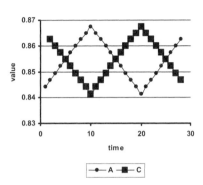

Parallel Assets   Mirror-Image Assets

volatility as Asset B and an equally weighted portfolio of the two has the same volatility. In the right panel, however, Assets A and C have mirror-image patterns. When A's return rises, C's falls, and the reverse is also true. This example has been constructed so that the two exactly offset one another and the volatility of an equally weighted portfolio is precisely zero.

The statistical measure of the degree to which two assets tend to move relative to one another is known as *correlation*. Correlation is like an index that ranges between $+1$ and -1. The correlation can be either positive (one asset goes up, the other goes up), negative (one goes up, the other goes down), or zero (no relationship). Of course in practice it is difficult to find two assets that exactly offset one another (correlation equal to -1), but the principle still holds. Diversification among assets that are not perfectly positively correlated (less than $+1$) can produce portfolios that have less volatility than their constituent assets.

Once we see how the relationship between two assets affects portfolios, we can engineer those portfolios, taking advantage of the power of diversification to create better portfolios. The portfolio is better in the sense that it offers less variance and hence less risk than the sum of the variances for the individual assets taken separately. In this world, therefore, all investors will form portfolios to take advantage of risk reduction.

From this point on we will let the mathematical algorithm of mean variance optimization take over. It is not important that you know exactly how this optimization works as long as you understand the basic principles. Typical results are shown in Exhibit 2.4.

EXHIBIT 2.4

Efficient frontier

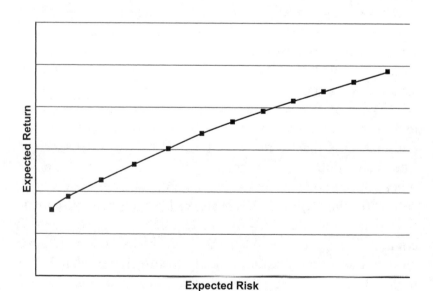

Exhibit 2.4 shows just those portfolios from a set of all possible portfolios that have the smallest variance for every given level of expected return. These portfolios all lie along a line. Some of the portfolios have been highlighted with squares for illustration. Given the expected returns and variances for the assets and all possible combinations of weights, these portfolios, which are the best you can do, are called *efficient portfolios*, and the collection is known as *the efficient set*.

Logically everyone would want one of these efficient portfolios and reject anything that was not in the efficient set. Which portfolio is right for a specific investor would depend on that investor's risk tolerance. Investors who do not want to take too much risk would choose portfolios from the lower left. Of course they would have to be content with lower rates of return, too. Similarly, investors who could tolerate more risk would pick from the upper right and have a chance to earn a higher return as well.

Actually we can do better than any of these efficient portfolios. William Sharpe shared the Nobel Prize with Markowitz mainly for his observation that if a risk-free asset (usually taken to be short-term Treasury bills) is available the graph will look like the one in Exhibit 2.5.

Now investors can allocate their money between the risky portfolio (M) and the risk-free asset (RF). Every portfolio along the line that connects RF and M has a higher rate of expected return for every level of variance than the original efficient frontier.

IMPLICATIONS OF THE QUANTITATIVE MODEL

We have already seen some of the implications of this quantitative model. By assumption, all investors make decisions

Efficient frontier with risk-free asset

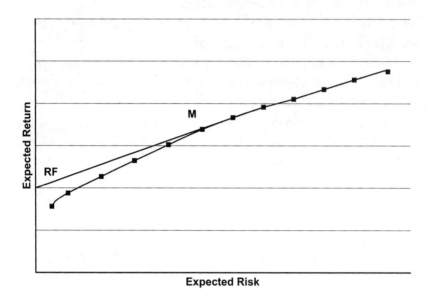

based on expected return and variance. All investors choose portfolios over individual assets because that gives them a better trade-off between expected return and risk. If investors can invest in a risk-free asset, they will all allocate their money between one risky portfolio and that risk-free asset. Because all assets can be summarized by their expected return and variance, we can compare investments based on their return per unit of risk. This measurement, developed by Sharpe and called the *Sharpe ratio*, is the return less the risk-free rate divided by the standard deviation.

The model is consistent with our intuition—there is a trade-off between risk and return. Investors, therefore, should expect to earn rates of return commensurate with the risk they take. That much is not too controversial. Experts disagree, however, about whether investors measure risk with standard deviation and whether market prices resemble those implied by this model.

EXTENSIONS OF THE QUANTITATIVE MODEL

The quantitative model has many other aspects. From the basics presented here analysts have developed the *beta coefficient* (a measure of a security's risk), capital market lines that describe the relationship between risk and return, and many more measurements. For our purposes these enhancements are not important. If you are interested, you can consult the references at the end of this chapter.

PROBLEMS WITH THE QUANTITATIVE MODEL

Markowitz himself realized that his model was an abstraction from reality and made assumptions that were not true. In particular he knew that assuming investors used variance to measure risk was unrealistic. He hoped to find a solution for the portfolio allocation problem that allowed investors to place more emphasis on losses than gains. Unfortunately this problem is very difficult to solve mathematically. That is too bad because many investors appear to feel the pain of a loss more than the joy of the same-sized gain. We are all probably more sensitive to losses than gains. Variance, however, treats losses and gains as equals. We also observe that many assets are asymmetric and do not follow bell-shaped curves. Exhibit 2.6 shows the historical distribution of small-company stocks. This pattern is not as bell-shaped as Exhibit 2.1. The fundamental assumption of risk measured by variance, therefore, falls short of describing reality.

EXHIBIT 2.6

Histogram of U.S. small-cap stock market returns,
1926–2003

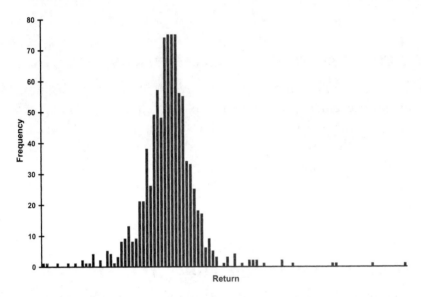

As we will see later, asymmetric return patterns are a
major characteristic of satellite asset classes. Chapter 10 discusses alternative ways of measuring their risk.

Empirical tests of the quantitative approach have also been
disappointing. If investors believed as Markowitz assumed,
then we would expect to see investors holding well-diversified
portfolios. Even if we allow for investors not having access to
the mathematical solution, we still see far too many individual
investors with poorly diversified portfolios. Extensions of the
model have fared even worse. Most of the empirical tests have
shown that variance is a poor description of risk, that variance
and return are not systematically related, and that investors do
not behave as if only expected return and variance are important to them. In a famous series of critiques Richard Roll (1977,

1978, 1980, 1981) pointed out that the model is essentially untestable because of our inability to measure all assets available to investors (like their human capital).

Of course the model is framed in terms of expectations not realizations. A true test of the model would use what investors expected to happen in place of historical observations about what actually happened. Some observers believe, however, that even expectations (if we could measure them) might not make the model fit reality very well.

Despite all these empirical and theoretical disappointments, many analysts continue to use the quantitative model. Perhaps that is because it is better than nothing—and it probably is. The difficulty is that the model has shortcomings that can lead us astray in some important directions.

PRACTICAL SHORTCOMINGS OF THE QUANTITATIVE APPROACH

The portfolios constructed by the mean-variance algorithm are optimal, but mathematics cannot respond to information it does not have. A prime example is that efficient portfolios try to include assets that have low correlation with each other. This attraction means that efficient portfolios often include illiquid or inappropriate assets. For example, some researchers have suggested that venture capital has high expected returns, high risk, and a low correlation with equity (Chen 2002). Without constraints an optimizer would almost always allocate a significant part of the portfolio to venture capital despite the fact that venture capital is highly illiquid and may be inappropriate.

Another very practical problem with efficient portfolios is that small changes in inputs can result in large changes in asset allocation.

EXHIBIT 2.7

Asset allocation: (A) 1926–2003. (B) 1926–1999

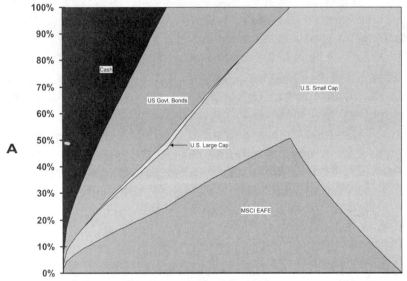

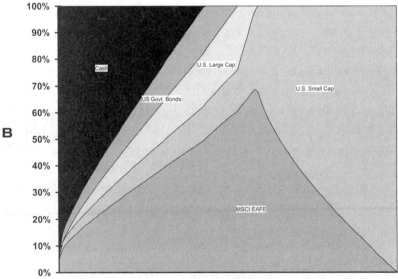

Exhibit 2.7 demonstrates how asset allocation changes with risk. The two graphs in this exhibit were created by using data from 1926 through 2003 (panel A) and 1926 through 1999 (panel B). These graphs allow us to see how differences in risk translate into differences in asset allocation.

In these graphs we used mean-variance optimization to create efficient portfolios from five asset classes: international equity (MSCI's Europe Asia Far East Index[1]), U.S. large-cap stocks (the S&P 500 Index), U.S. small-cap stocks (Ibbotson Associates' Small Stock Index), long-term government bonds (Ibbotson Associates' 20-year constant maturity U.S. government bond index), and cash (30-day Treasury bills). The efficient portfolios range from low to high standard deviation, arranged left to right along the horizontal axis in the graphs. The vertical axis represents the allocation of the portfolios.

For example, using data from 1926 to 2003, the lowest risk (standard deviation) portfolio lies to the far left of the graph and has small allocations to international equity, small-cap stocks, and U.S. government bonds, with most of its allocation to cash. As we move to the right the portfolios have decreasing amounts of cash, with more international and small stocks and more government bonds. The first observation pertains to both graphs (panels A and B). Notice how the allocation to international stocks (MSCI EAFE) rises and falls rapidly as the standard deviation changes. While we know that these portfolios are mathematically optimal, it seems a bit odd that the allocation to this asset class should change so much in such a narrow range. This phenomenon is not related to international equity—it can happen to any asset class. A major practical problem for investment managers who use an optimizer exclusively to build portfolios is justifying why the asset allocation should be so different with almost the same risk.

The second observation comes from comparing the two graphs. The only difference between the two is 4 years of historical data. The average annual return of MSCI EAFE dropped from 15% (through 1999) to 12% (through 2003) while the standard deviation changed very little. The correlation between large-cap stocks and the MSCI EAFE dropped from 0.6 to 0.5 without these 4 years. These changes are not that large and probably within the bounds of forecast errors. If we had built portfolios in 1999 with the data then available, we would have had to reallocate almost every portfolio to match the optimal 2003 asset allocations. Notice, too, that the sensitivity of the allocation to international stocks is even more acute in panel B than A because it changes so rapidly over such a narrow range. As estimates change, whether from the passage of time or improved information, asset allocations change. While evolutionary change is natural and appropriate, these graphs demonstrate how much allocations can change in response to modest changes in forecasts.

A final shortcoming that merits mention is that the model is especially ill-suited to accommodate assets that we know will have returns that are decidedly different than bell-shaped. As you will read in Chapter 10, the Sharpe ratio, while popular with some analysts, does not provide a good comparative measure when portfolios contain satellite asset classes like high-yield bonds, private equity, hedge funds, or illiquid small-cap stocks.

HOW RISK SHOULD BE MEASURED IN THE CORE

If expected variance is not a good measure of risk for fiduciaries, should we abandon risk and focus only on return? Are efficient portfolios an empty exercise? We think the answer to both these questions is no. First, efficient portfolios are a valuable tool for gaining insight into whether improvements to existing portfolios are reasonable. That is, an analyst could plot the existing portfolio along with the efficient frontier based on the constituent asset classes. If the portfolio is not efficient, which probably will be the case, the asset allocation in the efficient portfolio with the same amount of variance could be revealing. Perhaps the efficient portfolio has some merit and should be considered as an alternative. In our experience few fiduciaries build their portfolios with mean-variance optimization. Most portfolios are the result of a legacy or reasonable rules of thumb. Often these portfolios can benefit, however, from a comparison with their efficient counterpart. Second, we should not abandon risk just because it is hard to measure precisely. Prudent investor laws generally require fiduciaries to consider both return and risk. Even if you agree that variance is not a very good measure of risk, you are not excused from considering some alternate measures of risk.

While it might be tempting to try to minimize the risk exposure of the portfolio, this is unlikely to help the portfolio reach its goals. Remember "nothing ventured, nothing gained." The principle is that you cannot expect the portfolio to earn a healthy rate of return without taking some risk. Fiduciaries are supposed to take risk sensibly. At a minimum you should have a rough idea of what sorts of risks are embedded in the portfolio and monitor them to make sure they do not grow out of control. While commercial risk factor models[2] will help you measure and monitor risk, they are not perfect. They will, inevitably, miss something. That something will, inevitably, come back to haunt the portfolio. You cannot, nor do reasonable people expect you to, guard against every possibility. What they (and the law) expect is that you have taken reasonable steps, in consultation with experts as necessary, to understand and monitor the risk of the portfolio within the limitations of the tools available.

We now focus on risk measurement within the core, where asset classes, like those in Exhibit 2.1, tend to be symmetric and variance is appropriate. Measuring risk for satellite asset classes requires some special techniques covered in Chapter 10.

In our experience risk factor models are a reasonable approach for fiduciaries. Think of risk factor models like your homeowner's insurance. Your home can be damaged by wind, hail, rain, plumbing failure, and fire, to name a few risks. Risk factor models suppose that the portfolio will be exposed to a variety of risks, just like your home. Their purpose is to measure these exposures so you can consider them and monitor any changes. Even if the measurements are not perfect, they are a step in the right direction.

For example, changes in interest rates are a risk. If interest rates rise, bond and stock prices generally fall. Stock prices for some companies, like financial institutions, however, might rise. Fiduciaries should want to know how much interest rate risk their portfolio is facing. Similarly, changes in commodity prices will affect different companies in different ways. If oil prices rise, the stocks of airlines and trucking companies may fall while the stocks of oil companies will probably rise. As a final example, consider the level of business activity. Most companies profit in an expansion (and their stocks will rise, as well). Some companies, however, do well in a recession. The factors listed in Exhibit 2.8 are further examples of the kinds of risks a fiduciary would do well to monitor.

Risk factors can also be measured at the level of individ-

E X H I B I T   2 . 8

Examples of portfolio macroeconomic risk factors
fiduciaries should monitor

> Changes in long-term interest rates
> Changes in short-term interest rates
> Credit risk (economywide)
> Commodity prices
> Stage of the business cycle
> Economic growth rate
> Inflation
> Consumer confidence
> Exchange rates

ual companies. BARRA,[3] for example, sells a service that measures fundamental risks like trading activity, market capitalization, earnings growth, foreign income, and others—all of which are associated with return performance at the firm level. Because we assume fiduciaries will leave the selection of individual assets to the investment professional, we will not elaborate on these models.

Fiduciaries should either have their staff or an outside service conduct risk measurements periodically. Most of these services will provide a complete explanation of which factors they think are important and how they measure them. It is beyond the scope of this book to explore these services. Suffice it to say, however, that the provider must be able to explain what they do, and how they do it, in plain English. If they cannot help you understand exactly what they do, chances are they do not really understand it, either. Two things to watch for as you monitor the risk of the portfolio are the risks inherent in the portfolio and changes in the amount and distribution of those risks over time.

Risks Inherent in the Portfolio

Portfolios do not operate in a vacuum. Their goals and objectives are framed by the needs of the beneficiaries. For example, a pension fund is usually sensitive to changes in interest rates because they change the value of the liabilities as well as the assets. An endowment is less likely to have fixed liabilities but may want to preserve the portfolio's purchasing power. The portfolio architect should have expectations about the portfolio's inherent risk factors and plan accordingly. A pension portfolio, therefore, might have assets that gain as interest rates rise whereas an endowment portfolio may be more interested in inflation hedges. Either the staff or the professional managers should be able to help the fiduciaries identify all the inherent risk factor exposures so they can be sure the portfolio is positioned to counteract them.

Fiduciaries are also responsible for matching the return targets with the portfolio's risk. As we mentioned earlier, our intuition tells us that over a long investment horizon a portfolio's risk should largely dictate the return it earns. A return target that is high by historical standards is achievable but will require a higher than normal amount of risk, increasing the chance that the target will not be attained in the short run. Fiduciaries who intuitively understand this paradox (you have to take more risk to earn higher return, and the more risk you take the less likely it is you will actually earn high returns over any given time period) can contribute a great deal to the sponsoring organization's understanding of the trade-off between risk and return. Unfortunately, few organizations are content with the meager returns that a low-risk strategy produces.

Changes in Risk

Once the fiduciaries are comfortable with the risks inherent in their portfolio they need to monitor those exposures. Macroeconomic forces are not constant. As they change, we would expect changes in the risks faced by the portfolio. The things to watch for, however, are dramatic changes in the amount and distribution of risk across the portfolio. If the professional managers have changed their strategy, the fiduciaries should expect an explanation and the managers' expectations of how their new strategy better manages the risk factors. These expectations are all the more important when the portfolio is divided among several managers. It should be easy to see that changes in one manager's approach could be offset by or exacerbate changes another manager has implemented. Reviewing risk exposures at the manager and portfolio level should be a standard agenda item for each meeting of the fiduciaries.

This discussion is not meant to encourage fiduciaries to distract individual managers in their pursuit of tactics they think will enable them to provide the very best returns. Fiduciaries hire investment professionals for their expertise. Micromanagement serves no one well. The fiduciaries remain responsible for the overall health of the portfolio, however. Prudent fiduciaries monitor the experts they employ.

Styles and Style Drift—Another Source of Risk in the Core

We discussed style briefly in Chapter 1. Here we will provide a bit more detail. Many equity managers follow a specific investment style. Common styles include diversification by large, small, value, and growth stocks. Most professionals think of these as a matrix, shown in panel A of Exhibit 2.9.[4]

EXHIBIT 2.9

Equity-style matrix for the period 1928–2003:
(A) historical annual average return and risk; (B) historical
correlations.

	Large		Small	
	Average	Std. Dev	Average	Std. Dev
All	12.41	20.44	17.51	33.34
Value	15.30	27.83	19.42	32.68
Growth	11.21	20.49	14.42	34.10

A

	Large Value	Large Growth	Small Value	Small Growth
Large Value	1.00			
Large Growth	0.80	1.00		
Small Value	0.90	0.73	1.00	
Small Growth	0.80	0.80	0.87	1.00

B

Panel A of Exhibit 2.9 displays the commonly recognized equity styles. Managers might focus on large growth or small value or on growth or small stocks. They specialize to gain experience in the characteristics of these styles. When the equity portfolio is large enough, many fiduciaries allocate different asset classes to different managers. This approach allows each manager to use his or her special expertise.

The distinction between large and small stocks comes from their market capitalizations. Exhibit 1.3 in Chapter 1 showed the size and performance of large- and small-cap stocks and suggested that these stocks have offered different risks and returns with the more risky small stocks recording higher returns and higher risks. These results are summarized in the first row of panel A in Exhibit 2.9. The correlation between large and small stocks is 0.87, which is high, but with some room for diversification benefits.

In the same way portfolio managers consider growth and value as distinct asset classes. Exhibit 2.9 shows their historical risk and return (panel A) as well as the correlations (panel B). In this exhibit large is defined as capitalization deciles 1 through 5 and small as capitalization deciles 6 through 10 (see Exhibit 1.3 in Chapter 1).

Although the subject is controversial, many analysts believe that value stocks are inherently more risky than growth stocks. If nothing else, companies that have become value stocks because of internal difficulties are more likely to go out of business than companies that are registering strong earnings growth. The statistics bear this out for large-cap stocks where value had a higher historical annual return (15.30% versus 11.21%) with a higher standard deviation (27.83% versus 20.49%). If investors know that value is more risky they will demand a higher rate of return to hold these stocks. For small-cap stocks value again beat growth (19.42% versus 14.42%) but with a smaller standard deviation (32.68% versus 34.10%). The correlations suggest diversification benefits are available, especially between large growth and small value. While the question of growth and value styles is far from settled, we believe the large-cap numbers are more representative of what to expect in the future for two reasons: (1) Gathering enough small-cap value and growth stocks in the early years (1928–1940) is difficult and hence may not be representative; and (2) if small value were a risk-return bargain, alert traders would make sure it did not stay that way very long.

Style Drift

As mentioned in Chapter 1 many fiduciaries design the equity portion of their portfolios to take advantage of the diversification offered by large, small, value, and growth styles. Managers may be tempted, however, to stray from their asset class when their style is out of favor. For example, in the latter half of the 1990s large-cap growth stocks did extraordinarily well. Value styles did poorly, and managers who specialized in this asset class must have been sorely tempted to add a few (or a lot of) large-cap growth stocks to enhance returns. Fiduciaries who follow an asset allocation strategy—and especially a core-satellite approach—need their managers to be true to their assigned asset class. We can see that if the portfolio has an allocation to both small-cap value and large-cap growth and the small-cap value manager adds some large-cap growth, the portfolio will no longer perform as it was designed. Risk will no longer be under control.

Managers may consciously add popular asset classes when theirs is out of fashion. If these managers announce their intention to migrate between asset classes in search of high returns, we have no quarrel with them. The risk to a core-satellite portfolio, however, comes from managers who unconsciously stray from their mandate or who fail to disclose their style shift when returns have been disappointing. This is called *style drift*. Whatever the source, the fiduciary has lost control. While the term *style drift* was coined to describe managers who did not consistently follow a growth or value style, the meaning today is broad enough to encompass any deviation from the manager's assigned role in the portfolio. By designing a diversified core-satellite portfolio, the fiduciary has accepted responsibility for managing overall portfolio risk. Individual managers are given a mandate within that design. You can think of the core-satellite approach as a strategic plan with individual managers implementing tactics appropriate to their sector. If the individual managers are not working in concert with that plan, the strategy will probably fail.

Tools to Detect Style Drift

Two complementary tools are available to help the fiduciary detect style drift: holdings analysis and returns-based analysis.

Holdings analysis looks at each asset in the manager's portfolio and determines whether it is appropriate. If the manager's mandate is style-neutral small cap (balanced between growth and value), then each stock's market capitalization would be computed. If the holdings were predominantly within the small-cap range, the portfolio would be judged as within the mandate. This process is straightforward when the mandate is based on market capitalization. Holdings analysis is trickier when the mandate includes a style like value or growth. These styles are subjective and even investment professionals cannot agree on their definition. Holdings analysis consultants classify each holding according to their firm's definition of style (and capitalization, if appropriate). The dominant (capitalization-weighted) style of the portfolio is then declared to be that manager's style. It is easy to see that because holdings analysis necessarily includes judgments, the results are subjective. Even so, it is a good way to measure whether the manager is staying true to his or her mandate. For a portfolio invested in mutual funds, which only have to report their holdings every 6 months, the holdings analysis may be seriously out of date. This is not the case for dedicated managers who place each portfolio in a separate account. Measuring the portfolio only every 6 months can cloud much of the detail that would enable early detection of style drift.

Returns-based analysis is an alternative measure of a manager's style. Because mutual fund managers report their returns every month (and dedicated managers can do it even more often, if required), an analysis of the pattern of returns can detect style drift relatively quickly. In this procedure an equity manager's returns, for example, could be compared to indexes like small- and large-cap value and growth, long-term government bonds, corporate bonds, and Treasury bills. A statistical procedure is used to measure how closely the manager's returns mimic the returns to the various indexes. One would expect a small-cap value manager's returns to correspond pretty closely to the small-cap value index and not very closely to, say, the large-cap growth index. If the manager, consciously or unconsciously, drifts away from his or her mandate toward large-cap value, the analysis will show an increasing affinity for the large-cap value index.

Returns-based analysis has several advantages over a holdings analysis. First, the analysis does not require any judgment as to the classification of individual assets. Second, returns are typically available more often than holdings. Third, returns-based analysis can give a much better picture of the behavior of the manager's portfolio over time. Returns-based analysis, however, also has shortcomings. The most important key to success in returns-based analysis is to have timely indexes for each asset class that might be relevant. The calculations must employ more indexes than the manager's mandate so that any drift will show up. Managers may be legitimately following their mandate but using securities that are not in the index. This might be desirable as we do not want managers to slavishly follow an index. At the same time it might make the estimation of their style less precise. Also, as a statistical procedure, it is no better than the input data. The procedure assumes that all input data are correct, even if they actually contain incorrect returns. Data errors, of course, mean that the results will not be reliable.

Style drift is a significant risk that fiduciaries will be hard put to detect by inspecting their managers' holdings. We recommend that fiduciaries use both holdings and returns-based analyses to check for style drift. If both techniques come to the same conclusion, then the style is confirmed. If the techniques disagree (which happens fairly often) then further investigation is necessary.

SPECIAL CONSIDERATION FOR CORE BOND ALLOCATIONS

Chapter 4 addresses the issues involved in an allocation to core bonds. Here we will set the stage with some basics. Bond yields (and prices) are tied much more closely to prevailing interest rates than are stock prices. Bond yields vary with maturity. As you would expect, the longer the maturity, the higher the yield the market requires. While this is not always true, it holds true most of the time. The bond market refers to the relationship between maturity and yields (interest rates) as the *yield curve* (with rates on the vertical axis and maturity on the horizontal axis).

The risk in the core bond allocation depends largely on how much interest rates change. Managing that risk depends in part on understanding what happens to bond prices when interest rates change. When interest rates rise, all bond prices fall. When interest rates rise, however, the return on reinvesting coupons from those bonds also rises over time, counterbalancing the decline in price. A rise in interest rates brings good news (reinvestment returns rise) that offsets the bad news (bond prices fall). By judiciously choosing the maturity of the bond and the investment horizon these two effects balance each other. From this balance comes the gauge of bond risk called *duration*. You will hear most bond portfolio managers talk about the risk of their portfolio in terms of duration. Duration measures the sensitivity of bond prices (or the aggregate value of a bond portfolio) to changes in interest rates. If someone says the duration of a bond is 7.5, then a 0.50% change in interest rates should change the bond's price by 3.75% (7.5 × 0.50). While duration is only accurate for very small changes in interest rates, it is a handy summary measure of bond risk.

You will learn much more about core bonds in Chapter 4, but for now you only need an understanding of the basics of core bonds and bond risk.

SUMMARY

Risk is a key "control variable" for fiduciaries. The portfolio typically will not reach its goals and fulfill its obligations without taking some risk. The very fact that there is a portfolio suggests that investing all the money in low-risk, low-return Treasury bills will not be enough. Risk can be measured and managed to a rough approximation. While there is no single commonly accepted measure of risk, we have suggested several ways in which fiduciaries can get a handle on the risks their core portfolio faces and ways to monitor those risks over time. Two other risk considerations are addressed in later chapters: Tracking error risk is covered in Chapter 3 and risk measurement for asymmetric asset classes is the topic of Chapter 10.

N O T E S

1. This index tracks the equity markets in Australia, Austria, Belgium, Denmark, Finland, France, Germany, Greece, Hong

Kong, Ireland, Italy, Japan, Netherlands, New Zealand, Norway, Portugal, Singapore, Spain, Sweden, Switzerland, and the United Kingdom. The data begin in 1970.

2. See Connor (1995) for a review of some commercial models.

3. http://www.barra.com/ Barra, Inc., 2100 Milvia Street, Berkeley, CA 94704

4. Source: http://mba.tuck.dartmouth.edu/pages/faculty/ken. french/.

B I B L I O G R A P H Y

Chen, Peng, Gary T. Baierl, and Paul D. Kaplan (2002 Winter). "Venture Capital and Its Role in Strategic Asset Allocation," *Journal of Portfolio Management*, Vol. 28, no. 2, pp. 83–89.

Connor, Gregory (1995 May/June). "The Three Types of Factor Models: A Comparison of Their Explanatory Power," *Financial Analysts Journal*, Vol. 51, no. 3, pp. 42–46.

Ibbotson Associates (2004). SBBI: 2004 Yearbook (Chicago, Ibbotson Associates).

Markowitz, Harry (1952 March). "Portfolio Selection," *Journal of Finance*, Vol. 7, no. 1, pp. 77–91.

Markowitz, Harry (1959). *Portfolio Selection—Efficient Diversification of Investments* (New Haven, Conn., Yale University Press).

Roll, Richard (1977 March). "A Critique of Asset Pricing Theory's Tests," *Journal of Financial Economics*, Vol. 4, no, 4, pp. 129–176.

Roll, Richard (1978 September). "Ambiguity When Performance Is Measured by the Securities Market Line," *Journal of Finance*, Vol. 33, no. 4, pp. 1051–1069.

Roll, Richard (1980 Summer). "Performance Evaluation and Benchmark Error I," *Journal of Portfolio Management*, Vol. 6, no. 4, pp. 5–12.

Roll, Richard (1981 Winter). "Performance Evaluation and Benchmark Error II," *Journal of Portfolio Management*, Vol. 7, no. 2, pp. 17–22.

CHAPTER 3

Core Equity:

Constructing a Passively Managed Core Portfolio

James A. Pupillo, CIMA, CIMC

INTRODUCTION

For decades, academics, portfolio managers, and financial professionals have debated the benefits of active versus passive investment approaches. The core-satellite approach to portfolio construction reconciles both sides of this debate by showing investors how to reap the benefits of both active and passive investment strategies. The core-satellite method helps fiduciaries, such as the sponsors of qualified retirement plans, foundation and endowment trustees, state and local officials, hospital administrators, and family office executives to design their asset allocation strategies, reduce costs, control risk, and increase liquidity. Long advocated by institutional investors, the core-satellite approach also has become increasingly popular with private individuals, who find its ability to enhance after-tax performance an additional benefit.

Constructing any diversified portfolio means establishing risk and reward parameters, as risk tends to drive portfolio returns. Developing an appropriate asset allocation strategy is the first step in successfully implementing a core-satellite approach. The second step includes setting a "budget for active manager risk," explained in more detail in this chapter.

The third important component in implementing the core-satellite approach is to understand the major core U.S. indices and pick an appropriate benchmark, which will serve as the market's proxy and measure. In fact, index selection is paramount to nearly every component of the investment process, including those of the satellite asset classes, which are discussed in more detail in subsequent chapters.

Constructing a passively managed core equity component requires familiarity with commonly used broad market and style indices. Today, there are thousands of market indices, across virtually every imaginable economic sector or industry and every investment style or asset class, including some that represent entire sections of the globe or very specific geographic locations. One well-known U.S. market index, and one most readily known to investors, is the Standard & Poor's 500 Index; even broader measures include the Russell 3000 Index and the Wilshire 5000, among others.

The purposes of this chapter are to help fiduciaries understand the benefits of a passively managed core equity allocation, explain the concept of budgeting for active management risk, and provide a guide to the major market indices and their potential to serve as an accurate judge of the passively managed core component's performance.

BUDGETING FOR ACTIVE MANAGEMENT RISK

All investors should understand the differences between active risk (alpha risk) and market risk (beta risk). *Market risk* is the risk assumed by investing in the market for any particular period; it is commonly identified as the annualized standard deviation of the market return. On the other hand, *active risk* is the risk a portfolio assumes if its active managers underperform their designated asset class benchmark. Most active managers are hired to outperform a specific benchmark on a relative basis, both more positively on a market upswing and less negatively on a market downturn. This return, commonly measured against a specific preselected benchmark, is known as *active return.*

Likewise, active risk is calculated as the manager's annualized variability of returns relative to the benchmark and is called *active tracking error.* For active managers to beat their benchmark, they must own securities or have security or sector weightings that are different from the benchmark. Active managers can achieve their potentially higher active returns only with higher levels of active tracking error, because higher tracking errors reflect the differences between the manager's portfolio and the benchmark.

Passive managers in the core equity portfolio are also measured against their asset class benchmark index. While we expect active managers to generate active tracking error, in principle passive managers should not generate any tracking error. Their job is to mimic the benchmark. Of course passive managers will not match their benchmark exactly. Even though core equities in the popular benchmarks are usually liquid, technical factors like changes in index membership make it difficult to hold all the securities in the benchmark in exactly the same proportions as the index all the time. A passive manager, therefore, may generate risk in the form of passive tracking error, although it will be considerably less than an active manager's tracking error. As an example of the three kinds of risk, consider a portfolio devoted entirely to core equity and passively managed. This portfolio incurs market risk and passive tracking error. A portfolio divided between core equity and any actively managed satellite asset class faces market risk and passive tracking error on the passively managed core portion plus active tracking error on the actively managed satellite portion.

Market risk is largely unavoidable. Active management adds more risk than passive management but also offers potentially higher returns. The questions to address are: How can fiduciaries manage the risk that the satellite portions of their portfolio may *not* outperform their designated benchmark? What is an appropriate process to budget for active risk and make the basic allocation between core and satellite?

Active risk budgets help guide a portfolio's asset allocation policies—policies which not only set the strategic (long-term) allocation among stocks and bonds and the tactical (short-term) allocations among different types of investment styles (beta risk management) but also determine the allocation between active and passive investment strategies (alpha risk management).

Regardless of the active risk budget assignment, the core-satellite approach manages and measures active risk; however, it does not eliminate the opportunity to outperform the market through active return. Active risk budgets are subjective goals, customized to each portfolio's risk tolerance levels. A portfolio with a low tolerance for active manager risk may allocate a larger percentage to core (passive) asset classes to achieve low overall tracking error. Portfolios less sensitive to tracking error risk may allocate a greater percentage to satellite (active) asset classes for the opportunity to benefit from potential incremental active management returns.

Risk budgeting usually starts by considering matching liabilities and asset returns. A pension plan, for example, should have a good idea of the liabilities it owes to the plan participants as it assembles assets to meet those liabilities. An endowment also may have quasi-liabilities in the form of promises it has made to the beneficiaries or to meet the spending policy required to maintain its nonprofit tax status. Other fiduciaries may not have liabilities per se but they will usually have goals for the portfolio like funding a project or providing income for a charity. To start their risk budgets all these fiduciaries need to estimate the rate of return that will be required if the portfolio is to meet its goals. Either way it comes down to forecasting. If a portfolio needs to return 10% per year, the best place to look for guidance is capital market history. In Chapter 1 we saw that the S&P 500 Index posted an average annual return of 12.4% from 1926 through the end of 2003. During the same period U.S. government bonds averaged 5.8%. The annual standard deviations were 20.4% and 9.4%, respectively. A core portfolio of 100% stocks, therefore, should return in the neighborhood of 12% per year over the long run, easily meeting the 10% target.

Fiduciaries, however, must consider two other factors. First, the future might not be like the past and capital market returns may not be as high. Second, an average return of 12.4% with a standard deviation of 20.4% implies that a *loss* of 8% is within only one standard deviation of the mean. In other words, it is highly likely the portfolio will suffer a substantial loss in any single year (statistically about 32% of the time the return will be one standard deviation or more below the mean). Furthermore, nothing prevents a series of annual losses that might restrict the ability of the portfolio to meet its obligations or reach its goals. Achieving a return of 10%, therefore, may not be as easy as allocating 100% of the portfolio to passively managed core equity. We also saw in

Chapters 1 and 2 the power of diversification. With a diversified portfolio the changes in one asset class can balance out
changes in another. While bonds are not riskless, they are less
risky than stocks and tend not to move in lockstep with
stocks. The risk budgeting decision, therefore, needs to consider the returns and risks of the asset classes, the correlations
between them, as well as the portion of the portfolio to be
actively managed.

Because of the complexity of the interrelationships
between asset classes the active risk budget itself is most often
framed in terms of tracking errors. For a simplified example,
assume you are the fiduciary for a portfolio that has allocated
all its funds between one core (passive) and one satellite
(active) asset class. While you decide that the satellite portion
of the portfolio can tolerate no more than a 4% underperformance of its active benchmark, you also expect the satellite to
have a 5.5% tracking error against its benchmark. The risk
budget would be determined as:

$$\frac{\text{Tracking error tolerance}}{\text{Expected tracking error}} = \frac{.04}{.055} = 72.7\% \text{ allocation to the satellite} \\ \text{and } 27.3\% \text{ allocation to the core}$$

To see how this risk budget achieves the desired result,
consider how the portfolio would perform if the satellite allocation actually had a tracking error of 5.5% and the core
allocation had no tracking error.

Satellite allocation times its tracking error plus core allocation times
its tracking error = portfolio tracking error = 72.7% × 5.5%
$$+ 27.3\% \times 0\% = 4.0\%$$

This is the desired tracking error tolerance. Risk budgeting is not insurance against underperformance; rather, it is a
rational approach to managing active risk.

If the portfolio's tolerance for active tracking error is
lower, the risk budget would be more risk averse. Assum-

ing the tolerance is 2% rather than 4% the risk budget would be:

$$\frac{\text{Tracking error tolerance}}{\text{Expected tracking error}} = \frac{.02}{.055} = 36.3\% \text{ allocation to the satellite and } 63.7\% \text{ allocation to the core}$$

Higher expected tracking error would also cause the risk budget to be more risk averse. Assuming the expected tracking error is 10% rather than 5.5%, the risk budget would be:

$$\frac{\text{Tracking error tolerance}}{\text{Expected tracking error}} = \frac{.02}{.10} = 20\% \text{ allocation to the satellite and } 80\% \text{ allocated to the core}$$

Risk budgeting is easiest to comprehend with only one satellite asset class. With more than one satellite asset class the fiduciary should construct a composite by appropriately weighting benchmark indices for each of the constituent satellite asset classes. The tracking error for the composite (perhaps estimated from historical returns) then can be substituted for the expected tracking error in the calculations above. The tracking error tolerance depends on the amount by which the fiduciary is willing to let the portfolio underperform its benchmark. Even the most skilled active managers will underperform their benchmarks from time to time. These aberrations tend to be cyclical and risk budgeting should help maintain consistency over the long term. If, however, a manager continuously underperforms, the prudent fiduciary may consider switching to another manager.[1]

ESTABLISHING AN APPROPRIATE BENCHMARK FOR THE CORE EQUITY ALLOCATION

Constructing a passively managed core equity component requires a broad U.S. market index. The best-known U.S.

market index, and one most readily known to investors, is the Standard & Poor's 500 Index; other indexes, such as the Russell 3000 Index and the Wilshire 5000, are still broader in scope. In fact, index selection is important in nearly every component of the investment process, including those of the satellite asset classes, which are discussed in more detail in subsequent chapters.

The second important component to implementing the core-satellite approach is to understand how to pick an appropriate benchmark, which will serve as the market's proxy and measure.

ESTABLISHING THE CORE EQUITY ALLOCATION

The core-satellite approach quiets the debate over the benefits of active versus passive investment management. Fiduciaries pursuing active returns can select investment firms or funds that they believe will outperform a market index through the portfolio manager's skill in discretionary stock picking and selection of industry and sector weights. Active managers are expected to generate pure *alpha*, the portion of return that is not explained by market or beta risk exposures of the portfolio. In choosing the potential to generate alpha over a certain benchmark with an active manager, fiduciaries also choose to accept the risk of active tracking error.

Passive managers, on the other hand, hold securities similar to those in the particular index they are seeking to replicate. Indexed investments gained heightened popularity in the late 1980s as respected academics advanced the proposition that active management may not be worth the increased risk and higher transaction costs. Common flaws in this research were that all equity managers were lumped together and compared against the S&P 500 and that the research did not isolate managers into investment substyles (Trone, Allbright, and Taylor 1996). To successfully outperform their benchmarks, active managers conduct market and economic analysis in an attempt to exploit market mispricing; they also engage in active sector allocations and capitalization decisions based on their particular investment style.

Today, many investment professionals believe that active investment styles are best employed for asset classes such as small-capitalization stocks or international and emerging markets, where active management has a better chance of adding value—these are the likely candidates for the "satellites" of the core-satellite strategy. Passive investing, on the other hand, yields its best benefits in larger, established markets. With a passively managed core component in the large-capitalization space, investors can take advantage of the thousands of U.S. companies with a large to midmarket capitalization, possessing millions of outstanding and liquid shares readily available through efficient exchanges.

To take the passively managed core allocation process even further, some investment consultants may recommend splitting the core between large-cap growth and large-cap value investment styles. For example, Exhibit 3.1 illustrates the differences between the cumulative total returns on the two main growth and value indices, the Russell 1000 Growth Index and Russell 1000 Value Index, from December 1979 through December 2003.

Exhibit 3.1 shows the relative performances of the two styles as if they were in a race, beginning on December 31, 1979. A reading over 100% indicates the growth index had the better performance since December 31, 1979. A reading under 100% signals that the value index had the best cumulative track record. Value has been the cumulative leader over much

EXHIBIT 3.1

Relative performance cumulative return on the Russell 1000 Growth and Russell 1000 Value indices, 1979–2003

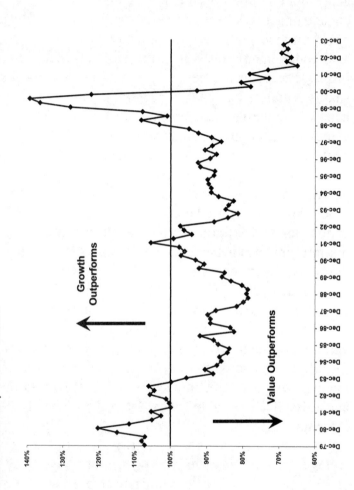

of the past 20 years. However, this result is heavily influenced by the inception date of the Russell indices. Value stocks enjoyed a powerful rally in the early- and mid-1980s, allowing them to build up a considerable lead. Periods of growth out-performance, on the other hand, have tended to be shorter but also more powerful.

One can identify six discrete style cycles since December 31, 1979. Cycles are defined as a move of 15% or more from a high or low in the return difference between the two major style indices. These cycles have ranged in length from 16 months to 8 years. The current cycle, a value cycle, began in March 2000. In Exhibit 3.2, note how frequently large annual differences have been followed by a sharp reversal in favor of the other style. There is no guarantee that extreme biases toward growth or value will not extend beyond a single year; indeed, investors would be wise not to expect them to last indefinitely.

Because it is nearly impossible to accurately predict when value or growth will outperform and for how long—and how to accurately determine the optimal weighting between the two styles—many fiduciaries have turned to core equity allocation, which balances growth and value stocks. However, other fiduciaries will seek additional alpha by attempting to over- and underweight value and growth as stocks pass through variable length cycles. Finally, a fiduciary may also elect an unbalanced blend of these strategies as a partial hedge. None of these approaches are right or wrong. Unless the fiduciary has some unique insight into these cycles, however, the most prudent approach is to invest broadly in large-cap stocks, covering both value and growth.

To summarize, the benefits of the core-satellite approach with a passively managed broad or large-capitalization U.S. equity index include:

EXHIBIT 3.2

Annual relative performance returns on Russell
1000 Growth minus Russell 1000 Value indices,
1983–2003

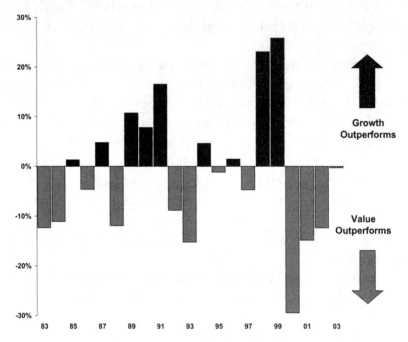

- *Liquidity.* With thousands of U.S. large-capitalization and midcapitalization companies and millions of shares available for purchase or sale through efficient and regulated exchanges, the large-cap markets are known for their trading liquidity.
- *Improved Diversification.* Once an appropriate core allocation has been determined, fiduciaries can easily replicate this very large basket of U.S. companies through a well-managed indexed mutual or exchange-traded fund. This fund then becomes the core around which the satellite asset classes are added.

- *Cost Control.* Active managers conduct regular analyses and use that data to buy and sell securities within the guidelines of their stated investment process. For doing so, they charge fees and incur increased trading costs. On the other hand, passively managed index fund managers simply replicate a benchmark and do not possess the same expense levels. By allocating a portion of the overall portfolio to passive management, fiduciaries can reduce their overall costs (at the expense of potential additional alpha).

- *Tax Efficiency.* For some fiduciaries and many private individuals and families, taxes are a significant concern. Passive investments have lower turnover and realized capital gains, which may result in smaller end-of-year tax bills.

- *Budgeting for Active Management Risk.* The risk budgeting process combines both active and index investments to achieve an overall diversified portfolio. Risk budgets are customizable according to each portfolio's risk tolerance levels, asset allocation strategies, and investment policies. As we have seen, a passively managed core component can help reduce the risk level of the entire portfolio.

CORE-SATELLITE PORTFOLIO MEASUREMENT

Thousands of indices have been created since the inception of the popular Dow Jones Industrial Average, first calculated by Charles Henry Dow in 1884. The first Dow Jones average was simply the average price of 11 railroad stocks. Published daily, the Dow provided investors with one of the first continually calculated and constantly updated measures of the market.

Over a hundred years ago, Mr. Dow helped investors answer such key questions as "What did the market do today?" and "How are my investments performing?" An index constructed on a consistent basis and measured across time allows investors to gauge their long-run rates of return and to compare those returns at different points in time. Properly constructed indices are important for three main reasons: (1) determining asset allocation policies, (2) calculating risks in specific asset classes, and (3) measuring the value of diversification.

Importance of Index Selection

While they may vary in their composition and construction, all of the broad-capitalization U.S. equity indices are indicators of market trends. Regardless of the indices ultimately selected, they are predominantly used as a proxy for an asset class, as a benchmark against which to judge active managers, and as the core component of a core-satellite approach. Indices are also used to conduct performance attribution analysis and to weigh both active and passive managers' performance after fees and expenses.

According to some researchers, "The best index is one that can be used for all three purposes simultaneously, so that one does not have to keep switching between indices, depending on the purpose to which one wants to put it at a particular time." (Enderle, Pope, and Siegel 2003)

The Benchmark Selection Process

Regardless of which benchmark is ultimately selected, it "should be a feasible alternative identified in advance of the period over which performance is measured." (Sharpe 1991)

Enderle, Pope, and Siegel (2003) cite seven key criteria that are useful in identifying an appropriate broad market benchmark for U.S. equities:

1. *Completeness.* The ideal index would include every single possible security in its asset class. For example, the Wilshire 5000 Index is considered by many professionals to be the broadest measure of the collective performance of all U.S. equities. In fact, as of June 30, 2003, it actually contained 403 more securities than its original 5,000, reflecting the increase in U.S. equity issuance.

2. *Investability.* The broader the index, the more securities it contains and measures. However, many issues are illiquid and may be difficult for investors to trade. Because it is not possible to invest directly in an index, that particular basket of securities is accessed through an index mutual or exchange-traded fund. In some cases, a complete replication of a particular index—for example, the Wilshire 5000—has yet to be made available to investors. An index can be considered appropriate only to the extent its securities can be easily accessed through an indexed mutual fund or exchange-traded fund.

3. *Objective Rules.* As noted below in the descriptions of the indices themselves, some benchmark constructors use rules that are fairly objective, while others use judgment when assembling their index's holdings. The availability of objective, published rules means that index fund managers can predict, with varying levels of accuracy, which stocks will be added or removed from a particular benchmark.

   On the other hand, the use of judgment—rather than rules—to select an index's components means that conscious steps are taken to construct an index of desired

characteristics. This means that an index fund manager
may or may not be able to predict with exact certainty
which securities will ultimately be held in the index on
the reconstitution dates. The result may be increased
passive tracking error in index mutual or exchange-
traded funds.

4. *Accurate Data.* The introduction of indexed mutual
   funds in the 1970s and their increasing popularity with
   investors in subsequent decades was facilitated by the
   improved availability of accurate market data made possible through technology. Both the index constructors
   and the index fund replicators rely on this same level of
   accurate and timely data about the individual securities
   held in their portfolios.

5. *Acceptance by Investors.* The selection of an index
   serves a number of purposes: as a benchmark for
   active management, as an index portfolio itself, and as a
   proxy for an asset class in asset allocation determina-
   tions. It can also be used to gauge after-fee performance. Investment professionals typically favor those
   indices judged to use the most accurate data, have the
   longest history, and maintain a consistent style and
   security substyles, among other criteria. The most popular benchmarks—and the most widely accepted—are
   consistently recognized for their ability to meet all of
   these criteria.

6. *Availability of Crossing Opportunities, Derivatives,
   and Other Products.* Most indices are selected for the
   key reasons previously mentioned; however, even if
   used only as a guideline to select an appropriate
   indexed mutual fund or exchange-traded fund, fiduciaries should be aware of thcir potential other uses and
   capabilities.

7. *Low Turnover and Related Transaction Costs.* Trading can be costly no matter how often or in what magnitude it is conducted. When selecting a benchmark, fiduciaries should be aware that less index-driven turnover is often more desirable.

Additional Index Considerations

Fiduciaries should consider three additional factors in the index selection process:

1. *Reconstitution Frequency and Turnover.* Reconstitution is the process of periodically deciding which securities meet the criteria for index inclusion. When an index is reconstituted, the indexed mutual fund or exchange-traded fund manager must then buy or sell securities to replicate the benchmark's holdings; this trading incurs fees for investors. Many of the indices described in more detail below have a set number of stocks. These indices are typically reconstituted as securities are added or removed due to changes in their capitalization rankings as their price fluctuates. When selecting an index, fiduciaries should be mindful that more frequent reconstitution typically incurs increased internal transaction costs for the mutual fund or exchange-traded fund tracking that index.
2. *Rebalancing Frequency and Turnover.* Rebalancing, as opposed to reconstitution, is the process of adjusting the weights of stocks held in the index for changes in the number of shares outstanding. Theoretically, the ideal index will continuously update its holdings based on the number of shares issued by a company; to accurately replicate the benchmark, the index fund

manager must simultaneously make these changes.
Most managers of major indices develop a prearranged
process for rebalancing frequency to create an orderly
flow of changes. Regardless of the frequency, index
managers must eventually replicate or optimize these
changes.

3. *Fees and Transactions Costs.* Benchmark indexes
   do not include management fees or transactions
   costs incurred by both active and passive managers. A
   passive manager who meets the benchmark return
   has earned his or her fees and covered trading expenses.
   Active managers, who typically charge higher fees
   for their services, have to overcome a greater hurdle
   to match the benchmark's return. These considerations are important when evaluating manager performance.

Broad-Capitalization Indices

Today, many investment professionals consider the leading
broad-capitalization benchmarks of the U.S. equity market to
be the Wilshire 5000, Russell 3000, Dow Jones U.S. Total
Market, and Standard & Poor's 1500 indices. At times, fiduciaries may also consider the narrower Russell 1000 and
Standard & Poor's 500 Index, although many professionals
believe they do not adequately capture the breadth of the
broader market. Each benchmark has different characteristics,
each is calculated differently, and each is rebalanced using different methods and time periods. Most of these indices are
published both with and without dividends. Some of the major
characteristics and distinctions of the U.S. broad market
benchmarks are:

- *Wilshire 5000 Index.* With monthly returns backdated to January 1971, the Wilshire 5000 Total Market Index represents one of the broadest measures of the U.S. equity market. Calculated daily since 1980, it measures the performance of all U.S.-domiciled equity securities for which price and shares outstanding are readily available; each issue must trade in the United States and must be the primary equity issue for the company. Additions to the index are made once a month after the month-end close with additions and deletions preannounced by the second day prior to the month end. Now containing over 5,400 stocks due to the growth in U.S. equity issues, the Wilshire 5000 is considered by many to be a very reasonable approximation of dollar changes in the U.S. equity market. Wilshire Associates, Santa Monica, California, a consulting and investment management firm, constructs the Wilshire indices series.

- *Russell 3000 Index.* The Russell 3000 Index measures the performance of the 3,000 largest U.S.-domiciled companies based on total market capitalization. It represents approximately 98% of the investable U.S. equity market as of the index reconstitution date. All companies listed on the NYSE, AMEX, and NASDAQ are considered for inclusion in the index; however, stocks that trade on the exchanges but are headquartered in other countries are excluded. Closed-end mutual funds, limited partnerships, royalty trusts, and ADRs are also excluded. Each stock must trade at or above $1.00 on May 31 to be eligible; however, if it falls below $1.00 intrayear it is not removed from the index until the date of the next annual reconstitution. The Frank Russell Company, Tacoma, Washington, a

consulting and investment management firm, constructs the Russell Index series. Historical data for the
Russell 3000 is available from January 1, 1979.

- *Dow Jones U.S. Total Market Index.* The Dow Jones
  U.S. Total Market Index is a relative newcomer to the
  list of broad market indices and represents the top 95%
  of the free-float capitalization of the U.S. stock market; it excludes some infrequently traded stocks. It
  contains slightly more than 1,500 stocks and is reconstituted quarterly; it is also subject to continuous
  review of each security's eligibility. The index is calculated by Dow Jones & Company, creators of the Dow
  Jones Industrial Average and other well-known market
  benchmarks. Price returns and total returns (including
  dividends) for the Dow Jones U.S. Total Market Index
  have been backdated to December 31, 1986.

- *Standard & Poor's 1500 Supercomposite Index.* The
  Standard & Poor's Supercomposite Index was introduced in 1994 and combines the S&P 500, S&P
  MidCap 400, and S&P SmallCap 600 indices to create
  a broad market portfolio representing 90% of the market cap of all U.S. equities. The S&P 500, S&P
  MidCap 400, and S&P SmallCap 600 indices are
  maintained by the S&P Index Committee, whose
  members include Standard and Poor's economists and
  index analysts. The committee's index policy attempts
  to maintain a broad representation of the U.S. economy. Standard & Poor's, New York, New York, a unit of
  McGraw-Hill, Inc., calculates the S&P indices.

- *Russell 1000 Index.* The Russell 1000 Index measures
  the performance of the largest 1,000 U.S.-domiciled
  companies and is reconstituted on an annual basis.
  Each security in the Russell 1000 is float-adjusted and

market capitalization–weighted to ensure investable positions. Low-priced shares, closed-end funds, foreign stocks, ADRs, and several other categories of stocks are excluded. Calculated by the Frank Russell Company, historical data for the Russell 1000 are available starting January 1, 1979. It represents approximately 92% of the total market capitalization of the Russell 3000 Index.

- *Standard & Poor's 500 Stock Composite Index.* For many investors, the S&P 500 is the most widely known gauge of the U.S. equities markets' performance. It consists of 500 stocks selected as representatives of the major industry groups. Stocks are weighted by their market capitalization. While the S&P 500 focuses on the large-cap segment of the market, it does not contain the largest 500 stocks because its goal is to match the broad economy. The index has been compiled since March 1957 (backdated to 1926 both with and without dividends) and represents over 80% of the market cap of U.S. equities. The S&P 500, along with its predecessor index, the S&P 90 (first calculated in the early 1920s), has been used in many well-known studies focusing on long-term stock market performance. It is constructed by Standard and Poor's, a unit of McGraw-Hill, Inc.

Exhibit 3.3 summarizes the key features of these six indices.

IMPLEMENTING THE CORE EQUITY STRATEGY

Fiduciaries can implement a core equity strategy in two main ways: through indexed mutual funds and through exchange-traded funds.

EXHIBIT 3.3

Broad market index comparisons

Index	Wilshire 5000*	Russell 3000	Dow Jones U.S. Total Market	Standard & Poor's 1500 Supercomposite Index	Russell 1000	Standard & Poor's 500
Measurement Objective	Broad Market	Broad Market	Very Broad Market	Broad Market	Mostly Large Cap	Only Large Cap
Investor Access	Partial replication index funds only	Institutional index fund and exchange-traded funds	Exchange traded funds	None; positions can be created out of combination of exchange-traded funds	Index funds, exchange-traded funds, and futures contracts with limited liquidity	Index funds, exchange-traded funds, and liquid futures contracts
Number of Stocks	5,400+	3,000	1,580+	1,500	1,000	500
Weighting	Full Market Cap	Float-adjusted Cap	Free-float Cap	Full Market Cap	Float-adjusted Cap	Full Market Cap
Reconstitution	Monthly+	Annual	Quarterly	Continuous	Annual	Continuous
Established	Dec. 1970	Jan. 1979	Dec. 1986	Jan. 1995	Jan. 1979	To 1957 with predecessor index to 1920s
Percent of Market	100% of U.S.-domiciled, publicly traded equities	89.5% of total U.S. Market Cap	87.5% of total U.S. Market Cap and 95% of Float-adjusted U.S. Market Cap	89.5% of Total U.S. Equity Market Cap (including some non-U.S. stocks)	83.3% of Total U.S. Market Cap	79.3% of Total U.S. Equity market Cap; Non-U.S. stocks about 0.67% of S&P 500 Cap

Turnover[†]	Approx. 3%	3.42%	3.54%	4.10%	3.53%	4.10%
Comments[‡]	Index construction rules are straightforward and objective. Available to public at www.wilshire.com	Index construction rules are detailed and objective. Changes to the construction rules are subject to Advisory Board approval. Available to the public at www.russell.com	Index construction rules are clearly stated, enabling investors to forecast changes in index constituents. Available to the public at www.djindexes.com	Index construction rules are somewhat subjective, leaving room for the Index Committee to apply its judgment. As a result, changes in index constituents cannot be easily predicted.	Index construction rules are detailed and objective. Available to the public at www.russell.com	Index construction rules are somewhat subjective, leaving room for the Index Committee to apply its judgment. As a result, changes in index constituents cannot be easily predicted. A methodological document is available at www.spglobalcom

Note: This exhibit is adapted from *Wilshire Broad Market Indexes*, Wilshire Associates, and *Broad-Capitalization Indices*, Barclays Global Investors.

* *Source:* Wilshire Broad Market Index Comparisons, data as of June 30, 2002, www.wilshire.com

[†] For the year ended December 31, 2002. *Source:* Wilshire Atlas, Wilshire Associates

[‡] *Source:* Francis Enderle, Brad Pope, and Lawrence Siegel The Investment Research Journal from Barclays Global Investors, 2003.

Mutual Funds

Mutual funds have experienced an unprecedented rise in popularity with American households since the Securities Act of 1933 formally regulated the registration and offering of new securities, allowing the creation of mutual funds. A mutual fund is basically an investment company that gathers assets from investors and collectively invests those assets in securities within a specific asset class and stated investment style. By investing collectively, each investor shares in the returns of the fund's portfolio while benefiting from professional portfolio management, diversification, liquidity, and other benefits.

Shareholders are provided with information through the mutual fund's prospectus, which details its goals, fees, and expenses, as well as its investment strategies and risks, among other data. A board of directors, elected by the fund's shareholders to govern the fund, is responsible for overseeing the fund's business affairs and management. Mutual funds are required by law to include independent directors, individuals who cannot have any significant relationship with the fund's adviser or underwriter so that they can provide an independent review of the fund's operations. These mutual funds are considered *open-end investment companies* under federal law for two reasons. First, they are required to redeem (or repurchase) outstanding shares upon a shareholder's request at a price based on the current value of the fund's net assets. Second, although not required, virtually all mutual funds continuously offer new fund shares to the public. Other features of mutual funds include:

- *Variety*. As of the end of 2002, 8,256 mutual funds were available to investors, in a wide variety of investment objectives and offering exposure to a wide range of securities.[2] Many of these funds replicate the broad

U.S. equity market benchmarks, making them appropriate for the passive component of a core-satellite approach.

- *Liquidity*. Mutual funds are required by law to redeem shares daily, making funds a very liquid investment with the processing of sales, redemptions, and exchanges conducted on a daily basis.

- *Accessibility*. Mutual funds are readily available to investors and may be purchased through an investment professional or directly from the fund company itself.

- *Shareholder Services*. Mutual funds offer a variety of services to shareholders, including telephone information, 24-hour telephone access to account information and transaction processing, consolidated account statements, shareholder cost basis information, exchanges between funds, automatic investments, check writing privileges on selected funds, automatic reinvestment of fund dividends, and automatic withdrawals.

- *Affordability*. Finally, mutual funds are available in a broad range of investment styles and asset classes—including passively managed components—and may offer many benefits and services at reasonable prices. This is particularly evident for the smaller portfolio (i.e., less than $1 million).

Mutual Fund Considerations

- *Rule 12b–1 fees*. These fees, named after a Securities and Exchange Commission (SEC) rule, are fees paid out of the assets of a mutual fund share class on a continuing basis to cover marketing and distributions costs. The amount of the 12b–1 fee is expressed as a percentage of the fund's total assets. A fund also deducts certain other ongoing fees from its assets to pay firms that provide various services to the fund, such as the fund's investment adviser, transfer agent, custodian, and administrator. The 12b–1 fees, management fees, and other ongoing expenses are described in each mutual fund's prospectus. These fees will vary from fund to fund and for different share classes of the same fund.

■ *Share Classes.* A single mutual fund, with one portfolio and one investment adviser, usually offers more than one "class" of its shares to investors. Each class represents the same interest in the mutual fund's portfolio; however, the key difference between the share classes is based on different sales and distribution fees charged. Purchasers of Class A shares are typically charged a front-end sales charge or commission (sales charges on mutual funds are also referred to as *loads*) that is included in the price of the fund shares. Investments in Class B shares typically are not subject to a front-end sales charge. Instead, purchasers of Class B shares are normally required to pay a contingent-deferred sales charge (CDSC) if they sell their shares during a specified time period (typically 6 years). In addition, Class B shares are generally subject to higher 12b–1 fees, which result in higher ongoing expenses than Class A shares. For this reason, Class B shares are not, and should not be, viewed as "no-load" shares. Investments in Class C and L shares usually are subject to a smaller front-end sales charge than Class A shares, or no front-end sales charge at all. Purchasers of Class C and L shares are typically required, however, to pay a CDSC if the shares are sold within a short time of purchase, usually 1 year. The 12b–1 fees associated with Class C and L shares are typically higher than those of Class A shares, and these fees continue indefinitely, because the Class C and L shares do not convert into Class A shares. In most cases owning Class C or L shares will be more expensive than owning Class A shares or Class B shares over longer holding periods. Higher expenses will mean reduced investment performance.

- *Pricing.* Mutual fund pricing takes place once at the end of each business day; this price is generally calculated at the close of the New York Stock Exchange, normally at 4:00 p.m. Eastern time. For a fund's share price to be published in the next day's morning newspapers, it must be delivered by 5:55 p.m. Eastern time to NASDAQ.[3] This late-day pricing process often leaves investors "blind" as to the exact value of their fund throughout the day.

Exchange-Traded Funds

Since their creation in 1993, exchange-traded funds (ETFs) have become an attractive alternative to mutual funds. Like mutual funds, they can be used to replicate an index, but with additional benefits such as intraday pricing, unique creation and redemption capabilities, and other features.

Many investment professionals and fiduciaries alike consider exchange-traded funds as a "new and improved" index vehicle because their benefits include:

- *Intraday Pricing and Increased Liquidity.* Exchange-traded funds trade intraday on stock exchanges at

market-determined prices. They are listed on an
exchange and can be bought and sold throughout the
day. Traditional mutual funds, on the other hand, are
always bought and sold at a price equal to the closing
net asset value (NAV), which is based on the closing
price of the fund's investments. In periods of market
volatility, intraday pricing can be an important advantage, offering immediate liquidity and increased trade
flexibility.

- *Low Expense Ratios.* The embedded expense for
  exchange-traded funds can be considerably lower than
  mutual funds because they do not require the services of
  a transfer agent to track shareholders. Exchange-traded
  funds are held in street names and in book entry form
  with the Depository Trust Company, and is placed
  responsibility for accounting with a broker-dealer rather
  than a transfer agent. While this method precludes
  investors from obtaining a physical certificate of ownership, these factors, coupled with the lack of constant
  cash inflows and outflows, can lead to very low expense
  ratios in many cases.

- *Creation and Redemption.* Exchange-traded funds are
  created or redeemed on a daily basis, which means
  that one of the exchange-traded fund's major players is
  the specialist. For example, if there is a strong demand
  for a particular stock, the specialist will move the price
  higher to find sellers. If there is significant selling
  pressure, the specialist will lower the price in an
  attempt to find buyers. In the case of an exchange-
  traded fund, the specialist has another option: to create
  new shares to meet demand or terminate old shares to
  quell supply. This option helps maintain exchange-
  traded funds at or close to their NAV.

- *Tax Efficiency.* The managers of traditional indexed
  mutual funds must meet the need for daily redemptions for cash. This in turn leads to the selling of securities and the possible realization of capital gains. On
  the other hand, cash redemptions in exchange-traded
  funds are for the underlying stocks in the index. In
  exchange-traded funds, individual investors are buying
  and selling shares of the exchange-traded fund on the
  exchange, which also avoids realizing gains within the
  fund. By shipping out the stock, the fund does not
  realize gains.

  Even more important, traditional index mutual fund
  managers will avoid realizing gains by selling their
  highest cost basis stock to meet redemptions. This
  leaves the lowest cost basis stock in the portfolio—
  along with the larger future tax liability. Conversely,
  when an exchange-traded fund receives a redemption
  order, it will ship out is lowest cost basis stock, leaving the highest cost basis stock in the fund—along
  with the lower future tax liability. The redeemer
  assumes the cost basis as of the redemption. When a
  change is made to the constituent of the index and
  turnover is required, the exchange-traded fund should
  realize less in gains as a result. In exchange-traded
  funds the portfolio's exchange-traded fund cost basis is
  based on the actual purchase and sale date and its price
  (which reflects the cost and net asset value of the
  underlying stocks of the exchange-traded fund on
  those purchase and sale dates).

- *Trading.* Finally, exchange-traded funds are margin-
  able, can be shorted (even on a down tick), and,
  because they are listed on an exchange, allow investors
  to use stop and limit orders. Professional managers

often use exchange-traded funds where in the past they would have used futures.

Exhibit 3.4 summarizes the key features of exchange-traded funds and traditional mutual funds.

ADDITIONAL ISSUES FOR MUTUAL FUNDS AND EXCHANGE-TRADED FUNDS

It should be noted that indexed mutual funds and exchange-traded funds might not track their benchmarks perfectly due to cash drag, trading spreads, premium/discount levels, and issues resulting from implementing changes based on index reconstitution or rebalancing. Additionally, some indexes cannot be replicated perfectly due to legal restrictions. These factors all contribute to passive tracking error, discussed earlier.

- *Replication and Optimization.* Because funds are registered investment companies, they must comply with the rules of the Investment Company Act of 1940 (40 Act). In many cases, 40 Act rules may force a fund to deviate from the exact holdings of its underlying index. For example, the 40 Act requires that no fund invest more than 25% of its assets in any single issuer (appreciation can bring that percentage higher); in some cases an index may be composed of more than 25% weighting in any particular security. This rule could result in the fund "optimizing" its holdings by purchasing another security or multiple securities in a similar industry and of a similar style; these replacement securities are judged as closely correlated to the original security. Replications such as this could result in at least a moderate degree of passive tracking error to the benchmark.

EXHIBIT 3.4

Comparison of mutual funds and exchange-traded funds

Exchange-Traded Funds	Mutual Funds
Offer intraday pricing and trading	Typically priced and traded at end-of-day NAV
"In-kind" creation/redemption process can reduce like-lihood of tax-consequent transactions for shareholders	Net redemptions can generate taxable distributions to nonexiting shareholders
Investors purchase/sell shares through an exchange; this does not result in activity in the underlying portfolio and reduces the likelihood of tax consequences for other shareholders	Individual investor transactions—redemptions—with the fund may result in a capital gains tax distribution for nonexiting shareholders
Can be traded with limit orders, stocks, or stock limits (buys and sells) per exchange rules	Limit order pricing not available; transactions typically completed at end-of-day NAV
Standard margin rules apply to purchases	Funds cannot be directly purchased on margin; can be considered "good collateral" only after being held fully paid for 30 days
Offer low-to-moderate expense ratio	Offer low-to-moderate expense ratios depending on fund
Can be traded through any brokerage account	Mutual fund availability through brokers predicated upon negotiated selling agreements; however, funds can be purchased directly from fund company
Normal brokerage account fees apply	Some funds charge sales load; some no-load funds pur-chased through fund supermarkets and brokers may be subject to transaction fees
Early sales/redemption fees do not apply	Fund company may impose fees for "active" trading

(*Source: Barclays Global Investors, www.ishares.com.*)

■ *Cash Drag and Expenses*. Exchange-traded funds typically pay their dividends on a quarterly basis, but the stocks within the fund may pay dividends sporadically throughout the quarter. Therefore, the fund may hold cash in the portfolio while the index is calculated assuming full investment. Most exchange-traded funds hold very little cash, so the drag is moderate, but can cause passive tracking error nonetheless.

Indexes are calculated assuming no fees or trading expenses; however, in the real world, funds have management fees. As a result, all indexed funds will exhibit some level of passive tracking error due to fees.

■ *Fund Implementation*. Finally, indices are calculated, not implemented. When Standard & Poor's makes a change to its S&P 500 Index, the company does not adjust the index actively or alter a portfolio, it simply changes the constituents. Meanwhile, index mutual funds that replicate the S&P 500 must implement the change by trading securities. Given the large amount of assets invested in index funds, a surge in demand— or a glut of a particular security being sold—can add or detract from the ultimate price received for a particular purchase or sale within the fund.

CONCLUSION

The key questions for fiduciaries to address in using the core-satellite approach are:

■ How can an asset allocation strategy be constructed to leverage the benefits of both active and passive investment strategies?

- How much active risk is too much risk?
- Which broad market or style index will serve as an appropriate benchmark for my core allocation?
- Which index strategy, a mutual fund or exchange-traded fund, will best meet my needs for diversification and reduced costs?

The debate fiduciaries should address is not which strategy is the best way to achieve their goals; instead, it should be how to allocate their portfolios between both active and passive management. Fiduciaries should gauge and set their active management risk budgets for their portfolio as a whole and for each active portion. Larger or smaller core investments should depend on their tolerance for risk. Ongoing monitoring—at both the investment policy level and for each individual asset or subasset class component—should be regularly conducted and periodic rebalancing strategies should be implemented.

To conclude, both passive and active investments have an important position in both institutional and private fiduciaries' portfolios. The key steps to implementing a core-satellite approach are to develop a prudent asset allocation strategy, determine an appropriate risk budget, select the ideal broad-market U.S. equity indices, and choose an appropriate passively managed index mutual or exchange-traded fund. Through this process, the risk and return levels of both the core component and satellite portfolios can be manipulated to reach desired goals. The careful implementation of a core-satellite strategy will enable fiduciaries with all types of responsibilities to match their choices about risk and return with their investment objectives.

Investment management consultants may assist fiduciaries in blending active and passive management strategies into a core-satellite portfolio construct. Portfolio expense or an individual fiduciary's active and passive bias preference should not solely drive the decision making. The choices should depend on the portfolio's risk/return profile and investment objectives. A subliminal objective of this chapter is to dispel the myths (usually created for marketing purposes) that exist around the active versus passive arguments that plague fiduciaries. The reality is that both active and passive management strategies may provide synergy to fiduciaries' portfolios. The decision fiduciaries should make regarding active versus passive management need not be selecting one strategy over another. Rather, the primary issue is determining the blend of active and passive strategies in the core-satellite portfolio. A close second issue is selecting appropriate benchmarks for the core. This chapter has focused on the large-cap equity part of the core. The final step considered here was implementing the core equity allocation with index mutual funds or exchange-traded funds. With this framework in mind fiduciaries should be able to set a reasonable course toward achieving the portfolio's investment goals and objectives.

The views expressed herein are those of the author and do not represent the views of the broker-dealer for whom he is employed, its officers, directors, or other employees.

NOTES

1. This section follows a similar discussion in Waring, et al. (2000 Spring), pp. 96–97.
2. 2003 Mutual Fund Fact Book, Investment Company Institute.
3. 2003 Mutual Fund Fact Book, Investment Company Institute.

BIBLIOGRAPHY

Enderle, Francis J., Brad Pope, and Laurence B. Siegel (2003 Spring). "Broad-Capitalization Indices of the U.S. Equity Market," *The Journal of Investing*, pp. 11–22.

Sharpe, William F. (1991 January–February). "The Arithmetic of Active Management," *Financial Analysts Journal*, pp. 7–9.

Trone, Donald B., William R. Allbright, and Philip R. Taylor (1996). *The Management of Investment Decisions*, McGraw-Hill, 1996.

Waring, Barton, Duane Whitney, John Pirone, and Charles Castile (2000 Spring). "Optimizing Manager Structure and Budgeting Manager Risk," *Journal of Portfolio Management*, pp. 90–105.

Core Fixed-Income Management

Ken Volpert, CFA
The Vanguard Group

INTRODUCTION

Over the years, the difficult balancing act that fixed-income managers must perform has hardly become any easier. In fact, the quest to control risk while trying to outpace the market and rivals has grown more challenging as technology and analytics have improved and competition has heightened. But recently, an increasing number of managers have changed their point of attack, moving toward a strategy that combines a relatively predictable "core" with a riskier group of "satellites." This core-satellite approach has gained acceptance because it takes advantage of the benefits of indexing—and indexing-like strategies—but does not forfeit the possibility of outperformance. The key is that this approach acknowledges what piles of data and years of experience have taught many portfolio managers: adding value is possible in certain segments of the fixed-income market, but virtually impossible in others. Essentially, the core-satellite strategy focuses on putting effort in to adding value where it is most likely to succeed.

Though the core-satellite approach is fairly simple in theory, its application requires an in-depth understanding of the various ways to construct a fixed-income portfolio, the strengths and shortfalls of index benchmarks, and the best ways to manage the primary risk factors inherent in fixed-income securities.

TRADITIONAL APPROACHES TO FIXED-INCOME MANAGEMENT

The core-satellite approach marks a significant departure from traditional fixed-income management, but it incorporates many of the time-tested principles. Historically, fixed-income portfolio management has focused on managing a bond portfolio against a high-grade bond index. Risk is managed against a range of risk factors, primarily term structure (interest rate) risk and credit (sector) risk. Active managers generally try to outperform the high-grade benchmark by taking interest rate risk relative to the benchmark, by overweighting mortgage and/or corporate sectors, and by investing outside the index; for example, placing a portion of their portfolios in high-yield and emerging-markets debt. Some of the more sophisticated fiduciaries employ a strategic allocation to the high-yield sectors and the emerging markets, managed by specialist managers.

The spectrum of managing traditional fixed-income portfolios as shown from left to right in Exhibit 4.1 generally includes:

- Pure indexing, or very close to pure indexing, through which the manager attempts to match—as close as possible issue for issue—the weights within the respective benchmark.
- Matching the primary risk factors to the index in a credit-diversified portfolio.

■ Allowing for minor mismatches relative to the index in factors such as cash-flow distribution, sectors, and quality in an attempt to add value.

In these three cases, duration bets are typically nowhere to be found.

But as a manager moves to the more "active" end of the spectrum, larger mismatches are common. They center around cash-flow distribution, sector, quality, callability, and interest rate risk or duration risk. The hope, of course, is that this added risk is paid off by returns which are meaningfully greater than those of the benchmark and which, therefore, offset the higher active-management fees and larger transactions costs.

MOVING TO THE CORE-SATELLITE APPROACH

Though many of these traditional approaches are alive and well, many fixed-income managers have moved a few steps beyond this conventional model and are building portfolios

EXHIBIT 4.1

Traditional bond management spectrum

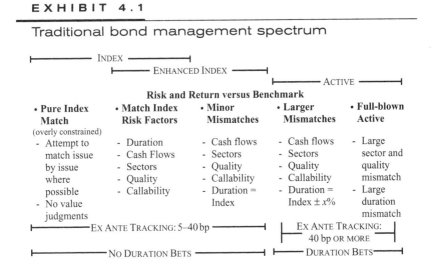

with a conservative, low-cost (often index-based) core, and satellites that may encompass a variety of active strategies. As shown in Exhibit 4.2, a core portfolio is typically managed against a broad, liquid benchmark within a tight risk budget (generally under 40 basis points ex-ante tracking error versus the benchmark).[1] The first investment approach within the core classification is the "risk-factor matching" approach. In this strategy the manager creates a broadly diversified portfolio that closely replicates primary index risk factors such as duration, cash-flow distribution, sectors, quality, and callability. The ex-ante tracking error is expected to be below 20 basis points, because this high-quality, liquid bond market is assumed to be competitively priced.

The expected opportunity to outperform the index is very limited. Therefore, the objective is to match and replicate the risks and generate the returns of the target benchmark at the lowest possible cost (management fee and transactions costs).

The second investment approach within the core classification is the "minor mismatching" approach. Here, the man-

EXHIBIT 4.2

Core-statellite risk spectrum

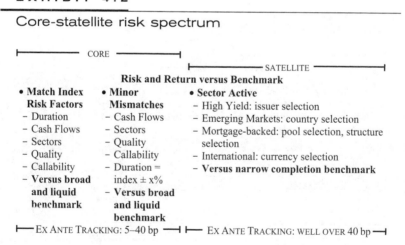

ager is given a larger risk budget (20–40 basis points) to mismatch relative to broad liquid benchmark characteristics such as cash-flow distribution, sector and quality weightings, and even duration, to a limited extent. The expectation is that the manager will add value relative to that broad benchmark. As a result of this expected added value, the manager would also have a higher fee structure.

The satellite portion focuses on the less-liquid sectors that have lower correlations with the broad liquid core. This manager is given a smaller pool of assets and a much larger risk budget relative to the narrow benchmark. This bigger risk budget provides opportunity for the manager to take meaningful selection, sector, and quality risk relative to the benchmark, with the expectation of adding considerable value.

Examples of such narrow, less-liquid markets include high-yield and emerging-market bonds.[2] In the case of the high-yield market, issuer and sector selection are primary determinants of added value versus the benchmark. Within emerging markets, country selection is a driving force in adding value. In many cases, the mortgage-backed market is also viewed as a satellite market due to the many structural complexities that are based on interest rate volatility risk. Securities with exposure to foreign currencies may be considered satellites, as could inflation-protected securities.

A key requirement of the satellite component is that it acts as a diversifier and that it has a higher expected return due to its illiquidity and lower credit quality.

THE BENEFITS OF THE CORE

The beauty of the core portfolio is that it generates the full market return for taking on the market's undiversifiable primary risks, namely, interest rate and credit risk. Naturally, an investor is not paid for taking risks that can be diversified away.

An effectively managed core portfolio should be broadly diversified at the issuer, sector, and quality levels relative to the benchmark, such that the idiosyncratic (issue specific) credit risk and any other specific risks are minimized. The result is a portfolio that compensates the investor for market risk. Such a core provides risk control and competitive performance.

- *Risk control:* The Lehman Brothers Aggregate Index, which is designed to capture the entire U.S. investment grade bond market, is an excellent example of a broad liquid index. As of June 30, 2003, it had well over 7,000 issues and more than $8 trillion in market value. A broad bond portfolio designed to track this index would replicate closely the exposures across sectors— and even closely among many of the largest issuers— such that the returns would be closely matched to the returns of that broad market benchmark. This high level of diversification minimizes exposure to uncompensated risk.

- *Competitive performance:* Because the cost structure of core management is considerably lower than the average cost structure within the fixed-income markets—and certainly within the traditional style of fixed-income management—the after-expenses (net) return that is earned by core investors is higher. Here's why: By definition, the sum of all investments within fixed-income portfolios is "the market" index. Core investors are able to invest in that market portfolio at a far lower cost (operating expenses and transaction costs), resulting in a portfolio that should meaningfully outperform the average manager within the same universe. A corollary argument is the consistent *relative* performance that the core provides. The cost advantage works for the investor year in and year out, providing competitive performance annually, and especially over longer periods of time, as the advantage compounds. Exhibit 4.3 shows how difficult it has been for active managers to outperform this broad market index.

Moreover, the core portfolio also provides a significant but often overlooked benefit for investors. It allows them to focus their attention on the most important decisions: asset allocation and satellite-manager selection. Very often, fiduciaries (plan sponsors, foundations, etc.) are unwisely focused on trying to add a few basis points in competitive core markets (and paying high fees to do so). In reality, they should be spending their energy on making an effective and appropriate

EXHIBIT 4.3

Percentage of intermediate investment-grade bond funds outperformed by the Lehman Aggregate, 1989–2002[3]

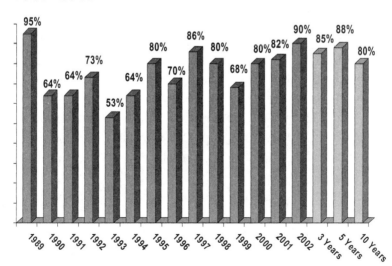

asset allocation decision and on evaluating the important qualitative factors of their satellite managers.

THE BENCHMARK SELECTION

As strange as it may seem, both the core and satellite slices rely heavily upon index benchmarks. For the core portion, an index benchmark serves largely as a target; for the satellite portion, an index serves as a reference point to help identify opportunities for differentiation. That's why it's important to understand the composition of various benchmarks and to select those that best represent the segment of the market that a portfolio is trying to match—or beat.

Most bond indices are rules-based. These rules typically specify minimum standards or levels for such characteristics as quality, maturity, and issue size to determine whether an issue is included in the index. The issues that meet the rules are then aggregated together into a theoretical portfolio, with the weights based on the outstanding market value of each issue.

The most widely used U.S. investment-grade benchmark is the Lehman Aggregate Bond Index. The Lehman U.S. Aggregate, as of June 30, 2003, was composed of 34% government bonds, 34% mortgage bonds, and 32% corporate and asset-backed securities. The quality distribution for the Lehman U.S. Aggregate and other broad Lehman indices are shown in Exhibit 4.4. Other less widely used broad U.S. indices include the Citigroup U.S. Broad Investment-Grade Bond Index (BIG) and the Merrill Lynch U.S. Broad Market Bond Index.

Exhibit 4.4 displays the percentage allocation of four broad Lehman bond indices by quality ratings. These ratings are widely used by the bond market as indicators of credit risk.

Four major private, independent companies provide these bond ratings: Moody's Investors Services, Standard & Poor's Corporation, Duff and Phelps Credit Rating Company, and Fitch Ratings. Many regulators and fiduciaries rely on these companies to assess credit risk. While there are some important differences in technique, these four companies essentially calculate their ratings the same way—by analyzing the company's financial information to determine how likely investors are to receive promised interest and principal payments over the life of the bond. Their ratings use similar symbols and are structured from investment grade with high creditworthiness (Aaa through Baa), to distinctly speculative with low creditworthiness (Ba through B), to predominately speculative with substantial risk or already in default (Caa through D).[4] These credit ratings are changed as the rater's perceptions of underlying risk change. The markets respect these ratings and accord a higher yield to lower-rated bonds. Notice that in Exhibit 4.4 these broad indices generally avoid any significant allocation to bonds below investment grade.

An index that is even broader than the Lehman U.S. Aggregate (but not as widely used, due to the below-investment-grade holdings) is the Lehman U.S. Universal Index. This index also includes emerging market and high-yield debt, 144a securities, and eurodollar bonds. The Lehman Aggregate represents 88% of the market value of the U.S. Universal, so the returns and risks of the Lehman U.S. Aggregate Index drive that of the Lehman U.S. Universal.

From a global fixed-income standpoint, the Lehman Global Aggregate Bond Index is a tremendously broad, liquid benchmark. This index includes government, corporate, and mortgage securities. Broader still is the Lehman Multiverse Index, which like the U.S. Universal also includes high-yield and emerging-market bonds. About 96% of the Lehman

EXHIBIT 4.4

Benchmark selection: Lehman index quality analysis

Quality Rating	Core: Broad U.S. Dollar*	Composite: Broad U.S. Dollar†	Core: Broad Global‡	Composite: Broad Global§
Aaa	74.8%	68.2%	57.4%	55.9%
Aa	5.1	5.4	12.6	11.8
A	10.3	9.8	24.6	23.1
Baa	9.8	9.3	5.4	5.1
Ba	0.0	3.1	0.0	1.7
B	0.0	3.1	0.0	1.8
Caa	0.0	0.8	0.0	0.3
Ca	0.0	0.2	0.0	0.1
C	0.0	0.0	0.0	0.1
D	0.0	0.0	0.0	0.0
Not Rated	0.0	0.1	0.0	0.1
Total	100.0%	100.0%	100.0%	100.0%

* Lehman U.S. Aggregate Bond Index
† Lehman U.S. Universal and Inflation Protected
‡ Lehman Global Aggregate Bond Index
§ Lehman Multiverse and Global Real

Source: Lehman Brothers Index Data (U.S. Universal and Multiverse Indices, June 30, 2003)

Multiverse Index is represented by the Lehman Global Aggregate Index.

A core portfolio is designed to be managed against the most liquid segments. It is these high-quality, liquid sectors that are most competitive and where opportunities to outperform the market through security selection are limited.

The less liquid sectors (high yield, emerging markets, etc.) can then be used as satellite benchmarks, sometimes called *completion benchmarks*. Typically, these benchmarks are weighted so that the overall risk and sector weights map to the broadest U.S. or global benchmarks. Broad benchmarks can also be customized to include additional satellite sectors such as inflation-protected securities or mortgage-backed securities, or can be tilted in accordance with the investor's desired risk preference. Exhibit 4.5 shows an example of both domestic and global care-satellite portfolios using the core and composite indices from Exhibit 4.4.

As you would expect, combining a broad composite benchmark with lower-correlation components reduces the

EXHIBIT 4.5

Benchmark selection: core, satellite, and composite

Broad U.S. Dollar Benchmark Domestic Example	% of Bench- mark	Market Value $ billion
Core: U.S. Aggregate + other		
U.S. Universal Investment Grade	90.9%	$8,609.6
Satellite: U.S. High Yield	5.2	493.5
Satellite: U.S. Emerging Markets	2.0	188.5
Satellite: U.S. TIPS	**1.9**	**179.3**
Composite: Total U.S. Universal + TIPS	**100.0%**	**$9,470.9**
Broad Global Benchmark Global Example		
Core: Global Aggregate	93.8%	$18,171.1
Satellite: U.S. High Yield	2.6	507.9
Satellite: Pan-Euro High Yield	0.3	64.9
Satellite: Global Emerging Markets	2.0	224.6
Satellite: Global Inflation Protected	1.8	400.6
Composite: Total Multiverse + Global Real (Inflation Protected)	**100.0%**	**$19,369.1**

Source: Lehman Brothers Index Data (U.S. Universal and Multiverse Indices, June 30, 2003)

volatility of returns. For example, Exhibit 4.6 shows that adding a high-yield index to the Lehman Aggregate Index reduced
the return volatility by 5% for the period January 1999 through
June 2003. Adding nondollar investment-grade markets
(Lehman Global Aggregate and Lehman Multiverse Index),
hedged against currency fluctuations, reduced return volatility
by 22% and 24%, respectively. Similar risk reduction is available for euro-based investors.

The driving force behind this reduced volatility is the low
correlation among major bond markets of changes in relationships between securities with different maturities (slope of the
yield curves). Exhibit 4.7 shows that the correlation between

EXHIBIT 4.6

Benchmark risk comparison

U.S. Investor (USD hedged)	Monthly Return Standard Deviation	Risk Reduction vs. U.S. Aggregate
Lehman U.S. Aggregate	0.99	
Lehman U.S. Universal	0.94	−5%
Lehman Global Aggregate (USD hedged)	0.77	−22%
Lehman Multiverse (USD hedged)	0.75	−24%
Euro Investor (EUR hedged)	**Monthly Return Standard Deviation**	**Risk Reduction vs. EUR Aggregate**
Lehman Euro Aggregate	0.91	
Lehman Global Aggregate (EUR hedged)	0.79	−13%
Lehman Multiverse (EUR hedged)	0.77	−15%

the daily "slope" changes of the three major global bond markets (U.S., Euro region, and Japan) is between 0.29 and −0.04. This low correlation results in risk reduction as large unfavorable moves in one market are partially offset by less significant moves or opposite moves in another market. Because of their broad diversification, global investment-grade (currency-hedged) benchmarks such as the Lehman Global Aggregate or the Lehman Multiverse Index are the most mean-variance efficient bond benchmarks available. Too often, however, the international aspects of the risks discourage investors from seriously considering these benchmarks.

PRIMARY "CORE" BOND PORTFOLIO RISK FACTORS

The key to effectively managing the core bond portfolio is matching the primary risk factors of the benchmark in a credit-diversified portfolio. Exhibit 4.8 lists the risk factors that are inherent in the government, corporate, and mortgage sectors. The following section includes suggestions for ways to

EXHIBIT 4.7

Global term structure diversification, 10-year to 2-year curve slope changes: daily from 1/1/1999 to 6/30/2003

	Standard Deviation	Correlation of Daily Slope Changes		
		U.S.	Euro	Japan
U.S.	0.034	1.000	0.294	0.024
Euro	0.029		1.000	−0.044
Japan	0.026			1.000

effectively manage these risks. Though each factor differs in composition and complexity, a common theme runs through all of them: During tumultuous periods, even minor mismatches can result in major performance gaps.

Modified Adjusted Duration

The modified adjusted duration (or option-adjusted modified duration) is a simple measure of interest rate risk. For full management of the term-structure risk, however, it is entirely too rough of a measure. (*Duration* is defined in Chapter 1.) Duration gives the manager a rough approximation of the price change observed if interest rates immediately rise or fall (in a parallel fashion) by 1%. If rates rise by 1%, a 5-year duration

EXHIBIT 4.8

Primary "core" portfolio risk factors

	Government	Corporate	Mortgage Bond Sector
Modified Adjusted Duration	✓	✓	
Present Value of Cash Flows	✓	✓	
Percent in Sector and Subsector		✓	
Percent in Quality		✓	
Duration Contribution of Sector		✓	
Duration Contribution of Credit Quality			
Sector/Coupon/Maturity Cell Weights		✓	✓
Issuer Exposure Control		✓	

portfolio will experience a 5% decline in value [(+1% yield change) × (5-year portfolio duration) × (−1)]. If the yield curve does not move in a parallel fashion, then the duration is of limited value. For obvious reasons, an important but probably insufficient risk control technique is to match the duration of the portfolio to the duration of the benchmark index.

Present Value of Cash Flows

A more complete method of controlling yield curve risk is by matching the cash-flow distribution of the benchmark. Yield curve changes can take a variety of shapes: parallel shifts, curve twists (e.g., short rates down, intermediate rates unchanged, long rates up), and curve butterfly (e.g., short and long rates down, intermediate rates up) movements. The market value of the benchmark and the portfolio can be calculated by decomposing the benchmark and the core portfolio into a stream of future payments, discounting each payment to the present value, and then summing these values. By closely managing the portion of the core portfolio's present value that comes due at certain intervals in time with that of the benchmark index, the portfolio's *relative* performance will be largely immune to yield curve changes. See Exhibit 4.9 for an analysis of the cashflow distribution and duration contribution of the Lehman aggregate.

For callable securities, the cash flows need to be distributed to the time vertices in accordance with the probability that they are redeemed before maturity. A 10-year bond that is highly likely to be called in 3 years should have cash flows that are primarily allocated to the 3-year vertex.

Note: Because the portfolio's duration is equal to the benchmark index's duration (duration is the sum of all vertices, as shown in Exhibit 4.9) of the percent of present value

Cash flow distribution analysis for the Lehman
Aggregate, July 31, 2003

Time	% of Value	Duration Contribution	% of Index Duration
0	3.0%	0.00	0.0%
0.5	6.9	0.03	0.8
1	8.8	0.09	2.0
1.5	10.6	0.16	3.6
2	13.1	0.26	5.8
3	13.2	0.40	8.9
4	9.9	0.39	8.8
5	7.6	0.38	8.5
6	5.2	0.31	6.9
7	4.2	0.30	6.6
8	4.0	0.32	7.2
9	3.5	0.32	7.1
10	3.9	0.39	8.6
15	3.2	0.48	10.7
20	1.6	0.32	7.1
25	1.0	0.24	5.4
30	0.3	0.08	1.9
40	0.0	0.01	0.2
Total	100.0%	4.48	100.0%

multiplied by the vertex (time), this method will guard against
parallel changes in yield. Because all points in time are closely matched, any local term structure movements (nonparallel
changes) will not affect performance relative to the benchmark.

Percent and Duration Contribution by Sector (and Subsector)

The sector and subsector risk is effectively managed by matching the portfolio's duration contribution in the various sectors and subsectors with that of the index—assuming that all maturity categories are fully accounted for by the core portfolio. During most periods of spread volatility, managing the duration contribution exposure is adequate. Exhibit 4.10 lists the sector and quality exposures and their duration contributions for the Lehman aggregate.

Using July 2002 as an example, Exhibit 4.11 illustrates the risk that sector volatility can introduce into a portfolio. It presents the range of excess returns (return above or below a Treasury security of similar maturity) for BBB-rated issues that have 5- to 6-year durations. The vertical bars represent 1 standard deviation above and below the mean for each sector. (The longer the bar, the wider the range.) The obvious message is that during periods of economic stress and market illiquidity, the range of sector performance varies widely.

Percent and Duration Contribution of Credit Quality

The yield of the index is largely replicated by matching the percentage weight in the various quality categories, assuming that all maturity categories are fully accounted for by the core portfolio. As in sector risk management, both duration contribution and absolute differences are important.

During most periods of spread volatility, managing the duration contribution to the benchmark works well. However, during periods of severe market turmoil, such as in July 2002, managing the percentage difference versus the index, especially for BBB-rated securities, takes on the utmost importance.

EXHIBIT 4.10

Sector and quality distribution analysis for the
Lehman Aggregate Bond Index, June 30, 2003

Sector	Market Value ($ billion)	% of Present Value	Duration	Duration Contri-bution	% of Duration
Treasury	$1,782.7	21.9%	5.92	1.29	32.78%
Agency	991.2	12.2	4.22	0.51	12.99
Industrial	959.8	11.8	6.76	0.80	20.15
Finance	750.5	9.2	5.09	0.47	11.86
Utility	182.8	2.2	6.35	0.14	3.61
Foreign Agencies	54.1	0.7	2.99	0.02	0.50
Sovereign	131.5	1.6	5.83	0.09	2.38
Foreign Local Govts	58.5	0.7	7.23	0.05	1.31
Supranational	100.8	1.2	3.85	0.05	1.20
GNMA	434.1	5.3	0.69	0.04	0.93
FNMS	1,379.2	16.9	1.08	0.18	4.63
FHLMC	971.5	11.9	1.10	0.13	3.32
ABS	147.8	1.8	2.70	0.05	1.24
CMBS	204.9	2.5	4.86	0.12	3.09
Total	$8,149.5	100.0%		3.95	100.00%
Quality					
AAA	$6,090.1	74.7%	3.24	2.42	61.3%
AA	417.8	5.1	5.35	0.27	6.9
A	840.9	10.3	5.86	0.60	15.3
BAA	800.7	9.8	6.62	0.65	16.5
Total	$8,149.5	100.0%		3.95	100.0%

EXHIBIT 4.11

Sector and subsector risk, July 2002. Range of
excess returns (average ±1 standard deviation)
BBB-rated issues, 4- to 6-year duration with over
5 issues in the sector bucket (430 issues)[5]

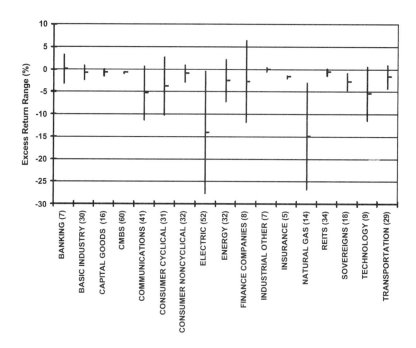

Exhibit 4.12 shows the range of excess returns for July 2002
for 4- to 6-year duration BBB-rated credit securities. Here we
see a very wide range of returns between the higher rated
bonds and BBB-rated bonds.

Sector/Coupon/Maturity Cell Weights

The call exposure of a benchmark index is a difficult risk
factor to control. The convexity value (*convexity* measures how
a bond's duration changes as yield levels change) alone is

EXHIBIT 4.12

Quality rating risk, July 2002. Range of excess
returns (average ±1 standard deviation), all credit
issues, 4- to 6-year duration by rating category
(1,313 issues)[6]

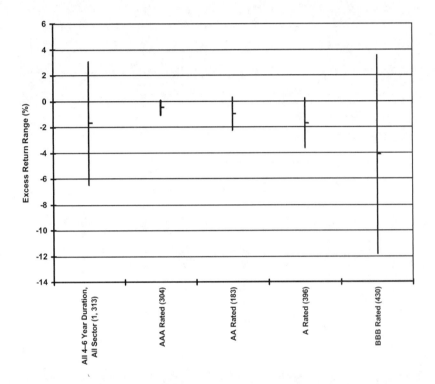

inadequate as it measures expected changes in duration over a
small change in yield. In addition, the change in convexity can
be very different as yield levels change. Managers who attempt
only to match the benchmark's convexity value often find
themselves having to buy or sell highly illiquid callable securities to effectively manage this risk. In the process, they generate excessive transaction costs. A better method of matching
the call exposure is to manage exposure to the sector, coupon,
and maturity weights of the callable sectors. By managing the

exposure to these factors, the convexity should be effectively controlled relative to the benchmark. In addition, as rates change, the changes in call exposure of the portfolio will closely approximate that of the benchmark, requiring little or no rebalancing.

In the mortgage market, call (prepayment) risk is very significant. The volatility in the option-adjusted duration of the Lehman Brothers Mortgage Index, which measures the extent of the call exposure of the mortgage market, is shown in Exhibit 4.13. Also shown is the Mortgage Bankers Refinancing Index (inverted), which measures mortgage refinancing activity. Clearly, the greater the refinancing activity, the shorter the index duration. This is because of the greater likelihood that the higher-coupon securities will be replaced with lower-coupon debt. For this reason, matching the coupon distribution of the mortgage index is critical. The best risk management is accomplished by managing the portfolios versus the benchmark's exposure in a multidimensional matrix of the maturity (balloon, 15-year, 30-year); sector (FNMA, FGLMC, GNMA); coupon (0.5 percent increments); and seasoning (new, moderate, and seasoned). This level of detail is easily accomplished in a large portfolio (more than $1 billion in assets), but far more difficult in smaller portfolios.

Issuer Exposure

It is possible to match an index's major risk factors but still leave a core portfolio open to significant risk. Simply put, the fewer issues that are used for matching, the more susceptible the portfolio to the risk that a single—or several—issues dent a portfolio's relative and absolute performance. To properly manage such risk, a portfolio manager must measure and control both "event" risk, which occurred most notably during the

EXHIBIT 4.13

Mortgage call exposure analysis

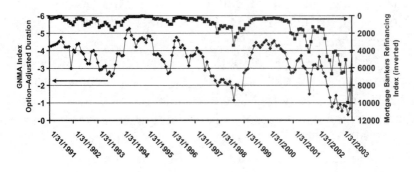

leverage buyout frenzy of the late 1980s, and "default" risk, which is widely experienced during periods of economic weakness (e.g., July 2002). As with sector and quality exposure, issuer exposure is best measured in terms of both percentage and duration contribution.

Setting boundaries for deviations versus the benchmark in any one issuer provides protection from these unlikely—but potentially damaging—risks. Periods such as July 2002, illustrated in Exhibit 4.14, point to the importance of such limits on the commitment to specific issuers. In that month alone, nearly 15% of the issuers in the credit index had excess returns (the difference between the issuer's return and that of a similar duration Treasury) below −5%. Almost 80% of the issuers had excess returns below 0%. Owning overweight positions in too many of the hardest-hit issuers would have significantly hurt the performance of the core portfolio relative to the benchmark—even if the high-level matching was sound.

Spread-widening risk that occurs due to occasional negative earnings surprises or supply-driven factors can be managed effectively by calculating how much of the portfolio duration ("duration contribution") comes from the holdings in

EXHIBIT 4.14

Issuer selection risk, July 2002 distribution of credit excess returns by issuer

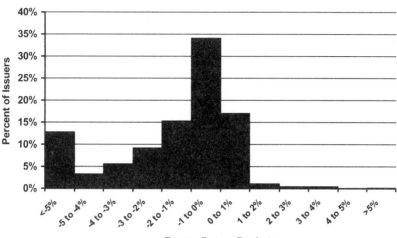

each issuer. This calculation should also be figured for the benchmark. The basis point impact of a spread-widening event on performance of the core portfolio relative to the benchmark is calculated this way: the spread change (of the issuer) is multiplied by the difference in duration contribution (portfolio − index) multiplied by −1. Exhibit 4.15 contains an example of this analysis. Issuer XXX Corp. has an equal percent weight (4% of market value) to the index, but its duration contribution is 0.16 greater (0.32 versus 0.16). If an event occurred that would widen the XXX Corp spread by 100 basis points, the portfolio would suffer an unfavorable tracking difference of 16 basis points versus the index (100 basis point spread change × 0.16 duration contribution overweight × −1). If the same widening were to occur to XYZ Corp. bonds, the tracking difference would be a favorable 8 basis points (100 basis point spread change × −0.08 duration contribution underweight $\times$ -1), even though the percent weight is matched to the index. The bottom line: For effective index fund management, duration contribution exposure limits (versus the index) need to be set at the issuer level.

CONCLUSION

The core-satellite approach is an effective method of managing fixed-income exposure. It recognizes that there are markets that are competitively priced, where active management is unlikely to add value over the long run. In these markets, the best course of action is to follow a core portfolio management strategy that attempts to gain the market's exposure at a low cost, through either matching the benchmark via indexing, or trying to modestly beat the benchmark through structured active bets within a tightly constrained risk budget.

When effectively managed, the core approach has the advantage of gaining the full market return with uncompensated risk minimized, at the lowest cost.

For the markets that are not as competitive or liquid, the satellite approach is used. Satellite managers employ active security selection strategies with the goal of meaningfully outperforming more narrow benchmarks. The combination of the two approaches results in a broadly diversified portfolio that offers the potential for enhanced performance—but also a limited amount of risk.

ACKNOWLEDGMENT

The author thanks Ian A. MacKinnon, who recently retired as head of Vanguard's Fixed Income Group, for his many years of mentoring, wisdom, leadership, and friendship. Thanks, Ian!

EXHIBIT 4.15

Issuer exposure comparison percent of market value versus duration contributions

	Portfolio			Index			Portfolio-Index	
	% of Market Value	Duration	Duration Contribution	% of Market Value	Duration	Duration Contribution	% Difference	Contribution Difference
XXX Inc.	4	8	0.32	4	4	0.16	0	0.16
ZZZ Inc.	4	4	0.16	4	4	0.16	0	0.00
XYZ Inc.	4	2	0.08	4	4	0.0	0	-0.08

N O T E S

1. See Chapter 3 for an extended discussion of tracking error and risk budgeting.
2. These and other satellite asset classes are discussed in Chapter 5.
3. *Source:* Lipper Inc. and The Vanguard Group. Aggregate index return is less 20 basis points estimated index fund expense ratio.
4. These rating classifications and those in Exhibit 4.4 follow Moody's system. The other companies are similar.
5. *Source:* Lehman Data.
6. *Source:* Lehman Data.

PART II

Satellite Asset Classes

CHAPTER 5

Satellite Bonds– Opportunities in High Yield and Distressed Debt

Clifford A. Sheets, CFA

In this chapter we provide a general description of the high-yield bond market so that the fiduciary can assess its potential role in a core-satellite portfolio. The high-yield bond market is a very complex segment of the overall bond market, with several unique aspects that distinguish it from the much larger and more liquid investment-grade sectors of the bond market covered in Chapter 4. While many of the same characteristics are shared across the leveraged finance spectrum, they tend to be more apparent and heightened within the high-yield corporate market. Later in the chapter we discuss in broad terms the market for distressed debt, an even more esoteric market that lies at the far end of the quality spectrum, as its name suggests.

Bond quality ratings are used as the technical basis for demarcating the high-yield spectrum.[1] Bonds rated below investment grade (i.e., below Baa3 by Moody's or BBB– by Standard & Poor's) are considered high yield because investors demand a higher yield to compensate for the higher default risk. Generally speaking, the term *high yield* is used in reference to high-yield domestic corporate bonds, though a smaller universe of below-investment-grade debt exists issued by various other entities such as sovereigns (national governments) or various structures which issue asset-backed debt. Another term synonymous with high yield is *junk bonds*, which invokes the negative connotation that at times seems quite appropriate given the risks associated with high yield.

TYPES OF HIGH-YIELD DEBT

The most common form of high-yield debt encountered in the marketplace is publicly traded notes issued by corporations that are rated below investment grade by one of the major bond rating agencies. These bonds or notes are generally senior unsecured obligations within an issuer's capital structure. That is, they represent a general obligation of the company issuing the bonds, the payment of which is dependent on the general creditworthiness of the issuer. No specific collateral is pledged against this type of issue (i.e., they are unsecured). They have the highest claim on assets of the company within the spectrum of unsecured debt, hence are termed *senior*. The ranking within the capital structure is critical in the assessment of a high-yield bond's value because the outcome in terms of recovery value in the event of bankruptcy on the part of the issuer will be highly influenced by the bondholder's status. If multiple levels of debt are issued they are called *subordinated* or *junior subordinated bonds*. Any convertible bonds are generally junior to the senior unsecured debt of the issuer as well.

The phrase *publicly traded* simply means that these bonds are readily traded, usually between large institutional buyers and sellers via a brokerage firm. While many of these bonds are registered with the SEC, most new high-yield issues will come to the market in a more expedited fashion as *144a securities*. This term refers to an exemption from registration requirements if the bonds are sold to "qualified institutional buyers," as opposed to the general public. This exemption saves the issuer the up-front time of meeting all of the SEC registration requirements, with the presumption the buyers are sophisticated enough to know what they are doing when they buy such securities. The bond will generally include a provision requiring the company to register the notes within a certain time, say 6 months, or face some penalty such as a higher coupon rate. Many "144a issues" remain as such and yet, because of the size of the issue and visibility of the borrower, usually a large corporation with publicly traded stock, these bonds are liquid and trade as easily as fully registered issues of comparable quality.

Often a high-yield issuer will also have bank loan agreements in place and the company's most liquid assets, such as inventory and receivables, usually secure any borrowings under these agreements. Bank debt is generally considered senior secured and any public unsecured bonds would be subordinate in claim to an issuer's bank loans. Bank loans for a high-yield issuer tend to carry fairly onerous covenants which require the issuer to meet certain financial objectives within specific time parameters or risk slipping into technical default.

The bank loan market for leveraged loans, or loans to high-yield-rated issuers, is a large over-the-counter market. These so-called syndicated bank loans are those sold to parties outside the original lending group of banks, mostly large non-banking credit lending institutions, including mutual funds (such as "prime rate funds"), insurance companies, hedge funds, and trusts set up to hold bank loans. The loans that trade are generally Term B loans which represent the longer-term portion of a loan package and are typically structured essentially with a single maturity date (bullet maturity), with minimal amortization prior to maturity. Leveraged loan packages will also typically consist of Term A loans which are shorter in maturity and generally retained by the original banking group. Bank loans are almost always structured as a floating-rate obligation with the rate based on LIBOR (London InterBank Offer Rate) usually with 1 or 3 months to maturity, with the pricing set as a spread above this base rate. They also generally lack call protection and can be repaid by the borrower at par at any time, which gives the borrower some flexibility should they obtain longer-term financing. By virtue of their structural characteristics, including their senior secured status, bank loans are often viewed as an attractive high-yielding alternative to the public high-yield bond market, especially for those lenders who prefer to receive a floating rate.

Another less sizeable component of the high-yield market consists of private placement loans that are made by large institutions such as insurance companies or private fund managers on behalf of fiduciaries to companies with less than investment-grade ratings. Occasionally a borrower and lender will negotiate directly, but these loans are usually arranged by investment bankers working for the borrower and distributed to a few large sophisticated lenders. Traditional private placements are not registered with the SEC and are purchased with the intent of being held to maturity by the lender. In recent years many of these issues contain "144a language," though they still remain much less liquid than the larger market of public high-yield debt. Private placements can be an attractive alternative to the borrower if they are a more obscure company that would have difficulty appealing to the public market, or are borrowing for a special purpose or in a smaller amount than is typical of the public market. The advantage to the lender is generally in the form of an enhanced set of financial covenants required of the borrower, and a yield premium for the lack of secondary market liquidity of the issue.

Lastly, in completing a review of the various types of high-yield debt, it is important to acknowledge emerging-market debt rated below investment grade. This is a market consisting of bonds issued by foreign countries as sovereign obligations and, to a lesser extent, high-yield-rated corporations domiciled in such countries. The countries making up this market are those classified as *developing* and are represented by countries with less advanced economies and financial systems than are typical of the larger industrialized economies. Most of these countries consist of those located in Central and South America, Southeast Asia, and the Eastern Europe region. Some of the larger issuers of debt include countries such as Brazil, Russia, and Argentina, all of which have a history of defaults. This is a large and viable market, providing attractive yields associated with lower-rated issues. Moreover, the issuing sovereign governments, being noncorporate entities, differ from U.S. high-yield corporate borrowers in the factors driving their ability and willingness to pay their debts. While presenting an element of diversification of risk within the broad high-yield market, and thus another potential satellite asset class, suffice it to say this is a unique sector requiring specialized management. For our purposes we will not go into depth on this market, but rather concentrate on the more mainstream U.S. high-yield corporate bond market.

MARKET HISTORY

High-yield bonds represent a relatively young segment of the fixed-income market. The asset class became recognized more broadly during the mid- to late-1980s when many marginal credit issuers (*credits* in market parlance) were first able to access the public market, having previously found acceptance only among bank lenders. The increased issuance of high yield was associated with the surge in highly leveraged financial restructurings that were occurring at that time, often as part of a leveraged buyout (LBO). The development of this market was spurred by the efforts of an upstart investment bank, Drexel Burnham Lambert, a West Coast–based firm which handled many of the LBO transactions of that time. This firm and its lead investment banker, Michael Milken, pioneered the market for high-yield corporate bonds. The controversy associated with the financial tactics of the LBO and its impact on the various constituencies of a corporation, combined with certain legal abuses, eventually led to the demise of Drexel in 1989. With the absence of Drexel as the primary market maker for many Drexel-originated bond deals and with the recession that began in the fall of 1990, the high-yield market experienced a dramatic decline, suffering poor returns in 1989–1990 as default rates escalated.

After defaults peaked in 1991 the sector began to grow as issuance increased with the economic rebound in the early 1990s. The mid-1990s marked an era of growing respectability for this market as default rates ebbed and returns were very compelling. As the economy picked up steam in 1996 we began to see the great boom in new issuance, with the telecom sector particularly popular as emerging telecom companies came to the public equity market and they began to expand in a challenge to the Baby Bells. Other technology credits were also beginning their dramatic expansion, though issuance in this sector was limited, given their greater reliance on equity capital and less need for debt-financed capital expenditures when compared to telecoms. This boom in debt issuance led to a dramatic increase in the proportion of the high-yield market represented by the telecom and cable sectors. At its peak in mid-2000, the telecom sector represented approximately 25% of most U.S. high-yield indices. This growth in telecom sector representation presented a potential conflict for benchmark-driven managers who may have felt compelled to own large holdings of telecom which exposed their portfolio to large losses when this sector suffered its dramatic downturn.

Beginning in 1999 the corporate debt bubble started to erode, with high-yield debt feeling the initial impact. This seeming inconsistency of poor debt performance during a still-growing U.S. economy at the time was explained by a combination of factors which speak to the complexity of forces that can impact high yield. Some of the primary factors explaining this decline were simply the economic realities faced by many of these companies after a debt-financed binge. First, the issuers in this market, given their lower credit quality, were vulnerable to any erosion in profits and cash flows as industrial America suffered in the wake of the Asian fallout in 1997–1998 and its attendant deflationary pressures. This slowdown in the industrial economy resulted in a moderate pick-up in defaults after a period of below-average default experience during the middle part of the decade. Another important factor leading to rising default trends was simply the surge of issuance in the seemingly benign period of 1997–1998, when many marginal credits that should not have come to market were able to because of the easy-money environment of the time. Defaults began to escalate in 1999 as the high-yield market entered the second major default wave of its lifetime. This default wave peaked in 2001, but economic distress during 2002 and at the time of this writing has caused default rates to remain at historically high levels. These default trends are shown in Exhibit 5.1.

The high-yield market has grown dramatically since the mid-1990s, both through new issuance and the rating agencies'

EXHIBIT 5.1

Issuer defaults, 1987–2002[2]

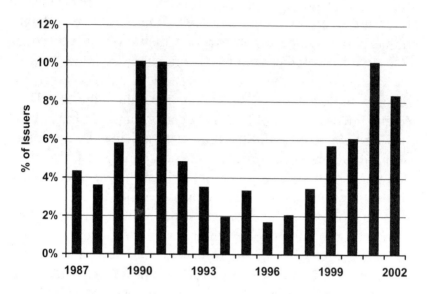

downgrade of investmcnt-grade-rated names. In 2002–2003 this downgrade effect created a record volume of so-called fallen angels. According to Moody's the number of investment-grade credits that were downgraded to high-yield status in 2002 reached a record 5.2% of issuers, up dramatically from just over 2% in 2001. As a proportion of the high-yield market these fallen angels represented 11% of issuers as of the end of 2002, the highest proportion since 1986.

Based on the Lehman index the U.S. corporate high-yield market consisted of $548 billion at face value and $552 billion at market value as of the end of May 2004. This compares to a market size of only $69 billion at face value as of the end of 1991, after the market had just weathered the last major default wave. Market growth is a function of new issue supply less redemptions, as well as downgrades and defaults, and depends largely on financing conditions. Because of the difficult market environment and general lack of demand in 2002, there was only $24 billion of net supply. This compares to a peak of $111 billion in 1998. The market recovered dramatically in 2003, with lower financing costs and strong demand spurring a surge in both originations and redemptions for a net supply of $71 billion. This is a large and viable market, though at times it may feel a lot smaller when liquidity is impaired during times of market stress.

COLLATERALIZED DEBT OBLIGATIONS

A relatively new type of financial structure has created an important factor in the demand for high-yield debt. Collateralized debt obligations (CDOs) are special purpose trusts created to hold various types of collateral and fund themselves by issuing debt obligations. The concept is based on an arbitrage between the yield earned on the collateral and the cost of funds from borrowing the needed capital. While these structures were initially used in the case of high-yield collateral, there also have been many large structures created for the purpose of holding investment-grade corporate debt as well as asset-backed securities. High-yield-backed structures consist of both collateralized bond obligations (CBOs) and collateralized loan obligations (CLOs), depending on the type of underlying collateral held within the structure. The bonds issued by these structures range across the quality spectrum and typically consist of a most-senior tranche[3] that is AAA-rated, followed by one or more subordinate classes, which may be rated from investment grade to high yield, plus a tranche of equity capital. This capital structure is accomplished by credit-tranching the various issues so that even high-yield-rated collateral can produce a tranche with a high rating. The process is complicated and depends on a host of assumptions, the primary one being the default rate of the underlying collateral. The structures are designed to absorb a certain number of expected defaults, with returns to the equity capital being hit first, followed by the subordinate debt tranches. The AAA tranche will presumably be insulated even under the worst of circumstances.

Many professional high-yield managers sponsor CDOs and act as collateral managers, receiving an asset-based management fee for their efforts. This business has been growing for investment managers specializing in credit management during the late 1990s, as mandates for pure high-yield asset management assignments slowed while demand for CDO debt grew, in part because of the ostensible safety of the investment-grade-rated debt issued by the structures. This market's emergence and ability to flourish would not have been possible without the benign default environment of the mid- to late-1990s. The complexity of managing a pool of collateral backing a CDO obligation should not be underestimated. To obtain ratings for the debt issued in support of such structures, the rating agencies impose a number of tests. These tests are designed to protect the buyer by imposing certain restrictions on the manager's actions with respect to the collateral. Some of the common tests involve measures of overcollateralization, diversification, ratings, and industry limits. These often hamper the ability to actively manage the collateral and as a result these structures are sometimes more susceptible to credit deterioration than a fully discretionary portfolio of high-yield bonds.

While these instruments can be purchased as an apparent investment-grade-rated bond, it is important to understand that the underlying performance of the high-yield collateral will ultimately determine how much will be returned to its various forms of capital. While the most senior tranche is highly protected from loss, given the underlying subordination in the structure, even it can still suffer significant market deterioration if collateral performs poorly. Many of these former AAA- and AA-rated bonds have suffered poor market price performance as collateral default rates exceeded the original assumptions when the structure was created, leading the agencies to downgrade the various CBO or CLO bonds. Some have even experienced realized losses of principal if collateral defaults were so excessive that insufficient cash was available in the structure to meet maturities. This is particularly true for structures created in the 1997–1998 period when default rate assumptions were unrealistically low and the quality of many issuers was poor. For fiduciaries who allocate a portion of their satellite portfolio to high yield, it is important to understand whether their manager will use any high-yield-rated debt issued by a CDO structure because credit risk is magnified with these holdings by virtue of the structure itself.

ASSET CHARACTERISTICS AND RETURNS

The high-yield bond market has changed over time as issuers have come and gone, influencing the characteristics of the outstanding debt that make up this market, though certain features remain in place. The market is predominantly made up of industrial companies. The communications sector represents about 83% of the market value as compared to 50% of the investment-grade corporate bond market. The utility sector represents the next largest major sector at 15%. The dearth of financial sector issuers in this market is simply based on the realities of that sector which make it very difficult for an issuer with a high-yield rating to achieve a sufficiently low enough cost of funds to survive. Another key feature of the market is its maturity profile. It tends to be a market dominated by bonds with an intermediate term to maturity of 5 to 10 years. Moreover, the bonds making up this market generally carry weak call protection, with a typical new issue having a 10-year maturity and only 5 years of call protection. As a result it is unusual to see the market trade at a substantial premium to par value as interest rates decline, even when bonds in general trade at a small premium to Treasuries of similar maturity.

Returns for the high-yield asset class are largely driven by expectations of credit quality and thus the likelihood of receiving promised interest and principal payments. These expectations in turn derive from general macroeconomic conditions, the access to capital by lower-rated credits which may depend on equity market conditions, and the willingness of the banks to lend. Times of poor market liquidity and higher risk premiums are generally associated with poor high-yield returns. Ironically, while defaults were peaking in 1991, the market experienced the highest return on record, as prices rallied in anticipation of better times ahead. Exhibit 5.2 shows historical returns for high-yield debt overall by rating class within the market and returns for U.S. credit, a proxy for the investment-grade corporate market

As can be seen in Exhibit 5.2, high-yield returns from 1984 through 2002 have been volatile compared to U.S. credit and have suffered over the last 5 years. The data in Exhibit 5.3 suggest, however, that high-yield returns have been competitive with investment-grade bonds (U.S. credit) and stocks (the S&P 500) over longer time periods.

For example the high-yield composite index had a higher return and higher risk (standard deviation) than U.S. credit from 1984 through 2003 and for all listed subperiods except

E X H I B I T   5 . 2

Historical returns on high-yield assets and U.S. credit, 1984–2003.[4]

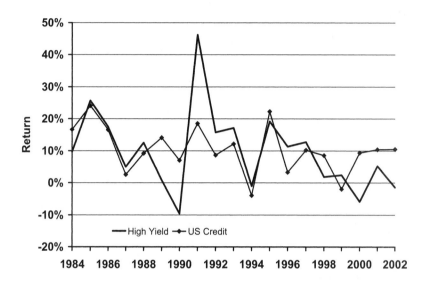

1984 through 1989. Note, too, that high yield's component rating categories (B, Ba, and Caa) were not all that similar, with Ba occasionally providing a higher return than Caa, while Caa almost always had a higher risk. The returns and risks from 1984 through 2003 in Exhibit 5.3 are plotted in Exhibit 5.4, which emphasizes the differences in the rating categories that make up high yield and shows that, for this period, the rating categories within high yield generally reflected higher return for higher risk.

The correlations in Exhibit 5.5 suggest that high yield often moves in the same direction as equities, but not always. The historical correlation between high yield and stocks was positive, although weak, with a correlation coefficient of 0.463 over 20 years.[5] The correlation with investment-grade

EXHIBIT 5.3

High-yield returns and risks by rating category compared to U.S. credit and stocks, 1984–2003[6]

Average Return	High Yield	Ba	B	Caa	U.S. Credit	S&P 500
1984–2003	11.66%	11.76%	11.17%	12.72%	10.59%	13.24%
1984–1989	11.86%	14.63%	11.52%	3.35%	13.85%	18.30%
1990–2003	11.58%	10.54%	11.03%	16.73%	9.19%	11.07%
1992–2003	10.46%	10.20%	9.98%	14.48%	8.59%	10.64%

Standard Deviation	High Yield	Ba	B	Caa	U.S. Credit	S&P 500
1984–2003	15.11%	9.47%	14.28%	35.32%	7.20%	17.06%
1984–1989	7.89%	8.93%	6.76%	8.33%	8.19%	10.92%
1990–2003	17.41%	9.84%	16.53%	41.41%	6.94%	18.87%
1992–2003	14.40%	9.23%	13.86%	38.46%	6.94%	19.18%

EXHIBIT 5.4

Risk and return from high-yield rating categories and other asset classes, 1984–2003[7]

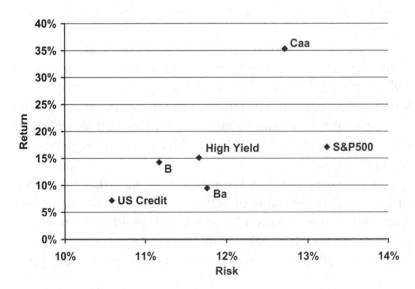

Historical correlations between high yields, U.S. credits, and stocks, 1984–2002

	High Yield	Ba	B	Caa	Ca-D	US Credit	S&P 500
High Yield	1.000						
Ba	0.897	1.000					
B	0.994	0.869	1.000				
Caa	0.938	0.756	0.933	1.000			
U.S. Credit	0.538	0.737	0.502	0.332	0.369	1.000	
S&P 500	0.463	0.537	0.461	0.323	0.145	0.374	1.000

credit was similar at 0.538. These correlations suggest an allocation to this sector should provide diversification benefits in a core-satellite portfolio.

When considering expected returns for this asset class it is important to bear in mind that the sector has a high level of volatility when compared to other debt classes. This volatility derives naturally from the increased level of risk associated with lower credit quality and is exacerbated by periodic bouts of poor liquidity that can hurt returns. This variable can work both ways as was witnessed in 1991 when the Fed was flooding the financial system with liquidity. Another important characteristic to remember is that high yield is an over-the-counter market that does not provide an exchange-based degree of pricing transparency. Secondary market prices are determined by the demand and supply for specific issues as buyers and sellers transact through security dealers. Pricing transparency is particularly poor with less actively traded issues or those suffering from distress due to specific company developments. As a result, pricing accuracy is poor during periods of heightened anxiety as spreads widen and liquidity becomes more constrained. This can lead to opportunity for astute managers, but also suggests that short-term returns be taken with a grain of salt when market conditions are especially volatile.

DIFFERENCES BETWEEN HIGH
YIELD AND CORPORATE BONDS

As explained at the outset of this chapter, the spectrum of corporate credit quality is divided in terms of market classification into investment-grade issues, generally referred to as *corporates*, and the below-investment-grade issues, or high yield. While the market for corporate debt is divided based on rating, it remains a continuum of credit quality, with certain features more predominant at the ends of the spectrum. A key dimension in which high yield differs from corporates is in terms of its interest rate sensitivity. While the market prices of all bonds are influenced by changes in benchmark U.S. Treasury yields, or swap rates, the lower-quality bonds that make up the high-yield asset class are much less sensitive to these changes than higher-rated corporates. Instead, the credit sensitivity of the asset class dominates its price behavior, with the lowest end of the spectrum driven almost entirely by the unique fundamentals of the issuers and the likelihood that they will survive and meet their obligations.

At the crossover point of the ratings spectrum, or low Baa/BBB, a corporate bond is most vulnerable to poor performance if expectations turn negative for the issuer and the prospect for a rating downgrade increases. If perceptions of a negative credit outlook grow, the bond may behave more like high yield than investment grade. Ratings often will lag the reality of a bond that trades like high yield, meaning simply that the market is anticipating a downgrade below investment grade. By the time many of these issuers reach official high-yield status they have already experienced the bulk of their price deterioration. As noted earlier, these so-called fallen angels increase in occurrence as credit quality deteriorates in the wake of a weaker economy and access to capital becomes more difficult. Typically the propensity for downgrade and potential default is most prevalent within the high-yield spectrum, as one would expect given their lower ratings. Yet credit conditions deteriorated so dramatically in 2002 that we saw a dramatic spike in the downgrade rate for investment grade, reaching a record 22% of issuers. This almost equaled the downgrade rate within the high-yield market, which peaked at 27% in 2001 and fell slightly to 25% in 2002. These figures are a record for high yield as well, which experienced its previous peak downgrade rate of 24% in 1990 at the worst of the last credit cycle.

This environment increases the importance of active credit management. The heightened level of downgrades experienced by issuers do not always lead to default, though lower ratings are clearly associated with a higher probability of default. Moody's reports on the U.S. cumulative default rates, as measured by dollar volume, not issuers, over 5-year intervals during the period 1994–2002, show that 4% of outstanding investment-grade corporate debt suffered default as compared with 24.8% of outstanding high-yield debt. The volume of B-rated defaults was over twice that of Ba-rated debt at 27.7% as compared to 11.3%. This seemingly natural tendency for corporate debt to deteriorate over time underscores the importance of active credit management, particularly within the high-yield market. While the emphasis of late has been on avoiding downgrades, both from investment grade and within the high-yield spectrum, in better times the ability to spot potential upgrades can add substantial value to a managed high-yield portfolio.

Another typical distinction between high-yield-rated issuers and investment grade borrowers is that bank loans provided to more highly rated credits are typically unsecured and rank equally with the outstanding bonds of the company. As noted earlier, with a typical high-yield issuer the bank loans have seniority and receive a higher recovery value in the event of bankruptcy. This is well understood by professional high-yield managers and an accepted reality of the asset class. However, when a previously investment-grade borrower falls into the high-yield spectrum due to downgrade, the bankers become very nervous given their lack of security, and thus advantage over the bondholders, as credit risk escalates. In a variety of recent cases involving downgrades of large investment-grade borrowers with substantial outstanding bank debt, the credit decline has been so precipitous that the company has been forced to renegotiate with its banks to avert a liquidity crisis. In such cases the bank lenders are more inclined to provide liquidity in the form of a maturity extension or additional credit only if they can attain priority status over the bondholders. When this occurs, and if the borrower eventually defaults, the now high-yield bondholders are in a subordinate position and their recovery prospects will suffer. Understanding an issuer's capital structure and where the bonds stand is critically important in the high-yield market, particularly as that borrower's credit quality deteriorates.

One important management technique that applies to any prudently managed credit portfolio is diversification, in terms of both industry and company exposures. In the wake of several individual company blowups during 2001–2002, many professional managers have an even greater appreciation for this strategy. As the degree of defaults increased in this time period and secondary market liquidity became more limited for several deteriorating credits, having a very diverse portfolio has been one way to minimize the effect of an individual company surprise. These negative surprises have been most apparent within the investment-grade arena, where fraudulent accounting practices were revealed, as with Enron and WorldCom, leading to downgrade and almost immediate default. Similar events have hit the high-yield market (e.g., Adelphia), but within this market the uncertainty has always been higher. Nevertheless, the high level of defaults and negative ratings trend in high yield has increased the importance of holding a very diverse portfolio. To control these risks, a manager will typically hold less than 0.5% of the portfolio in any one credit, especially for names rated less than Ba/BB.

DISTRESSED DEBT

If *high yield* is a polite way of referring to junk bonds, then *distressed debt* is a nice way of describing nuclear waste. These are bonds or loans that conventional owners do not want because the companies that have issued them have descended into bankruptcy, liquidation, or have a high risk of ending up in either position. Broadly speaking, there is a heightened probability these debt obligations will see their original contractual terms modified or voided, usually via a Chapter 11 bankruptcy filing. Yet in times of severe credit market stress, as witnessed in 2001–2002, distressed opportunities may arise that do not involve a bankruptcy. A general definition that is sometimes used to define this asset category is any bond trading at a spread greater than 1,000 basis points above Treasury yields, or at a yield-to-maturity above 20%. During the most recent credit cycle downturn the proportion of the high-yield market that met this definition exceeded 20%. While typically rated at the bottom of the high-yield spectrum, ratings do not always tell the story because they often tend to lag market realities. Sometimes even an investment-grade-rated bond will temporarily fall out of favor and represent a distressed opportunity. However *distressed* is defined, it does not mean these assets do not have value. In fact if bought at the right price and managed appropriately, these instruments can offer very attractive double-digit returns. The key is to be able to look out beyond the issuer's current difficulties and make an assessment of the underlying value, whether in terms of a surviving franchise or assets worth more than the cost of the debt in question.

This is an opportunistic asset class. While there is always some troubled company with outstanding debt even in the best of times, recessions in the wake of a debt bubble like that witnessed in the second half of the 1990s will produce a vast number and dollar volume of opportunities, as we have painfully learned. A similar process of destruction in the credit market occurred in the 1990–1992 period in the wake of the prior recession. The symptoms leading up to a high level of downgrades and defaults are almost always easy to recognize after the fact, but it is difficult during good times to envision such a negative scenario.

Banks and insurance companies invest in the credit markets and have historically embraced credit-related assets as a primary holding. To varying degrees they take on credit risk to support their own returns sufficient to pay their cost of capital and hopefully earn a positive return for their shareholders. Through prudent management practices most of these firms have internal limits on credit risk exposure, both to investment-grade and high-yield-rated assets. Many of these institutions are also highly regulated or have their own rated debt outstanding and thus face external restrictions that limit their exposures. As a result of these institutional preferences, biases, and restrictions, a downturn in the credit cycle can accelerate as these lenders stop providing additional liquidity and in some cases sell the assets they own that are at risk of downgrade or default. A fundamental shift in the supply and demand for corporate debt occurs, creating the ideal conditions for a distressed-debt manager. Unfortunately their opportunities and potential profits come at the expense of the original owners of these debt obligations who absorb the brunt of the credit losses that occur. Forced selling by institutional holders of distressed debt creates the imbalance that can drive asset prices to extreme lows, setting up opportunities for a distressed-debt buyer. These sellers might be an investment-grade bond mutual fund, an insurance company, or a bank which may believe the bond will eventually recover but still must sell because of restrictions or fears that limit their ability to hold such debt.

The nature of distressed debt almost always creates a market condition in which it is murky and difficult to maneuver in any size. A cloud of uncertainty usually surrounds a distressed credit and trading can be sporadic and difficult to track. Remember that the market for the vast majority of corporate debt is an over-the-counter market where pricing is less transparent than with listed securities such as common stocks. As a result of these factors the distressed market is more volatile than the high-yield market. Dedicated distressed-debt managers must have nerves of steel to stick to their positions in the face of the uncertainty surrounding a distressed credit, particularly in the early stages of a problem when asset values and survivability are more difficult to judge. As a result of the often-limited trading activity and poor pricing transparency, the returns for a fund of distressed debt are very difficult to assess over a short time frame. Quarterly returns are almost meaningless. A fiduciary allocating to distressed debt must have a multiyear horizon. The manner of participating in this market and manager attributes will be discussed later in this chapter.

The recovery rate on defaulted debt issues is a critical variable driving distressed debt returns. Ultimate recovery of value from a defaulted obligation is difficult to measure because the resolution of bankruptcy often involves the distribution of new debt, equity, and assets over time frames that vary after the date of default. Therefore, a common method of measuring recovery rates is to use prices 1 month after default as the best proxy. Obviously for any seller or buyer of defaulted debt, the recovery rate will vary depending on when the trade occurs. While every situation is different, the most important variables influencing recovery on a default are the obligation's position within the company's capital structure and the amount and form of assets backing the claim. Thus, secured bank loans averaged the highest recovery rate, at 62% of face value between 1982 and 2002, according to Moody's. This falls to only 37% for senior unsecured bonds. The level of recovery suffered during the 2001–2002 period, as one might expect given the increased supply of distressed debt, with the average issuer-weighted recover price for senior unsecured bonds falling to 34% in 2002.

Recoveries can also be heavily influenced by industry-specific fallouts. This was apparent in 2002 as the implosion of the telecom sector culminated in the bankruptcy of WorldCom. The volume both in dollar terms and number of issuers defaulting in this industry pulled recovery rates down. On an issuer or equal-weighted basis the 2002 recovery rate for all defaulted bonds was 34%, but this rises to 39% when telecom debt is excluded. On a dollar-weighted basis the recovery rate looks even worse given the large size of many defaults in 2002. On this basis the average for all bonds was 26%, but rises to 34% when telecom is excluded.

A competent distressed-debt manager will beat the averages by selectively acquiring debt positions representing varying levels of claim at prices that ultimately prove profitable. Their holding periods are often longer than the arbitrary 30 days used in determining recovery rates for statistical purposes. Further, it is important to note that a portion of their holdings may not even be in default but have suffered some blow to their credit outlook that provides a trading opportunity as an imbalance in market supply and demand occurs.

MANAGEMENT OF HIGH YIELD AND DISTRESSED DEBT

High-yield asset managers can be found among a variety of institutions that have a broad capability of managing credit-related assets. While many financial intermediaries own credit-based loans and bonds, this does not mean they are prepared to offer professional management services to fiduciaries. Some organizations, typically smaller banks and insurers, may own loans and bonds that were purchased with the intent to hold them to maturity as a core asset with limited up-front due diligence and analysis. On the other hand, larger organizations have very capable internal credit management units that focus strictly on their own proprietary assets. Large banks, for example, will underwrite leveraged loans for their own use with no intent of offering fee-based services to outside entities.

Many large banks and insurance companies will offer high-yield management services through an affiliated money management organization that benefits from the firm's skill set. Banks and brokerage firms generally set up these organizations as stand-alone units that deal only with third-party funds. They are required to avoid the legal improprieties of gathering nonpublic information from the banking side. In the case of many large insurance companies the distinctions may not be so clear organizationally. Even though the company may have created a registered investment adviser, they may also act as manager of the company's own proprietary assets.

While the synergies of sharing a dedicated credit staff may add value to the process, these organizations must be careful to treat all clients, both affiliated and external, with fairness. There are also many competent independent fee-based money management companies. Some of these may also offer a family of mutual funds which includes a high-yield fund. Managers organized as mutual fund companies will many times offer a separate institutional management service which provides dedicated separate high-yield account management for mandates of substantial size. Depending on the manager, a separate account minimum would typically fall around $30–50 million. Thus for fiduciaries with a smaller allocation to high yield the most practical alternative may be to find a registered mutual fund or other form of commingled account[8] that will accept large investment amounts.

Many high-yield managers will leverage their core credit management capabilities to act as the manager of CDOs as discussed earlier in this chapter. The trusts set up to hold the managed collateral are nothing more than an innovative way to source assets by creating a structure that is self-funded by issuing its own liabilities and equity in the institutional marketplace. Typical CDO managers include large insurance companies, independent money managers, and hedge fund operations. While CDOs do not represent a practical high-yield investment vehicle for a fund sponsor, you will often see a high-yield manager tout its role as a sponsor and manager of a CDO as evidence of its capabilities in this arena. If this is the case, it is important to ask about the status of the CDO and its underlying collateral. While these structures have their own idiosyncrasies and require specialized management skills, their track record will help demonstrate a high-yield manager's general level of competence.

Distressed debt managers primarily consist of privately owned firms within the hedge fund universe that have a core skill set focused on managing leveraged finance. Periodically these organizations will offer limited partnership (LP) interests to their investors, with the manager acting as general partner. The partnership provides a means of participating in a large pool of distressed debt since all capital is combined and used to acquire positions, much like a mutual fund but without the regulatory oversight. These LP offerings tend to be more prevalent and larger in size at times when default rates are high and therefore distressed debt supply is high, even though distressed does not always mean defaulted. Often it does, and these funds play an important role in providing the demand for these assets as they go through workout and some level of eventual recovery. These partnerships are generally set up as either controlling or noncontrolling, with *control* meaning the intent of accumulating the debt to obtain control of the ultimate ownership of the issuer or a substantial enough position to control any restructuring. The tactics and types of positions acquired in the case of a control-oriented manager may be quite different than those of the noncontrolling manager where the focus is typically over a shorter horizon. A control-oriented partnership will often take positions that are less liquid and require a longer workout. Some firms operating in this arena will invest globally, requiring foreign restructuring management skills, though the bulk of these offerings will focus on the U.S. debt market, which has provided plenty of supply in recent years, unfortunately.

Another important consideration in allocating funds to distressed debt involves liquidity or the lack thereof in this case. Limited partnerships are a long-term investment and generally require investors to lock up their funds for the term of the partnership. Some general partners may allow a secondary sale of an LP interest at their discretion, but it is discouraged and is not a practical exit strategy. The typical term of a distressed debt LP fund is 7 to 10 years, consisting of an investment period of 3 to 4 years, followed by a distribution period over the balance of the life when underlying investments are liquidated and capital is returned and profits distributed.

It is also worth mentioning that even among the institutions that do not provide distressed debt management offerings to fund sponsors, there are often specialists on staff that deal with distressed debt. These institutional holders of distressed debt are usually the banks and insurance companies that owned the same bonds and loans before these assets fell out of favor. They can be viewed as involuntary holders that simply want to work their way out of the positions with the best recovery values possible. While holding such debt may not have been the best experience on the way down, these holders do not want to give away the paper when events are expected that will lead to some recovery above the fire sale prices that they would otherwise be forced to accept.

An important attribute in looking for a dedicated high-yield manager is the degree of organizational commitment to the management resources involved, whatever the type of firm. As I hope I was able to convey earlier in this chapter, the successful management of high yield and distressed debt requires specialized skills. A good manager must have enough critical mass under management that they can afford the talent needed to be effective. This talent entails a solid group of experienced credit analysts that understand the variety of industries and companies that exist in this market. Their capabilities must include not only the ability to perform rigorous financial statement analysis, but also the skills to assess management capabilities and industry prospects. In many respects a good high-yield or distressed debt analyst must also be an equity analyst. In addition to the analytical talent, competent portfolio manager skills are needed to construct and oversee a portfolio. Most portfolio managers are former analysts who have a broad background and good sense of market dynamics that can affect pricing beyond the basic knowledge of whether a credit is good or bad. Many of these skills are only gathered over many years of hard lessons in the marketplace.

As with all investment decisions, not all work out as expected, even with the best talent available; therefore, it is important to look at the manager's capabilities and track record over time. Another critical skill set within a competent money management shop, particularly one specializing in distressed debt, is legal support, whether internal or external to the firm. Any workout scenario entails an assessment of the legal standing of the debt holder and the relative priority and control presented by a particular niche in the capital structure. Understanding how the bankruptcy process works is fundamental to any workout and will shape the expectation of the amount and timing of any recovery.

FEES

The management fee for a separate high-yield account will primarily depend on account size, with the larger an account the lower the percentage fee since most managers offer a graduated fee structure. Generally the fee is for advisory services only and the fund sponsor also must pay the associated custodial fees associated with the portfolio. Custodial fees are typically quite minimal, and range 2–5 basis points. The fee for advisory services for a large high-yield portfolio will typically range 20–50 basis points. In the context of a mutual fund the underlying fees are likely to fall in a much broader range depending on the particular investment firm offering the fund. The total expense ratio for a high-yield fund will typically range from 25 to 100 basis points. Smaller fund sponsors that choose to participate in this asset class via a mutual fund should be careful to avoid funds that carry a sales charge or load, whether structured as an up-front or deferred load. There are plenty of respectable mutual funds to choose from without having to pay this unnecessary cost. In some cases the mutual fund sponsor may offer an institutional class of shares with lower underlying costs. Advisory fees for high yield will always run higher than for investment-grade fixed-income management because of the unique skills required to be successful. Nevertheless, these costs can be justified given the value provided by a good manager. Performance over a given time period will normally exhibit a wide range across managers, making the selection of the manager an important decision, much as with an actively managed equity allocation decision.

In the case of distressed debt, the investment expense is imbedded in the partnership structure. Typical hedge fund fee structures apply which involve a base management fee of 1 to 2%, based on the amount committed, and a performance-based fee on the amounts funded. This incentive fee, also called *carried interest*, will depend on the particular LP and is generally 20% of profits. In many cases these partnerships offer a preferred return, say 8%, over which any profits are shared between the general partner and limited partners in a 20/80 ratio. While these costs look exorbitant on the surface, and indeed they are high, they represent the price of participating in this asset class, which if managed successfully, can provide attractive returns in the 15–20% area net of expenses.

SUMMARY

High-yield debt is a viable satellite asset class within the fixed-income arena. It offers a return and risk profile that can provide a diversification benefit with large portfolios. While sharing many fundamental similarities with investment-grade bonds, its lower quality rating makes the asset class more sensitive to economic conditions and specific company factors that will drive returns, independent of the trend in interest rates. Distressed debt is a special asset class within the credit-related arena and should be considered only by large fund sponsors in small quantities as part of an alternative asset allocation. While it shares some of the characteristics of the high-yield market, it operates in a marketplace that is even less transparent. It is a more opportunistic sector that provides the best return prospects after a major credit cycle downturn. Both high yield and distressed debt require specialized management skills that are best found among dedicated credit management organizations.

N O T E S

1. See Chapter 4 for a description of bond ratings.
2. Source: Moody's Investor Services
3. Tranches are created by directing the cash flows from the underlying collateral to different classes of bondholders. In the case of high-yield debt different tranches accept different levels of credit risk.
4. Source: Lehman Brothers.
5. See Chapter 2 for a discussion of correlation.
6. Source: Lehman Brothers.
7. Source: Lehman Brothers.
8. Commingled accounts are like mutual funds in that they pool the assets and offer shares to more than one investor. They differ from mutual funds in that they are not sold to the general public and are not governed by the same registration requirements.

Separate accounts that receive funds from only one investor are a common alternative.

9. See Chapter 2 for a discussion of mutual funds and loads.

B I B L I O G R A P H Y

Lehman Brothers, *High Yield Monthly Review*, May 7, 2003.
Moody's Investor Services, *Default and Recovery Rates of Corporate Bond Issuers*, February 2003.

Management of Currency Fluctuations Associated with International Investments

Ranga Nathan, CFA
Principal, InvestMatrix Inc.

INTRODUCTION

Returns on investments that are denominated in a foreign currency are dependent on two factors: (a) asset returns as measured in that foreign currency; and (b) the exchange rate fluctuations between the foreign currency and the investor's domestic currency. This chapter deals with the impact that currency fluctuations can have on overall returns. As a fiduciary you should be aware of the effect of hedging or not hedging your portfolio's currency exposure. We will assume for the purposes of this chapter that the exposure comes from satellite investments in foreign equities or bonds. We will also examine the circumstances under which active currency overlay programs are feasible. Finally we will touch on measuring the effectiveness of generic overlay programs.

SAMPLE INDEX PORTFOLIOS

To illustrate the concepts in this chapter, we use as examples two foreign-currency–denominated portfolios, across the 10-year period ending in 2002. The portfolios are: the Dow Jones UK Index (DJU) and the Dow Jones Japan Index (DJJ). Because the context is the core-satellite approach, we will be measuring these equity investments (satellite allocations) against the S&P 500 Index (S&P), the widely used U.S. equity benchmark (core).

These two foreign portfolios were chosen deliberately to represent widely different characteristics:

- During the 10-year period, the DJJ lost about 24% of its value, whereas the DJU gained about 88%, both measured in their respective currencies. Exhibit 6.1 shows the performance of these indexes, as well as that of the S&P (values set to 100 on December 31, 1992).
- As suggested by the closeness of their paths in Exhibit 6.1, the DJU has a relatively high correlation with the S&P (0.90), whereas the DJJ has a low correlation (0.31).
- Exhibit 6.2 shows the year-by-year currency values for the two currencies, pound sterling (STG) and Japanese yen (JPY) (values reset to 100 on December 31, 1992). Even though they both appreciated over the 10-year period by approximately the same extent, they arrived there via two different paths. The correlation between the two was only 0.29.

IMPACT OF FOREIGN
CURRENCY FLUCTUATIONS

Exhibit 6.3 summarizes the impact of foreign currency fluctuations on the DJU and DJJ, as seen from the viewpoint of a

Dow Jones U.K. (DJU) and Dow Jones Japan (DJJ)
index performance versus the S&P 500 Index

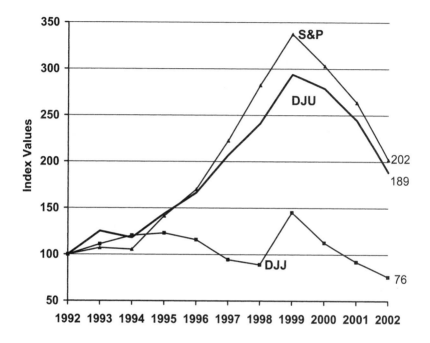

U.S. investor. The exhibit shows the overall return and the two
constituent components: the asset index return in its home currency and the currency return for both portfolios. The overall
return is the product of the two components.

When analyzing the impact of a component, we do not
look at the overall return. For example, in 1993 the overall
return from investing in UK assets was 22.4%. However, the
currency fluctuation had a 2.2% impact (in this case, negative
impact) while the assets contributed 25.1% (positive). The
overall return hides the separate effects of the two components.
The impact, therefore, of each component (exchange rate fluc-

E X H I B I T   6 . 2

Relative performance of pound sterling (STG)

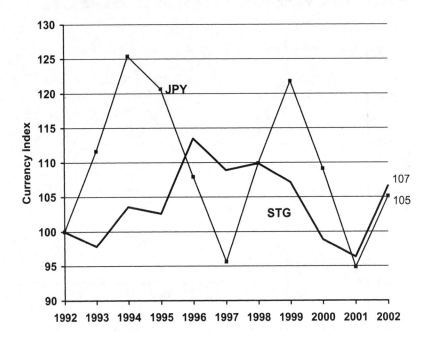

tuation and index of assets in the foreign currency) for any year is better measured as the *absolute* value of the change in that component. Over time the average impact (e.g., 4.8% for sterling and 17.2% for the Dow Jones UK Index in sterling) is the average of such absolute values for each component over the 10 years. Relative impact is the average impact of a component divided by the total of the average impacts of the two components, e.g., 22% = 4.8/(17.2 + 4.8).

As can be seen in Exhibit 6.3, in the case of the DJU, the STG fluctuations had a relative impact of 22% on the overall returns for a U.S. investor. The currency impact was 39% for the DJJ. It has been shown that the currency impact is sub-

E X H I B I T   6 . 3

Impact of asset index returns and foreign currency fluctuations (FX) on overall returns, 1993–2002 (all returns in percent)

| | Dow Jones UK (DJU) | | | Dow Jones Japan (DJJ) | | |
Year	Overall Return	Index in STG	FX STG/USD	Overall Return	Index in JPY	FX JPY/USD
1993	22.4	25.1	−2.2	24.0	11.1	11.6
1994	−0.2	−5.7	5.9	21.6	8.3	12.3
1995	20.7	21.9	−1.0	−1.7	2.2	−3.8
1996	28.1	15.8	10.6	−15.7	−5.7	−10.5
1997	19.4	24.4	−4.0	−27.8	−18.5	−11.4
1998	17.5	16.5	0.9	8.4	−5.7	14.9
1999	18.9	21.9	−2.5	80.5	62.9	10.8
2000	−12.6	−5.2	−7.7	−30.5	−22.5	−10.4
2001	−14.4	−12.2	−2.6	−28.9	−18.1	−13.1
2002	−14.7	−22.9	10.7	−8.5	−17.4	10.8
Average Impact	17.2	4.8		17.2	11.0	
Relative Impact	78.0	22.0		61.0	39.0	

stantially higher (40 to 70%) for international fixed-income portfolios. Any component that has such a large impact on overall returns deserves to be analyzed and, if possible, managed.

CURRENCY OVERLAY MANAGEMENT

The factors driving fluctuations in foreign securities (e.g., Sony) and those affecting fluctuations in exchange rates (JPY/USD) are quite different. Even the same factor usually has different effects on the two fluctuations. For example, Japanese interest rates might affect the price of Sony stock, but what seems to have the most pronounced effect on the

USD/JPY exchange rate is the *difference* between the interest rates in the two countries. Thus, it has been argued that two entirely different types of analyses are required to manage these two different components of total return and risk.

Management of currency fluctuations as a separate activity has come to be known as currency overlay management. Some large international asset management firms have a team to manage exchange rates separate from the team that performs security analyses. In addition, a subindustry of currency overlay managers has come into being. Many large institutional investors hire currency overlay managers when they find that their managers of foreign securities, while very good at stock selection, are not proficient in currency management.

Prudent fiduciaries should, therefore, understand how currency exposures are managed and how such management should be evaluated, so that they can decide whether separate overlay management should be pursued to improve their returns.

PASSIVE METHODS OF MANAGING CURRENCY FLUCTUATIONS

The two passive methods of dealing with exchange rate fluctuations are no hedge and full hedge as outlined in Exhibit 6.4. See the box at the end of this chapter for an explanation of hedging with forward contracts.

The term *forward differential* in boxes Q1 and Q2 of Exhibit 6.4 describes the possible net results of the fully hedged situation. With passive asset management and hedging, investment gains and losses will depend on the forward differential as shown in these boxes.

No hedge entails doing nothing at all (boxes P1 and P2).

EXHIBIT 6.4

Results of not hedging and hedging when currency movement is favorable or unfavorable

| | **Currency Movement** | |
	Favorable	**Unfavorable**
No Hedge	**Box P1** FX Change — Gain Hedge Result — None Net — Gain	**Box P2** FX Change — Loss Hedge Result — None Net — Loss
Hedge	**Box Q1** FX Change — Gain Hedge Result — Loss Net — Fwd Diff*	**Box Q2** FX Change — Loss Hedge Result — Gain Net — Fwd Diff

* Fwd Diff = forward differential.

- Because there is no hedge, the entire favorable foreign currency appreciation accrues to the investor (box P1: net = gain). This benefit enhances the positive foreign portfolio returns or mitigates negative foreign portfolio returns.
- Conversely, the entire unfavorable impact of the foreign currency depreciation also accrues to the investor (box P2: net = loss). This either worsens negative or reduces positive foreign asset returns.

Full hedge entails hedging the exchange rate risk throughout each year (boxes Q1 and Q2). Hedges are assumed to be placed using 12-month forward contracts and depend not on the value of the currency 12 months out (which is unknown), but on the forward interest rate differential between the two currencies.

- When there is no forward differential, gains from the hedge would completely offset the negative impact of adverse currency movement; similarly, any loss from the hedge would completely offset the positive impact of a favorable currency movement. The result is no net gain or loss as a result of currency fluctuations.

- When the forward differential is positive, hedge gains are larger and hedge losses are smaller, by this differential (premium). Hedge gains exceed the negative impact of adverse currency movement and hedge losses are less than the positive impact of favorable currency movement. The result is a net positive value equal to the forward premium (positive differential), regardless of currency movement.

- When the forward differential is negative, hedge gains are smaller and hedge losses are higher by this differential (discount). The negative impact of an adverse currency movement exceeds the hedge gain, and the hedge gain is lower than the positive impact of a favorable currency movement. The result is a net negative value equal to the forward discount (negative differential), regardless of the extent or direction of the currency movement.

With passive no hedge, the benefit is found in box P1, where the portfolio realizes the full currency translation gain. The risk is found in box P2, where the portfolio suffers the full currency translation loss. With passive full hedge, the benefit is found in box Q2, where hedge gains offset transaction loss, and the risk is found in box Q2, where hedge losses offset translation gains.

Actual results of the above passive methods applied to the two foreign portfolios are summarized in Exhibit 6.5, which shows the gross returns, the S&P returns, and the excess returns (gross returns minus corresponding S&P returns).

■ Returns when no hedges are in place are computed by combining the index change and the currency change.

■ Returns for the full hedge are computed by combining the index change and the forward differentials (forward differentials are not shown).

The bottom section of Exhibit 6.5 shows excess return mean and standard deviation. Also shown is a statistic *probability of underperformance*, explained below.

The intent of any management is to either: (a) increase the return without a commensurate increase in risk or (b) decrease the risk, without a commensurate decrease in return. In Exhibit 6.6 we see the probability distributions of two hypothetical investment alternatives, X and Y. Alternative X has a mean of 2.8 and a standard deviation of 2.5. Alternative Y has a mean of 5.2 and a standard deviation of 4.0. Compared to Alternative X, Y has a higher mean, but it also has a higher standard deviation. Is the increase in risk worth taking? In other words, does the return increase sufficiently, given the additional risk? The answer is yes, because the probability of loss is decreased from 13% to 9%. Alternative X has more area under the distribution curve to the left of the 0 return, hence a higher probability of loss.[1]

Returning to Exhibit 6.5, we see that the no-hedge strategy has higher excess returns in some years while the full hedge does better in other years. For the entire 10-year period the mean excess return was worse for the full hedge in the case of the DJU (−0.6% unhedged versus −2.1% hedged) but better for the full hedge for the DJJ (−6.9% unhedged versus −5.3% hedged). The probability of underperformance is higher for full hedge in the case of the DJU and does not change at all in the case of the DJJ.

EXHIBIT 6.5

Portfolio gross and excess returns with passive currency management, 1993–2002 (all returns in percent)

| | Dow Jones UK (DJU) | | | | | Dow Jones Japan (DJJ) | | | | |
| | Gross Returns | | | Excess Returns | | Gross Returns | | | Excess Returns | |
Year	No Hedge	Full Hedge	S&P	No Hedge	Full Hedge	No Hedge	Full Hedge	S&P	No Hedge	Full Hedge
1994	-0.2	-6.9	-1.5	1.4	-5.3	21.6	10.4	-1.5	23.1	11.9
1995	20.7	21.8	34.1	-13.4	-12.3	-1.7	7.5	34.1	-35.8	-26.6
1996	28.1	14.9	20.3	7.8	-5.3	-15.7	-1.2	20.3	-35.9	-21.4
1997	19.4	23.4	31.0	-11.6	-8.0	-27.8	-14.2	31.0	-58.8	-45.2
1998	17.5	14.7	26.7	-9.1	-12.0	8.4	-0.5	26.7	-18.2	-27.1
1999	18.9	21.4	19.5	-0.7	1.9	80.5	70.7	19.5	61.0	51.1
2000	-12.6	-5.3	-10.1	-2.4	4.8	-30.5	-17.6	-10.1	-20.4	-7.5
2001	-14.4	-11.9	-13.0	-1.4	1.1	-28.9	-13.6	-13.0	-15.8	-0.5
2002	-14.7	-24.4	-23.4	8.7	-1.1	-8.5	-15.5	-23.4	14.9	7.9
Mean				-0.6	-2.1				-6.9	-5.3
Standard Deviation				9.3	8.3				35.4	27.0
Probability of Underperformance				52.4	60.1				57.7	57.8

Comparison of two hypothetical distributions

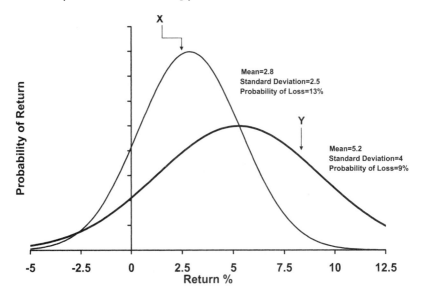

In summary, no clear pattern emerges as to which of the two passive methods is clearly preferable to the other. These results are typical and not unique to the time period used here as an illustration.

ACTIVE MANAGEMENT OF CURRENCY FLUCTUATIONS

An active currency overlay program involves a periodic decision by the manager (daily, weekly, etc.) as to whether or not a hedge is required. Given no specific constraints, the manager initiates a hedge when the foreign currency is projected to depreciate and removes the hedge when an appreciation is projected. Some managers (for example, those using option replication methods) do not explicitly form their own views as to currency appreciation or depreciation. For purposes of this discussion, we can assume their implicit market projections are reflected in their hedge/no-hedge actions. The quality of the research underlying such projections determines the outcome over a period. The manager's objective during each subperiod is either protection or enhancement, depending on whether the currency movement is adverse or favorable.

To study the efficacy of such management, let's start with two hypothetical active programs:

1. Efficiency of 100%.[2] This hypothetical program assumes the availability, at the beginning of each year, of a perfect directional forecast of exchange rate movement during that year. Given a forecast of a depreciation of a currency against the U.S. dollar (USD), the exchange rate risk is fully hedged for the year (box Q2 of Exhibit 6.4). When the currency is forecast to appreciate, the risk is accepted with no hedge during the year (P1). Therefore, the result in each year is the *better* of the two results from the no-hedge and full-hedge methods.

2. Efficiency of 0%. This hypothetical program assumes that the manager is consistently wrong in making directional forecasts. Hedges are established in years during which a currency appreciates (Q1), denying the investor the positive currency impact. No hedges are in place during years of currency depreciation (P2) accruing to the investor the negative currency impact. The result in each year is therefore the *worse* of the two results from no-hedge and full-hedge methods.

Exhibit 6.7 summarizes these two levels of efficiency.

Efficiencies of 100% and 0% might appear to define the logical boundaries. These are the boundaries if only one deci-

Active programs—hedging, efficiency, and currency movements

% Efficiency	Currency Movement	
	Favorable	**Unfavorable**
100	No hedge	Hedge
0	Hedge	No hedge

sion is permitted at the beginning of each year. But, because active management permits many decisions within each year, these are not the absolute boundaries. Efficiency in excess of 100% can occur, especially when a currency experiences both upward and downward trends within the same year. Similarly, efficiency below 0% is possible, especially when a currency moves within a narrow range throughout a year.

Next, let's consider various levels of efficiency between 0 and 100%, at intervals of 10%. For example, a program with an efficiency of 40% can be described as follows:

1. During a year of currency appreciation against the USD, the program wrongly hedges 60% of the net appreciation (box Q1 of Exhibit 6.4) and accrues correctly 40% of the net appreciation to the investor (P1).

2. During a year of currency depreciation against the USD, the program correctly hedges 40% of the net depreciation (Q2), and incorrectly accrues 60% of the net depreciation to the investor (P2).

3. The result in each year from this program equals 0.4 times the result from the hypothetical 100% efficient program, plus 0.6 times the result from the hypothetical 0% efficient program.

We can thus compute the results of active overlay management at various levels of efficiency. Exhibit 6.8 (for the DJU) and Exhibit 6.9 (for the DJJ) illustrate these results. These exhibits have probability of loss as the horizontal axis and return as the vertical axis. The southeast quadrant combines low return and high risk, and the northwest quadrant combines high return and low risk.

At one end of the line in each exhibit we have the results of 100% efficiency. The other end represents the 0% efficiency. The points between the two represent efficiencies at 10% intervals. Two points, representing the results of the no-hedge and full-hedge passive methods, are also labeled in the exhibits.

The following observations can be made from these exhibits:

1. The program with 100% efficiency produces a higher return *and* a lower risk (low probability of underperformance) than either of the passive methods.

2. The program with 0% efficiency generates a lower return *and* a higher risk (high probability of underperformance) than either of the passive methods.

FEASIBILITY OF ACTIVE MANAGEMENT PROGRAMS

If the overlay manager makes random decisions as to whether to hedge exchange rate risk or not, the results over any period would approximate the 50% efficiency performance, with returns and the probability of loss between those of the no-hedge and the full-hedge results.

Exhibit 6.8 (for the DJU) shows that no hedge has return and risk at about a 67% efficiency level, and full hedge at a

Efficiency of the DJU

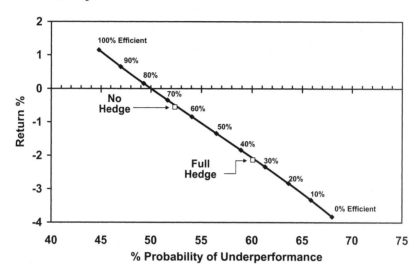

Efficiency of the DJJ

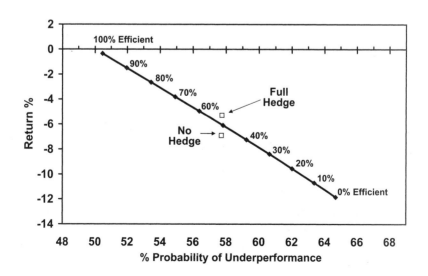

35% level. (We saw before that there is no pattern as to which passive method outperforms the other: this is unique to this specific currency and period.) To outperform both these passive methods would require efficiency in excess of 67%.

Exhibit 6.9 (for the DJJ) shows that both passive methods have a probability of loss at about the 50% efficiency level, with returns slightly above and below that level. To outperform both passive methods would require an efficiency of about 55%.

Exhibit 6.10 compares an efficiency of 75% (in the column headed "75%"). The period comparison is summarized at the bottom of the exhibit. In the case of each foreign portfolio, the excess returns are higher (-0.1 for the UK and -3.2% for Japan) than both the no-hedge (-0.6% for the UK and -6.9% for Japan) and full-hedge (-2.1% for the UK and -5.3% for Japan) returns. Additionally, the risk (probability of underperformance in each case) is lower than either the no-hedge or the full-hedge risk.

Investors want either a higher return without a commensurate increase in risk or a lower risk without a commensurate decrease in returns. When returns are increased while risk is reduced, this is indeed remarkable. But is this achievable?

The author's analysis of the performance of seven prominent overlay managers showed that efficiencies within the 60 to 90% range can be achieved. (Efficiencies exceeded 100% in some cases in some years and for some multiyear periods.) These results are supported in part by another empirical study of the actual performance of 11 active currency overlay managers managing 152 overlay accounts over a 10-year period (Strange 1998).

Such performance is possible because good active managers have models and procedures that are not constrained by

E X H I B I T 6 . 1 0

Excess returns for different levels of hedging efficiency, 1993–2002 (all returns in percent)

| | Dow Jones UK (DJU) | | | | | Dow Jones Japan (DJJ) | | | | |
| | Excess Returns | | Efficiency Levels | | | Excess Returns | | Efficiency Levels | | |
Year	No Hedge	Full Hedge	100%	0%	75%	No Hedge	Full Hedge	100%	0%	75%
1993	15.3	15.0	15.3	15.0	15.2	16.9	4.5	16.9	4.5	13.8
1994	1.4	−5.3	1.4	−5.3	−0.3	23.1	11.9	23.1	11.9	20.3
1995	−13.4	−12.3	−12.3	−13.4	−12.6	−35.8	−26.6	−26.6	−35.8	−28.9
1996	7.8	−5.3	7.8	−5.3	4.5	−35.9	−21.4	−21.4	−35.9	−25.0
1997	−11.6	−8.0	−8.0	−11.6	−8.9	−58.8	−45.2	−45.2	−58.8	−48.6
1998	−9.1	−12.0	−9.1	−12.0	−9.9	−18.2	−27.1	−18.2	−27.1	−20.5
1999	−0.7	1.9	1.9	−0.7	1.3	61.0	51.1	61.0	51.1	58.5
2000	−2.4	4.8	4.8	−2.4	3.0	−20.4	−7.5	−7.5	−20.4	−10.7
2001	−1.4	1.1	1.1	−1.4	0.5	−15.8	−0.5	−0.5	−15.8	−4.4
2002	8.7	−1.1	8.7	−1.1	6.2	14.9	7.9	14.9	7.9	13.1
Mean	−0.6	−2.1			−0.1	−6.9	−5.3			−3.2
Standard Deviation	9.3	8.3			8.4	35.4	27.0			30.7
PUP*	52.4	60.1			50.5	57.7	57.8			54.2

* PUP = probability of underperformance.

a need to make just one decision each year and to stand aside as spectators for the rest of the year. When a certain directional prediction proves to be wrong, these overlay managers change their posture. Further, some managers are able to detect and "ride" trends, which may last only a few months before changing directions.

These results do not mean, however, that all overlay managers exceed 50% efficiency in all periods and for all currencies. Furthermore, no single overlay manager outperforms all the others in every currency, in every year. Additionally, given possible personnel turnover within firms and changes to their analyses, there is no assurance that a certain manager selected based on superior past performance will continue such performance. For these reasons, prudent fiduciaries should consider employing three to five overlay managers.

Such "diversification" among several overlay managers avoids the risk of dependence on one manager's models and procedures. To further reduce the risk of underperformance, the fiduciary may consider a *risk containment program*. The purpose of a risk containment program is to minimize the possibility of undue underperformance in any subperiod (quarter, year, etc.). For example, the fiduciary may stipulate that the benchmark for the overlay management is half hedge, and further that in no year can the results be worse than, say, 5% below the benchmark. Risk containment would then entail:

1. Continuous monitoring of overlay performance in relation to the benchmark; and
2. Reducing the exposure to the active management program, in predefined stages, if and when predefined performance triggers are reached.

There are many layers of sophistication to this process. A detailed discussion is outside the scope of this chapter.

PERFORMANCE BENCHMARK
FOR ACTIVE MANAGEMENT PROGRAMS

As stated earlier, to achieve desirable results a professional manager should do better than a toss-of-the-coin approach. Random decisions produce, over a period of time, 50% efficiency, with returns that are the same as those of a half-hedge procedure. We suggest, therefore, that an appropriate benchmark to measure the effectiveness of an overlay manager's performance is a "half-hedge."

Asset managers who purport to manage the currency risk also should be asked to decompose their performance into *returns in foreign currency* and *effects of currency management*. While the former may have its own benchmark (perhaps a local stock index), the latter should be compared to the half-hedge benchmark, and the manager should report the associated efficiency results. If currency management is less than 50% efficient, the fiduciary should consider delinking this function and appointing overlay managers. In selecting overlay managers, the fiduciary should once again evaluate their performance using efficiencies as discussed previously.

Of course, the benchmark should be adjusted when constraints are imposed. For example, if investment guidelines call for a minimum hedge at all times of, say, 60%, then the benchmark should apply to only the portion of the fluctuations being actively managed (40%). In this case, the benchmark will be adjusted to an 80% hedge.

A "standard" currency exposure management program, then, should see either (a) no hedge (when the currency is expected to appreciate) or (b) a hedge in the form of a short position in the currency (when the currency is expected to depreciate).

Some overlay programs seek to add value to these standard results, by one or more of the following:

- Buying a currency long when appreciation is expected; a standard overlay program will not do that, because it recognizes that the investor is already long by virtue of the investment in the foreign portfolio and additional long positions increase exposure to the currency and add risk.
- Implementing short hedges that are larger than the exposure; once again, the standard overlay programs would not do this, since such a hedge creates a net short exposure to the currency and thus adds risk.
- Creating market positions in currencies that are not exposed. For example, given an exposure in STG resulting from an investment in the DJU, some overlay programs might include long or short positions in other currencies such as Swiss francs or Australian dollars.

These programs attempt to add value, in effect, by speculating in currencies. Currencies are volatile and currency trading might be acceptable for a sophisticated investor willing to assume the risk. Fiduciaries should look cautiously at proposed aggressive overlay programs and separate currency exposure management results from trading results. A fiduciary, however, who follows the core-satellite approach should probably stay with a standard currency overlay program to manage currency risk in the satellite foreign investments and avoid strategies that involve any currency speculation.

SUMMARY

The impact of currency fluctuations on overall returns from international investments is high enough to warrant considerable attention, and possibly a separate, specialized currency manager. Neither of the two passive management methods is decidedly superior to the other. An active management program requires an efficiency of at least 50% before it can consistently improve on the results of passive programs. Because good currency overlay managers have efficiencies in excess of 50% and because no one is the best at all times and for all currencies, it would be advisable to engage three to five currency overlay managers and allocate the portfolio-wide currency exposures among them. In addition, the fiduciary might implement a risk containment program (or appoint an overlay manager-of-managers for this function) to measure and control active management risk while pursuing its benefits. A "half hedge" with 50% efficiency is the logical benchmark against which to measure the performance of active currency overlay management programs.

HEDGING CURRENCY WITH A FORWARD CONTRACT

The essence of hedging is to use financial instruments on top of a basic asset holding to mitigate or offset some of the undesirable characteristics of that asset. Hedging candidates include all instruments that are correlated only with the undesirable characteristic. Forward contracts are highly correlated with exchange rates and give managers the opportunity to offset the foreign exchange risk of holding an asset denominated in another currency.

A forward contract is an agreement made today by which a certain amount of one currency will be exchanged for another currency, on a future date, for a specified exchange rate. It is described by the following elements:

- Date the contract is made
- Seller's currency (to be delivered)
- Buyer's currency (to be accepted)
- Amount of either currency to be exchanged
- Settlement date or the maturity date (term)
- Rate of exchange

The forward exchange rate is by no means a prediction by either party as to what the exchange rate will be on the maturity date. Rather, it is the result of arbitrage transactions, as described below.

Assume that the exchange rate today (spot rate) between the U.S. Dollar (USD) and the Swiss franc (SFR) is 2.0000, that is to say, USD 1.00 = SFR 2.00. Assume also that the 12-month interest rate in the USD is 5.00% and the 12-month interest rate in the SFR is 2.00%.

A Swiss investor holding SFR 1,000,000 has two choices:

1. The in investor can invest domestically and earn 2.00% (SFR 20,000) over a year, and end up at the year's end with the amount of SFR 1,020,000.
2. The investor can convert the amount into USD 500,000 (at today's spot rate of 2.0000), and invest it at 5.00% to end the year with the amount of USD 525,000. If the investor can convert this amount at the same exchange rate, the investor will have SFR 1,050,000.

The second option seems preferable, except that the investor does not know that USD will not have depreciated by 3% or more during the year. The investor can hedge this currency risk by entering into a forward contract to sell, at the end of the year, USD 525,000 for SFR. If this forward rate is such that the investor can receive more than SFR 1,020,000, he or she will do this transaction. Said differently, if the investor has to pay a forward differential (i.e., a forward discount) of less than about 3%, the investor will choose the second alternative.

A lot of other investors holding SFR will do the same thing. This will create a demand for spot USD, potentially increasing the spot exchange rate; and a supply of forward USD, potentially decreasing the forward exchange rate, thus causing an increase in the forward discount. When the discount reaches about 3%, no more Swiss investors will find it advantageous to go to USD to invest.

If the differential gets to more than 3%, U.S. investors would find it favorable to invest in SFR. This is because a forward discount from the Swiss point of view is a forward premium from the U.S. point of view. Even though the interest earned in SFR is 3% below the domestic interest rate, the forward exchange rate will pay a premium of more than 3%, resulting in a net advantage over a domestic (i.e., USD) investment. As many U.S. investors resort to this process, the spot and forward rates will converge to a premium of about 3%.

These arbitrage transactions will thus keep the forward differential at equilibrium, near 3%. That equilibrium rate is simply 1,020,000 divided by 525,000, or 1.9429. This is very close, but not exactly equal, to a 3% discount.

Note that the actual spot exchange rate at the end of the year might be 1.5000 or 2.5000 or any other rate. Where the exchange rate ends up at the year-end does not affect the results for the hedger, since the contract at the beginning of the year calls for an exchange of currencies at a certain rate.

In the context of this chapter, when we calculate the results of a fully hedged foreign portfolio, we can ignore the exchange rate movement during the year and adjust the index returns by just the forward differential.

N O T E S

1. Probability of loss can be calculated as the area to the left of the zero return vertical of a normal distribution curve whose mean and standard deviation are the same as those of a given stream of annual returns. In the context of excess returns, probability of loss means the probability of underperformance compared to the benchmark.
2. For a more detailed description of efficiency, see Nathan (1997).

B I B L I O G R A P H Y

Nathan, Ranga (1997 Fall). "Performance Measurement of Active Overlay Programs," *Derivatives Quarterly*, pp. 58–65.

Strange, Brian (1998 June). "Currency Overlay Managers Show Consistency," *Pensions & Investments*, pp. 26–31.

CHAPTER 7

Treasury Inflation Protected Securities

Peng Chen, PhD, CFA
Director of Research, Ibbotson Associates

While inflation was quiescent as this chapter was being written, it probably will not remain so for the life of your portfolio. Inflation is an increase in the general price level. For people on a fixed income, like a pension, inflation reduces their purchasing power and lowers their standard of living. Many firms take steps to protect their pension recipients from inflation, just like the government protects social security recipients from inflation by indexing their social security payments to inflation. When your portfolio has an explicit or implicit promise to protect the beneficiaries from inflation, you will want to consider inflation-sensitive assets. These are assets that prosper under inflation and should provide income to fund the inflation protection. In that sense they are an inflation hedge.

Some people believe that equity investments are a good hedge against inflation. The argument runs something like this: During inflation companies face rising prices for their inputs of labor and material. In response they raise prices for the products they make. This price increase allows them to cover their increased costs and, therefore, they are largely immune from inflation. This might be true if companies could both raise their product prices and sell the same amount. Unfortunately this is rarely true as consumers typically buy less when prices rise. Sales revenue falls due to lower volume even though the price per unit is higher. Inflation can be good for some companies, especially those who have borrowed heavily. They can repay their borrowing with inflated (cheaper) dollars. Even though this is true, it is generally not widespread enough to overcome the disadvantage of higher input costs and lower sales revenue.

Inflation hedges are a good idea for funds that have obligations that are sensitive to inflation. Specialized instruments, like Treasury Inflation Protected Securities (TIPS) and natural hedges, like timber, hard assets, and real estate, are more appropriate than stocks to protect a fund against inflation. In this chapter you will learn about TIPS —how they work and the kind of inflation protection they offer. The history of TIPS in the United States is fairly short, having been introduced in 1997. These bonds' annual payments and return of principal go up based on the government's announced rate of inflation. You will also read about an empirical study that helps us understand how these bonds are likely to behave in the future, especially in relation to other asset classes in the core and satellite parts of the portfolio.

Although inflation-indexed bonds have existed in other nations (e.g., the United Kingdom, Israel, Australia) for a number of years, TIPS were first auctioned in January 1997. Since that time, the Treasury has issued over $150 billion of inflation-indexed securities with maturity dates ranging from 2002 to 2032. Unlike the Treasury's conventional debt, TIPS have a fixed real coupon rate. That is, the dollar coupon payment increases as the general price level increases. Additionally, the principal is adjusted semiannually by the amount of actual inflation over the period. Because of the inflation adjustment, nominal coupon payments, equal to the product of the real coupon rate and the inflation-adjusted principal, grow with inflation. By design, TIPS provide a hedge against inflation because the real yield, which equals the real coupon rate at issuance, is essentially constant. This hedge is an attractive characteristic for institutional investors, such as pension funds and endowments, because they are required to fund future expenditures. We will further investigate the role of TIPS in an institutional investor's portfolio in this chapter. The chapter is organized in the following way. First, we review current literature on TIPS and how fiduciaries should approach them. Then, we explain how TIPS work, especially compared to traditional Treasury bonds. We also study the TIPS currently on the market and how they have performed. Then, we analyze their role in a long-term asset allocation for a fiduciary's portfolio. Lastly, we summarize and interpret the analysis in the context of a typical portfolio.

Many researchers have studied inflation-indexed bonds and their role in long-term asset allocation for both individual investors and institutional investors. Bodie (1990) points out that inflation-indexed bonds have potentially far-reaching effects on individual and institutional asset allocation decisions because these securities represent the only true long-run hedge against inflation risk. Inflation-indexed bond make possible the creation of additional financial innovations that would use them as the asset base. For example, inflation index-linked bonds eliminate one of the main obstacles to the indexation of benefits in private pension plans. A firm could hedge the risk associated with a long-term indexed liability by investing in

index-linked bonds with the same duration as the indexed liabilities. Chen and Terrien (2001) studied the risk and return
characteristics of TIPS and concluded that TIPS should play a
significant role in a long-term strategic portfolio that cares
about performance on an inflation-adjusted basis. Sack and
Elsasser (2002) provide a comprehensive review of the short
history of U.S. inflation-indexed bonds.

Despite intermittent uncertainty about future U.S. government support for inflation-protected bonds, public interest in
them has broadened as individuals, endowments, pension
plans, and other fiduciaries have increased their purchases in
the past several years. Hammond (2002) pointed out that the
heightened public interest in inflation-indexed bonds may have
two motivations, one transient and the other more fundamental. One transient reason is that inflation-indexed bonds have
had high returns in recent years. The more fundamental reason
is that inflation-indexed bonds represent a new asset class.
They enable investors to (1) protect assets and future income
against inflation, (2) better match liabilities and assets when
both are affected by inflation, and (3) provide diversification in
combination with other asset classes.

According to the Citigroup U.S. Inflation-linked Security
Index, TIPS returned on average 11.4% annually from January
2000 to December 2003 (13.1% in 2000, 7.9% in 2001, 16.7%
in 2002, and 8.3% in 2003). This compares with annualized
returns over the same time periods of about -5.3% for the
S&P 500 stock index, 8.5% for the Lehman Aggregate index
of corporate and government bonds, and 3.1% for money market funds.

It is common to find that inflation bonds represent
between 5 and 10 percent of major endowments' portfolios.
As such, fiduciaries are beginning to use inflation bonds
and various investment options based on them in retirement
savings and endowment portfolios. Because of their special

characteristics and growing availability, inflation-protected bonds are and should be of special interest to retirees, retirement savers, endowments, and other individuals and institutions.

THE MECHANICS OF TIPS

Unlike conventional Treasury bonds that have fixed nominal coupon rates, the coupon payments of TIPS are fixed in real terms at the time of issuance. That is, over the life of the bond, nominal interest payments are adjusted based on the actual inflation rate, as measured by changes in the consumer price index (CPI-U). TIPS's par values are also adjusted in a similar manner, such that the principal is returned to the investor upon maturity, fully adjusted for inflation. An example may clarify how this process works. Assume a 10-year inflation-indexed bond is issued with a par value of $10,000 and guarantees a real yield of 3% per year. Suppose that the inflation rate is 5% in the first year. The face value of the bond will rise to $10,500 and the coupon payment would be $315 (i.e., 3% of $10,500).[1] If deflation occurs, the principal and the coupon payment will be adjusted down based on the falling CPI-U. However, if deflation reduces the principal below par, the investor will still receive the par value at maturity. As Wrase (1997) points out, though, "the Treasury does not expect to have to implement this 'minimum guarantee' because it does not expect a prolonged decline in consumer prices to occur."

TIPS ensure that neither the U.S. Treasury nor the investor faces the risk that an unanticipated increase or decrease in inflation will erode or boost the purchasing power of the bond payments. Thus, TIPS are structured in a manner that allows them to maintain their real value[2], thereby offering a long-term hedge against inflation.

The return on TIPS is often viewed in the context of the following equation:

$$R_N = R_R + E_{[I]}$$

where R_N is the nominal interest rate[3]

R_R is the real interest rate

$E_{[I]}$ is expected inflation

For a nominal bond investor, expected inflation, as well as the existing real rate, is locked in upon purchase. For a TIPS investor, the nominal rate received is:

$$R_N = R_R + I$$

where I is realized inflation

The real rate is locked in upon purchase, but the realized inflation return varies depending on the reported CPI-U. Changes in real rates affect nominal bonds and TIPS in the same way, but because TIPS are inoculated against inflation risk, changes in the CPI-U will be passed through directly to the investor. In contrast, changes in inflation will either increase or decrease the price of nominal bonds. For this reason, the price of TIPS can move in the opposite direction of nominal bond prices, depending on the direction of inflation. In other words, TIPS could have a negative correlation with nominal bonds. The different impacts of inflation on nominal bonds and TIPS imply that there are potential diversification benefits between nominal and real bonds.

The interesting feature of TIPS is that the investor does not know the final return that will be received until maturity. Only the "real return" is known upon purchase. This is why there is some risk in TIPS. If inflation declines, then TIPS would underperform comparable nominal Treasury securities of the same duration. In contrast to TIPS, nominal bonds pay a fixed coupon that incorporates the real rate as well as expected inflation. The investor knows exactly what will be received from issuance to maturity. Nonetheless, this leaves the nominal bond investor at risk from increased inflation. If inflation rises substantially, the nominal bond investor can be faced with real negative returns. This will never be the case for a TIPS investor who holds to maturity.

The difference between the yield on nominal bonds and TIPS is referred to as the *breakeven inflation rate*. This is the inflation rate that must occur if the return on TIPS is to equal that of nominal bonds. Breakeven inflation can be viewed approximately as the market's current inflation forecast. If one believes breakeven inflation is too low, then the appropriate strategy is to purchase TIPS in lieu of bonds. Similarly, one would buy nominal bonds if breakeven inflation were too high. As this chapter is being written, breakeven inflation (yield differential between TIPS and similar maturity nominal bonds) is about 1.7% per year for the 10-year horizon and 2.3% for the 30-year horizon (see Exhibit 7.1 for detailed numbers).

The guarantee of a real rate of return above inflation has value to investors. As a result, a small portion of the cost of TIPS reflects the premium paid for inflation protection. If inflation is volatile, the value of this premium should be high, and vice versa. Fortunately, following several years of very low inflation, the current inflation protection premium is very low—only about 0.1% by most estimates. Initially, following the introduction of TIPS, the market was small and bid-ask spreads fairly wide for TIPS. It was sometimes difficult to buy and sell, and investors took a "haircut" when they traded. This price concession reflected an illiquidity premium and represented one reason why investors did not move into the product.

Although TIPS are significantly more apt to preserve real purchasing power than traditional nominal bonds are, they do not provide a completely perfect hedge against inflation.

Semiannual coupon payments are subject to reinvestment risk. Also, a portfolio's specific liabilities may increase at a faster rate than the CPI-U, making TIPS a less than effective funding vehicle for such expenses. Taxable portfolios are partially exposed to inflation risk due to the tax code's current inability to distinguish between nominal and real income. An increase in a TIPS's principal value is taxable as normal interest income, even though the adjustment simply keeps the principal value fixed in real terms. This problem of taxes exposing a TIPS investor to inflation risk is dealt with more thoroughly by Shen (1998). Finally, as Wrase (1997) pointed out, "inflation-indexed bonds . . . are subject to an 'indexation lag'—bond payments are linked to a [3-month] lagged value of a price index. Because of the indexation lag, an indexed bond also lacks inflation protection for a short period right before it matures."

TIPS PERFORMANCE AND MARKET EXPERIENCE (1997–2003)

As of February 28, 2003, TIPS accounted for about 2.5% of total outstanding U.S. government debt. The total market value of TIPS is $152.6 billion, whereas total outstanding government debt is $6.45 trillion. There are currently 10 TIPS issues available. As outlined in Exhibit 7.1, the current breakeven inflation (yield differential between TIPS and similar maturity nominal bonds) ranges from 1.6% per year for a 5-year horizon to 2.3% for a 30-year horizon.

TIPS have outperformed the CPI-U measurement of inflation significantly since they were first auctioned in 1997. They have slightly underperformed the broader government bond market. Exhibit 7.2 illustrates these trends. As Sargent and Taylor (1997) point out: "The performance of TIPS compared

EXHIBIT 7.1

Yield comparison of TIPS issues and similar maturity nominal bonds

TIPS			Nominal Bonds			
Coupon	Maturity	Yield*	Coupon	Maturity	Yield*	Inflation†
3.38%	January 2007	0.96%	6.25%	February 2007	2.59%	1.63%
3.63%	January 2008	1.34%	5.50%	February 2008	2.95%	1.61%
3.88%	January 2009	1.64%	5.50%	May 2009	3.31%	1.67%
4.25%	January 2010	1.78%	6.50%	January 2010	3.52%	1.74%
3.50%	January 2011	1.97%	5.00%	February 2011	3.71%	1.74%
3.38%	January 2012	2.04%	4.88%	February 2012	3.89%	1.85%
3.00%	July 2012	2.10%	4.38%	August 2011	3.95%	1.85%
3.63%	April 2028	2.68%	5.50%	August 2028	5.04%	2.36%
3.88%	April 2029	2.67%	5.25%	February 2029	5.04%	2.37%
3.38%	April 2032	2.59%	5.38%	February 2031	4.91%	2.32%

* Yield figures represent yield to maturity on accrued principal as reported in *The Wall Street Journal,* March 20, 2003.
† Breakeven inflation rate (see page 175).

to nominal Treasury securities depends on the actual rate of inflation relative to expectations. If actual inflation ends up being less than what the market anticipates, TIPS will underperform conventional Treasury securities. Conversely, if actual inflation exceeds expected inflation, TIPS will pay a higher rate of return than conventional Treasuries. The main difference hinges on the accuracy of the market's predictions about future inflation. If inflation forecasts prove to be correct, then in theory, TIPS's performance will lag that of traditional Treasuries because the return on the latter includes a premium for inflation risk. However, because TIPS have liquidity problems, the difference in returns will depend on the relative sizes of the inflation risk and liquidity premiums." In other words, the expected return on Treasury bonds includes a premium for expected inflation while TIPS's expected return includes an

EXHIBIT 7.2

Yields on TIPS and nominal bonds, February 28, 2003

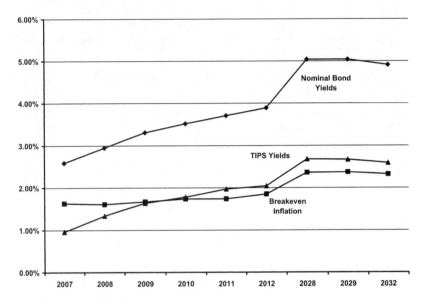

illiquidity premium. If expected inflation is low and the illiquidity premium is high, TIPS could have a higher promised rate of return than Treasury bonds of similar maturity. Most of the time, however, TIPS yields have been less than Treasury yields.

Let's take a brief look at the market experience over the past six years (see Exhibit 7.3). The TIPS program got off to an impressive start. The program's inaugural auction of a 10-year note in January 1997 was very well received by investors, creating a brief period of enthusiasm for the new asset class. The bid-to-cover ratio[4] at the first auction registered an impressive 5.3, compared to only 2.4 and 1.9 for the preceding and subsequent nominal 10-year-note auctions, respectively. Moreover, the stop-out rate[5] on the inaugural auction was

EXHIBIT 7.3

Historical performance of TIPS (February 1997–December 2002)

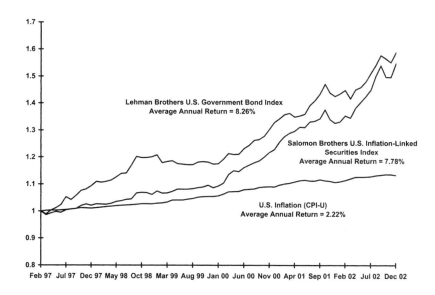

3.449 percent, which was more than 3 percentage points below the yields on comparable nominal Treasury securities. The spread between nominal and TIPS yields (breakeven inflation rate) that prevailed over the first several months would in fact be the widest level observed during the TIPS program to date.

The enthusiasm for inflation-indexed debt was not long-lived, though. Breakeven inflation fell steadily over 1997, reaching a level of about 2 percent during the first half of 1998. This decline may partly reflect that the strongest demand for TIPS—by those investors willing to give up the largest amount of yield to hold inflation-indexed rather than nominal securities—was quickly saturated. Additionally, the fall in inflation compensation may be partly attributed to a broad decline in inflation expectations. In the fall of 1998, financial market volatility abroad spread to U.S. financial markets, causing investors to place great value on the liquidity of their portfolios. The increased preference for liquidity at that time pushed down nominal yields relative to TIPS yields, given that nominal securities are more liquid and TIPS were reportedly viewed as too limited to provide the flexibility needed in such unpredictable market conditions. As a result, breakeven inflation fell to a remarkably low level, reaching a trough of 88 basis points in October 1998.

Over the first half of 1999, some of the factors that may have been limiting the appeal of TIPS began to unwind. CPI inflation turned higher and began to show some upward momentum, in part due to considerable increases in energy prices. Since the second quarter of 1999, movements in nominal and TIPS yields appear to become more correlated, and inflation compensation has remained in a narrower range—typically between 1.5 and 2.5%—in contrast to the wide swings seen during the first two years of the TIPS program.

Activity in the TIPS market has also evolved in the past 6 years. Interest in TIPS among investors has increased, particularly in 2000 and 2001. The investor base for TIPS has broadened, and secondary market liquidity has also improved. In dollar terms, trading volume increased dramatically, given that the supply of TIPS was increasing considerably over this period. Despite the reported increase in investor interest in TIPS, the average level of TIPS yields has been puzzlingly close to nominal Treasury yields. Indeed, the level of breakeven inflation rate has been consistently below many survey measures of expected inflation. On average, the market-based breakeven inflation has been about one-half of a percentage point below the survey measure. In other words, the market price of inflation-indexed bonds is low relative to the nominal bond and inflation expectations. Sack and Elsasser (2002) point to some factors that potentially explain the undervalue of inflation-indexed bonds from 1999 to 2002. These factors are (1) TIPS are new and likely require a nontrivial investment in a potential buyer's infrastructure (such as accounting and trading systems), thereby hindering the expansion of the investor base; (2) the investor base for TIPS is much more concentrated than that for nominal Treasuries; and (3) liquidity in the TIPS market has been limited, and this is a particularly challenging issue for fiduciaries.

In the next section, we turn our attention to analyzing the long-term return-risk characteristics of TIPS and their role in a long-term core-satellite asset allocation policy.

RETURN, RISK, AND CORRELATION OF TIPS

As discussed, inflation-indexed bonds should provide slightly lower returns and risk than traditional, nominal government bonds with comparable maturities. The explanation for this lies in the fact that inflation-indexed bonds hedge away the inflation risk associated with regular bonds. Therefore, investors should be willing to accept lower returns for the inflation protection. In other words, the investors are willing to pay an inflation premium.[6] An increase in inflation prompts investors to require higher yields from nominal bonds to compensate for the loss of purchasing power, resulting in a drop in the prices of these instruments. TIPS, however, have both their principal amount and coupon payments adjusted to reflect changes in inflation. The inflation protection received by TIPS investors is valuable, and this value is paid for in the form of lower yields as compared to regular bonds. Due to the fact that inflation impacts traditional bonds quite differently than TIPS, the correlation coefficient between the two is expected to be low. When inflation increases, the prices of both equities and nominal bonds decrease (as investors require higher discount rates for future dividends and coupon payments). Therefore, the correlation between equity and TIPS is also expected to be lower than the correlation between equities and nominal bonds.

Analysis of the Role of Inflation Indexed Bonds in Core-Satellite Asset Allocation

To incorporate inflation-indexed bonds in a long-term asset allocation framework using mean-variance analysis, it is necessary to analyze their expected return, standard deviation, and correlation coefficients with other asset classes. An examination of historical data would be helpful when estimating these mean-variance inputs. Inflation-indexed bonds, as discussed in the above sections, were introduced as recently as 1997 in the United States. The existing data, therefore, are insufficient for estimating long-term mean-variance inputs. Instead, a synthetic inflation-indexed bond series was created for the period 1970 to 1997. The synthetic return data were created based on historical inflation and Treasury bond yield data.[7] These synthetic return data are combined with market return data from 1997 to 2002 to form the basis for the analysis in this section. For the purposes of this study, a synthetic 10-year inflation-indexed bond was utilized.

Exhibit 7.4 provides the historical average returns, standard deviations, and correlation coefficients for the 10-year inflation-indexed bonds based on synthetic and market-return data, U.S. large-cap stocks, 10-year U.S. Treasury nominal bonds, and 30-day U.S. Treasury bills. The synthetic inflation-indexed bonds exhibited lower return and lower risk than 10-year Treasury bonds. The correlation coefficients between inflation-indexed bonds and the other asset classes were quite

Nominal return, risk, and correlations (1970–2002)

	Arithmetic Return %	Standard Deviation %	Correlation Coefficients			
			TIPS	S&P 500	10-Yr. T-Bond	30-Day T-Bills
TIPS (Synthetic 10-Year)	8.63	9.20	1.00			
S&P 500	12.23	17.52	−0.10	1.00		
10-Year Treasury Bond	9.42	10.15	0.02	0.31	1.00	
30-Day Treasury Bills	6.46	2.71	−0.06	0.09	0.09	1.00
Inflation	4.92	3.23	0.23	−0.21	−0.34	0.62

low. As expected, the correlation coefficient between synthetic inflation-indexed bonds and equities was lower than that between the regular 10-year Treasury bonds and equities.

Exhibit 7.5 provides the same statistics as Exhibit 7.4; however, the information in Exhibit 7.5 reflects inflation-adjusted (i.e., real) data. The synthetic inflation-indexed bonds exhibited lower real return and lower real risk than 10-year Treasury bonds. The inflation-adjusted correlation coefficient between synthetic inflation-indexed bonds and equities is slightly higher than it is in nominal terms; however, it is still considerably lower than the inflation-adjusted correlation coefficient between the regular 10-year Treasury bonds and equities. The low correlation coefficients between inflation-indexed bonds and the other asset classes (especially equities) suggest that potential diversification benefits exist from the addition of TIPS to a portfolio of core assets.

To evaluate the desirability of including inflation-indexed bonds in the asset allocation decision, mean-variance opti-

EXHIBIT 7.5

Real return, risk, and correlations (1970–2002)

	Arithmetic Return %	Standard Deviation %	Correlation Coefficients			
			TIPS	S&P 500	10-Yr. T-Bond	30-Day T-Bills
TIPS (Synthetic 10-Year)	3.57	8.65	1.00			
S&P 500	7.17	17.52	−0.01	1.00		
10-Year Treasury Bond	4.48	11.14	0.16	0.42	1.00	
30-Day Treasury Bills	6.46	2.71	−0.06	0.09	0.09	1.00
Inflation	1.51	2.49	−0.13	0.44	0.60	1.00

mization was performed in both a nominal and real (inflation-adjusted) setting. The four asset classes mentioned above were used in the analysis.

Historical Mean-Variance Analysis in Nominal Terms (1970–2002)

Exhibit 7.6 shows two mean-variance efficient frontiers; one with the synthetic 10-year inflation-indexed bond asset class, and one without.[8] The inputs used in this mean-variance analysis were presented in Exhibit 7.4. The lower efficient frontier excludes inflation-indexed bonds from consideration; the upper frontier includes them. This exhibit shows that adding TIPS improves the risk-return trade-off of the mean-variance efficient frontier. The improvement is most significant for the lower risk portion of the efficient frontier, where the portfolios are conservative and dominated by the fixed-income investments. Exhibits 7.7 and 7.8 show the allocations of these two efficient frontiers, respectively. The allocation to TIPS ranges from 0% for the highest-risk portfolio to over

EXHIBIT 7.6

Nominal mean-variance efficient frontier with and
without TIPS (1970–2002)

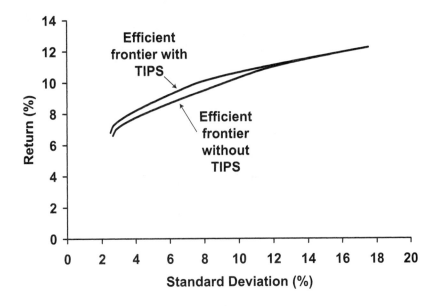

40% for a moderate-risk portfolio. The efficient allocation to
TIPS is greater than 0 for all portfolios on the efficient frontier
except for the highest-risk portfolio, which consists of 100%
U.S. large-cap equity. The efficient allocations to equities are
roughly the same with and without TIPS. The allocation to
TIPS mainly comes at the expense of bonds and cash. The allocations to regular bonds are still positive, albeit smaller, when
TIPS are included; thus, the inclusion of TIPS does not completely eliminate regular bonds.

Historical Mean-Variance Analysis
in Real Terms (1970–2002)

Exhibit 7.9 shows the results of the mean-variance analysis in
real-return space. In this scenario, return and risk are inflation-

EXHIBIT 7.7

Nominal efficient allocations with TIPS (1970–2002)

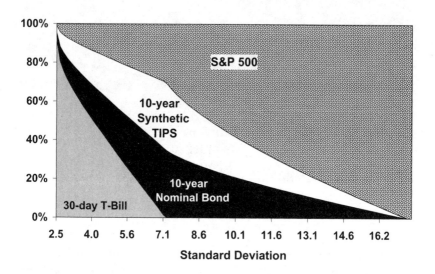

EXHIBIT 7.8

Nominal efficient allocations without TIPS
(1970–2002)

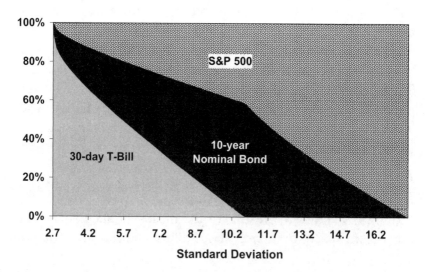

EXHIBIT 7.9

Real mean-variance efficient frontier with and without TIPS (1970–2002)

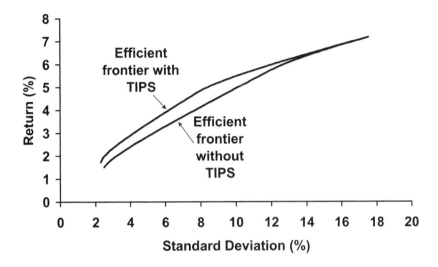

adjusted, which is appropriate for investors who are concerned about the purchasing power of their portfolios. The real-return, risk, and correlation coefficients of TIPS and the other three asset classes were presented earlier in Exhibit 7.5. The upper efficient frontier is the result of including TIPS in the efficient portfolios of traditional stocks, bonds, and cash. Including TIPS improves the real risk-return efficiency of traditional stock, bond, and cash portfolios. Exhibit 7.9 shows much the same picture as Exhibit 7.6. Adding TIPS improves the efficiency of the frontier for conservative portfolios in particular. Exhibits 7.10 and 7.11 provide the detailed allocations of the portfolios from the two frontiers shown in Exhibit 7.9. TIPS play an important role in the efficient portfolios. The allocations to TIPS range from about 10% in the minimum-variance portfolio to about 50% for moderate-risk portfolios. Allocations to bonds and cash are considerably lower after TIPS are included. Nominal bonds are almost completely replaced by TIPS. The allocations to equities are also lowered after the inclusion of TIPS in real-return space, especially for the moderate-risk portfolios.

Comparing the efficient allocations in real-return space with those in nominal-return space yields some interesting results. First, the allocation to TIPS is greater in real-return space than in nominal-return space. This indicates that the benefit of including TIPS in a portfolio is greater in real-return space (i.e., for investors whose objective is to maximize infla- tion-adjusted returns and minimize risk). Second, the alloca- tion to regular bonds is much smaller in real-return space than in nominal-return space regardless of whether TIPS are included or not. Third, the allocations to equities remain about the same in nominal-return space and are slightly lowered in the real space. Lastly, including TIPS improves the risk- return trade-off of the mean-variance efficient frontier in both

EXHIBIT 7.10

Real efficient allocations with TIPS (1970–2002)

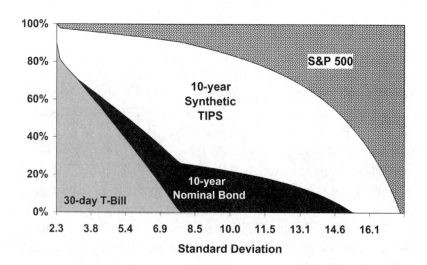

EXHIBIT 7.11

Real efficient allocations without TIPS (1970–2002)

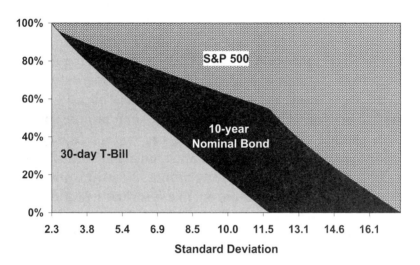

nominal and real terms. Investing part of a portfolio in TIPS helps investors achieve a higher expected rate of return and lower expected risk. The diversification benefits of TIPS are significant and deserve consideration in a core-satellite portfolio, especially when the portfolio's obligations are in part to preserve real purchasing power.

CONCLUSIONS

This chapter suggests that a satellite allocation to TIPS provides diversification benefits to a core portfolio that consists of cash, traditional nominal fixed-income securities, and stocks. This diversification benefit is more significant in the analysis of real-return space and, therefore, important to fiduciaries who have a responsibility to maintain their portfolio's purchasing power. TIPS also provide a unique opportunity for fiduciaries to hedge inflation risk. In the first few years that TIPS were available, the market for these securities was not as liquid as those for traditional nominal bonds, perhaps because TIPS are relatively new investment vehicles. TIPS's market size has also been small and their liquidity low compared to other fixed-income securities. This may have discouraged fiduciaries from allocating a significant portion of their portfolios to TIPS. As a result, the real yield of TIPS was over 4% at one time, which was well above the historical long-term real return of comparable nominal bonds.[9] The size and the liquidity of the TIPS market has improved significantly, and consequently, the TIPS yield has come down to around 2% as this review is being written, which is more in line with the historical real return of nominal bonds. With the improved size and liquidity, the TIPS market is better prepared to accommodate more investors than a couple of years ago.

TIPS offer fiduciaries an option for portfolio diversification that no other instrument can replicate. TIPS alone do not present a good opportunity for extraordinary returns, nor do they eliminate risk completely over the long run. However, as part of the satellite ring of a diversified core portfolio, their higher correlation with inflation and lower correlation with other assets offer great diversification benefits for stock, bond, and cash portfolios. For fiduciaries with most of their portfolios invested in core financial assets, the inclusion of TIPS reduces the risk and increases the return of the entire portfolio, especially measured after inflation. This study has shown that portfolios including TIPS offer better risk and return trade-offs in terms of both real and nominal returns than portfolios that neglect them.

APPENDIX

Theoretically, an inflation-linked bond series can be thought of as the price of the *real* yield of a bond (in contrast to regular bonds that price nominal yields). In other words, the price of an inflation-indexed bond is only affected by changes in real yields. When real yields increase, the inflation-indexed bond price will fall; when real yields decrease, the inflation-indexed bond price will rise. Therefore, it is critical to develop a historical real-yield series in order to construct the synthetic inflation-indexed bond series. To estimate historical real yields, we apply the Domestic Fisher Relation. The nominal yield, r_N, is the compounding of the real yield, r_R, and expected inflation, $E(I)$, over the investment time horizon.

$$r_N = (1 + r_R) \times [1 + E(I)] - 1 \approx r_R + E(I) \qquad (1)$$

Therefore, the real yield can be approximated by the nominal yield less expected inflation:

$$r_R = (1 + r_N) / [1 + E(I)] - 1 \approx r_N - E(I) \qquad (2)$$

Historical nominal yields can be estimated from the prices of bonds traded in the open market. However, a measurement of expected inflation is not so readily available. As Lucas and Queck (1998) pointed out, predicting inflation is a difficult job and perhaps this is why the market uses the year-to-year CPI as its inflation forecast; it is as good as any other method. As such, in our analysis, we use an adaptive expectations approach, whereby expected inflation is proxied by the most recent 12 months' inflation rate.

Both nominal yields and real yields can be observed from the current market prices for regular Treasury bonds and inflation-indexed bonds. According to the Fisher relation, the implied expected inflation would be the difference between the nominal and real yields. Several alternative models were explored as a proxy for market-expected inflation, including monthly and annual autoregression, a weighted average of recent inflation, and the inflation forecast by the Survey of Professional Forecasters (formerly ASA/NBER Economic Outlook Survey). However, the inflationary expectations formed through these various methods violated the Fisher relation in the current market; the expectations produced were much higher than the implied inflation from the bond yields. If the inflationary expectations from these models are correct, then there is an arbitrage opportunity, where investors should buy inflation-indexed bonds and sell nominal bonds. Because we believe the market is relatively competitive, there should not be such an arbitrage opportunity. Therefore, the inflation models inherent in these various approaches must be inaccurate. We determined to make the simplifying assumption that the inflation process follows a random walk:

$$I_t = I_{t-1} + \varepsilon$$

and

$$E(I_t) = I_{t-1}$$

where

I_t = inflation of period t

ε = random term with zero mean

Therefore, the expected real yield on a nominal bond is:

$$r_R = r_N - E(I) = r_N - I_{t-1} \tag{3}$$

Investors should be willing to accept a lower real yield for inflation-indexed bonds than nominal bonds, because inflation-indexed bonds provide an inflation hedge. Investors pay a premium for owning inflation-indexed bonds. Intuitively, the real return of an inflation-indexed bond will be lower than the implied real rate of return from a nominal bond, because an inflation-indexed bond guarantees that the return will keep pace with inflation. The current premium (IIP) is calculated as the difference between the expected real return of the nominal bond (r_N) and the current real yield of the inflation-indexed bond (r_{II}) with a comparable maturity. The following equation expresses this calculation:

$$IIP_t = r_{N,t} - E(I) - r_{II,t} = r_{N,t} - I_{t-1} - r_{II,t} \qquad (4)$$

As of March 5, 1999, the nominal yield on a traditional 10-year government bond and the yield on a 10-year inflation-indexed bond were:

$$r_N = 5.67\%$$

$$r_{II} = 3.89\%$$

The increase in inflation during calendar year 1998 was:

$$I_{t-1} = 1.61\%$$

The current inflation-index premium from (4) above = 5.67% − 1.61% − 3.89% = 0.17%.

This premium is assumed to be proportional to the standard deviation of inflation over the past 36 months. The idea is that the premium investors are willing to pay is tied to the recent volatility of inflation. If the inflation volatility is high, then investors are willing to pay a higher premium. The historical inflation index premium can be derived as follows:

$$IIP_i = \frac{S_i}{S_t} \times IIP_t \qquad (5)$$

where

i is any month in the past (since January 1970)

S_t is the standard deviation of inflation over the 36-month time period from February 1996 through January 1999

S_i is the standard deviation of inflation over the most recent 36-month time period from month i

Finally, subtracting the inflation index premium from the real yield produces a synthetic measurement of historical yields for inflation-indexed bonds:

$$r_{II,t} = r_{R,t} - IIP_t = r_N - E(I) - IIP_t = r_N - I_{t-1} - IIP_t \quad (6)$$

Several assumptions were made in the use of the above method:

1. The availability (i.e., presence or absence) of inflation-indexed bonds in the marketplace has no impact on the inflation rate or the market prices of bonds.
2. Expected inflation is assumed to be the most recent 12 months' inflation rate.
3. A nominal bond's expected real rate of return is equal to the difference between the bond's yield and expected inflation.
4. The expected real interest rate will always be greater than 2 percent.

Synthetic Historical Return Series

The objective of the analysis was to create a synthetic inflation-indexed bond series having a maturity of 10 years, as well as a series having a maturity equivalent to the assumed investment time horizon of 20 years. We calculate the total returns by utilizing the historical yields (derived via the methodology described above) of the inflation-indexed bonds. It is assumed that the manager of the portfolio buys a newly issued par bond at the beginning of each month, and then sells it at the beginning of the next month. We calculated the rate of return for the synthetic inflation-indexed bonds for each month from January 1970 through December 1998.

The income (IR) and total returns (TR) are calculated through the following formulas:

$$TR = \frac{\left[\dfrac{redemption}{\left(1+\dfrac{yld}{frequency}\right)^{N-1+\frac{DSC}{E}}}\right] + \left[\displaystyle\sum_{k=1}^{N} \dfrac{100 \times \dfrac{rate}{frequency}}{\left(1+\dfrac{yld}{frequency}\right)^{N-1+\frac{DSC}{E}}}\right]}{par} \times (1+I) - 1$$

$$IR = \frac{rate}{frequency} \times \frac{A}{E}$$

where

TR = Total return

IR = Income Return

DSC = number of days from settlement day to the next coupon date

E = number of days in coupon period in which settlement date occurs

N = number of coupons payable between settlement date and redemption date

A = number of days from beginning of coupon period to settlement date

$rate$ = annual coupon rate (yield when the inflation-indexed bond was bought)

$frequency$ = frequency of coupon payments per year

yld = yield to maturity (the current yield on the inflation-indexed bond)

I = inflation over the most recent calendar year

par = original face value of a bond

$redemption$ = proceeds from the sale of a bond

N O T E S

1. This hypothetical example assumes a single annual coupon payment. In practice, the interest payments on TIPS are made semiannually.

2. Real value here connotes the (unobservable) value that would prevail without inflation.

3. A nominal interest rate is the published rate and is presumed to incorporate both the real rate and expected inflation.

4. The bid-to-cover ratio is the sum of the quantity bidders said they would buy compared to the size of the offering. A bid-to-cover of 3 means there were $30 billion of bids for $10 billion of bonds offered. A bid-to-cover ratio of 5.3 indicates a very successful offering.

5. The stop-out rate is another measure of auction success. The stop-out rate is the lowest offered rate that was accepted. In this case the stop-out rate indicated bids in the TIPS auction were competitive and bidders were willing to buy at high prices (low yields) relative to comparable Treasuries.

6. Campbell and Shiller (1996) use the historical behavior of inflation and real interest rates in a CAPM model to estimate the inflation risk premium for the 5-year nominal bond. They estimated the inflation risk premium between 0.5 and 1 percentage point.

7. The method is first used in Chen and Terrien (2001). See the chapter Appendix for a summary of the method.

8. Efficient frontiers and portfolio allocations shown in this study are intended for illustrative purposes only. They do not necessarily represent Ibbotson Associates' advice.

9. The average annual real return on U.S. long-term government bond was 2.5% from 1926 to 2002. Source: 2002 SBBI Yearbook, Ibbotson Associates, 2003.

BIBLIOGRAPHY

Bodie, Zvi (1990 Winter). "Inflation, Indexed-Linked Bonds and Asset Allocation," *Journal of Portfolio Management*, pp. 48–53.

Campbell, John Y., and Robert J. Shiller (1996). "A Scorecard for Indexed Government Debt," *NBER Working Paper* No. 5587.

Chen, Peng, and Matthew Terrien (2001 Summer). "TIPS As an Asset Allocation," *Journal of Investing*, pp. 73–80.

Fabozzi, Frank J. (1999). "Handbook of Inflation Indexed Bonds," Frank J. Fabozzi Associates.

Hammond, P. Brett (2002 September). "Real Bonds and Inflation Protection for Retirement." TIAA-CREF Research Dialogues.

Ibbotson Associates (2003). "2002 SBBI Year-Book," Chicago.

Lucas, Gerald, and Timothy Quek (1998 December). "A Portfolio Approach to TIPS," *Journal of Fixed Income*, p. 77.

McCulloch, J., and Levis A. Kochin (2000). "The Inflation Premium Implicit in the US Real and Nominal Term Structure of Interest Rates." Working Paper #98–12. Ohio State University Economics Department.

Sack, Brian, and Robert Elsasser (2002). "Treasury Inflation-Indexed Debt: A Review of the U.S. Experience," *Working Paper*, Federal Reserve Bank of New York.

Sargent, Kevin H., and Richard D. Taylor (1997 July). "TIPS for Safer Investing." Federal Reserve Bank of Cleveland, *Economic Commentary*, (http://www.clevelandfed.org/Research/com97/0701.htm).

Shen, Pu (1998 First Quarter). "Features and Risks of Treasury Inflation Protection Securities," Federal Reserve Bank of Kansas City, *Economic Review*, pp. 31–33.

Wrase, Jeffrey M. (1997 July/August). "Inflation-Indexed Bonds: How Do They Work?" Federal Reserve Bank of Philadelphia, *Business Review*, p. 10.

Hard Assets

Peng Chen, PhD, CFA
Director of Research, Ibbotson Associates

Jeffrey M. Antonacci, CFA
Senior Consultant, Ibbotson Associates

Joseph Pinsky, CFA
Senior Consultant, Ibbotson Associates

This chapter continues the discussion of inflation-sensitive assets begun in Chapter 7. The research explained here explores the possibility of hard assets like oil and gas as satellite investments. These opportunities are typically not traded on exchanges, like stocks and bonds, but assembled and managed by skilled investment professionals. Commodities also fall into this category. If you are considering any of these investments, it is incumbent on you as a fiduciary to understand and interpret their historical record. By understanding their nature you will be in a better position to assess their role in your portfolio. In this chapter we explain some of the empirical research on hard assets and what it means for you as a fiduciary.[1]

In the past few years, investors have been paying more attention to alternative asset classes for better diversification of their core portfolio. This is partially due to the increase in the correlation between stocks and bonds. For the period of 1926 to 1970 the correlation coefficient between stocks and U.S. long-term bonds was −0.2. However, since 1970 the correlation coefficient has increased. From 1970 to 1980 the correlation between stocks and U.S. long-term bonds was 0.23, and from 1981 to 2002 the correlation was 0.32. Real assets include real estate, precious metals, commodities, and a variety of other items that have value independent of the monetary units in which they are denominated. By holding real economic assets as a satellite investment, fiduciaries can hedge against inflation much more effectively than with stocks. Real assets also tend to diversify away some of the risk of equities, with which they have low correlations. Hard assets can provide both diversification and inflation protection.

While financial assets garner the most attention from investors, nonfinancial (i.e., real or tangible assets) actually constitute the majority of the world's wealth. Some types of assets are difficult to place in either the financial or nonfinancial category, but in general nonfinancial assets tend to have intrinsic value (i.e., value in use). Typically this use is in some sort of manufacturing process or as a consumable. Real assets may be divided into "hard" and "soft" assets. *Hard assets* are nonperishable real assets and include real estate and commodity-related assets such as energy (e.g., oil and gas), precious metals (e.g., gold and silver), industrial metals (e.g., aluminum and copper), and timber. *Soft assets* are perishable and consumable and include the commodities of agricultural products and livestock.

In this chapter we focus on direct energy, a hard asset, and analyze its impact on a core investment portfolio. If you are considering adding other hard assets, you might want to consult some of the other studies that have investigated the portfolio benefits of real assets as satellite investments.[2] For the purposes of this chapter, *direct energy investments* are defined as a diversified portfolio of oil- and gas-producing properties. From a practical standpoint, direct energy investments are usually structured as limited partnerships, whereby long-term investors participate directly in the cash flows generated by the producing properties. The primary objectives of this chapter are to (1) define a viable methodology for modeling the historical returns of a generic direct oil and gas investment in the United States, (2) evaluate the behavior of direct energy investments relative to different macroeconomic variables, and (3) utilize mean-variance analysis to evaluate the impact on risk and return of including direct energy investments in core-satellite portfolios of financial assets.

DATA AND SYNTHETIC DIRECT ENERGY INDEX

One of the challenges of studying the risk-return characteristics of direct energy investments is the lack of reliable historical performance data, because most of direct energy investments are organized as private partnerships. Most of their operating information is not made public, nor is there a market where we can regularly observe the return and price fluctuation of these investments.

One of the primary objectives of this study is to explore the behavior of a synthetic historical return data series that represents a viable proxy for direct energy investments. We developed a unique method to synthetically generate returns for direct energy investments based on a discounted cash-flow method. We created a synthetic direct energy total return series (defined for the purposes of this study as a portfolio comprised of 50% crude oil and 50% natural gas) based on the theoretical model, data, and assumptions described in Appendix A at the end of this chapter.

Exhibit 8.1 shows the growth of a $1 investment made on

EXHIBIT 8.1

Growth of a $1 investment in various asset classes from 1970 through 2002

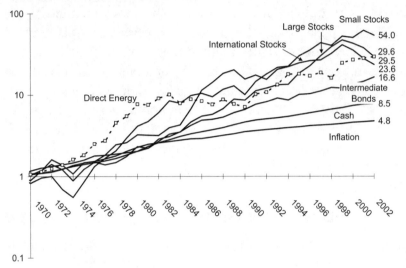

December 31, 1969, in various asset classes, including direct energy.[3] Direct energy underperformed U.S. equity investments, but outperformed international stocks, intermediate-term bonds, cash, and inflation.

Exhibits 8.2, 8.3, and 8.4 show asset class summary statistics in different economic environments:

- High inflation and increasing interest rates (1970–1981)
- Low inflation and decreasing interest rates (1982–2002)
- Entire period (1970–2002)[4]

In Exhibits 8.2, 8.3, and 8.4 return is measured by both historical arithmetic (average) and geometric (compound) means. Standard deviation is a proxy for risk and the Sharpe Ratio is the relationship between mean return and standard deviation. The higher the Sharpe Ratio, the more the asset class returned per unit of standard deviation risk. Not surprisingly, the higher-returning asset classes generally have higher risk. When viewed in isolation, direct energy has been slightly more volatile than large-cap stocks. It had a standard deviation of 21.5% over the 1970 to 2000 period, although it demonstrated less volatility over the 1982 to 2000 period. Direct energy exhibited a better Sharpe Ratio in the high-inflation scenario (Exhibit 8.2) than when inflation was low (Exhibit 8.3). Equities suffered in the inflationary period with, for the most part, lower returns and higher volatility, while cash kept pace with inflation with a high Sharpe Ratio. Measured by the highest and lowest returns, the statistics again suggest direct energy was more risky than bonds or large-cap equities, even though it compiled a record of positive and negative years that is very similar to the equity asset classes. Of course, only correlations can suggest how direct energy might have performed as a satellite investment in a core-satellite portfolio.

Direct Energy Correlation Coefficients

The correlation coefficient measures the degree to which two asset classes' returns change with respect to each other. Correlation coefficients can range between positive 1 (+1) and negative 1 (−1). Generally speaking, the lower the correlation coefficient of an asset class with the other asset classes in a portfolio, the more risk reduction benefit can be gained by including the additional asset class in the portfolio. Most traditional asset class correlation coefficients range between −0.2 and 0.9. Exhibit 8.5 shows the correlation coefficients of annual returns between the direct energy series and the other asset classes from 1970 through 2002. Direct energy, as expected, was fairly strongly correlated with the broad commodity index (0.34) and energy stocks (0.42). Direct energy had negative correlation coefficients, however, with tradition-

EXHIBIT 8.2

Historical statistics for high inflation and increasing interest rates—1970 through 1981

Asset Class	Arithmetic Mean	Geometric Mean	Standard Deviation	Highest Return	Lowest Return	No. of Positive Years	No. of Negative Years	Sharpe Ratio
Large-Cap Stocks	8.54	6.89	19.27	37.20	−26.47	8	4	0.44
Small-Cap Stocks	15.09	11.28	29.73	61.84	−34.41	9	3	0.51
International Stocks	12.18	10.24	21.30	37.60	−22.15	8	4	0.57
Direct Energy	25.29	24.48	14.86	47.85	5.31	12	0	1.70
U. S. Long-Term Bonds	4.59	4.39	6.81	16.75	−3.95	7	5	0.67
U. S. Intermediate-Term Bonds	7.01	6.93	4.41	16.86	1.41	12	0	1.59
Cash Equivalents	7.89	7.85	3.17	15.05	4.09	12	0	2.49
Inflation	7.96	7.91	3.43	13.31	3.36	12	0	2.32

EXHIBIT 8.3

Historical statistics for low inflation and decreasing interest rates—1982 through 2002

Asset Class	Arithmetic Mean	Geometric Mean	Standard Deviation	Highest Return	Lowest Return	# of Positive Years	# of Negative Years	Sharpe Ratio
Large-Cap Stocks	14.34	13.11	16.56	37.43	−22.10	17	4	0.87
Small-Cap Stocks	13.72	12.17	18.72	48.54	−21.60	15	6	0.73
International Stocks	12.28	9.95	23.85	69.94	−23.19	15	6	0.51
Direct Energy	25.29	3.67	21.64	75.47	−26.39	12	9	0.26
U. S. Long-Term Bonds	5.53	12.36	13.10	40.36	−8.96	17	4	1.00
U. S. Intermediate-Term Bonds	13.08	10.02	7.53	29.10	−5.14	19	2	1.36
Cash Equivalents	6.09	6.07	2.35	11.33	1.70	21	0	2.59
Inflation	3.17	3.17	1.20	6.11	1.13	21	0	2.64

EXHIBIT 8.4

Historical statistics for entire period, 1970 through 2002

Asset Class	Arithmetic Mean	Geometric Mean	Standard Deviation	Highest Return	Lowest Return	No. of Positive Years	No. of Negative Years	Sharpe Ratio
Large-Cap Stocks	12.23	10.81	17.52	37.43	−26.47	25	8	0.70
Small-Cap Stocks	14.24	11.86	22.88	61.67	−34.42	24	9	0.62
International Stocks	12.24	10.05	22.62	69.94	−23.19	23	10	0.54
Direct Energy	12.71	10.80	21.49	75.47	−26.39	24	9	0.59
U.S. Long-Term Bonds	9.99	9.39	11.85	40.36	−8.96	24	9	0.84
U.S. Intermediate-Term Bonds	9.08	8.89	6.69	29.10	−5.14	31	9	1.36
Cash Equivalents	6.74	6.71	2.77	15.05	1.70	33	0	2.43
Inflation	4.92	4.87	3.23	13.31	1.13	33	0	1.52

al equity and fixed income, ranging from −0.05 (small-cap stocks) to −0.42 (international stocks). This illustrates the potential diversification benefits from adding direct energy to core portfolios. Exhibit 8.5 also suggests the relationship between direct energy and inflation is not one-to-one, as might be expected.

Many studies have documented that broad market equity indexes tend to be negatively correlated with inflation.[5] Interestingly, the correlation coefficient between the direct energy series and inflation was 0.60 from 1970 through 2002. Because correlation coefficients below 1.0 suggest diversification benefits, this correlation indicates that direct energy has acted, to a limited extent, as an inflation hedge.

THE ROLE OF DIRECT ENERGY IN CORE PORTFOLIOS

We employed mean-variance optimization techniques to analyze the effects of including direct energy investments in core

EXHIBIT 8.5

Correlation coefficients between Direct Energy and other asset classes from 1970 to 2002

Asset Class	Correlation with Direct Energy
Large-Cap Stocks	−0.20
Small-Cap Stocks	0.02
International Stocks	−0.30
Public Energy Stocks	0.42
Commodities	0.34
Long-Term Bonds	−0.29
Intermediate-Term Bonds	−0.24
Cash Equivalents	0.40
Inflation	0.60

portfolios. Mean-variance optimization provides the set of portfolios that maximize return at any level of risk. This set of portfolios is known as the *efficient frontier*, and portfolios contained in this set are said to be mean-variance efficient. Given a set of asset classes or securities, it is not possible to construct a portfolio beyond the efficient frontier. However, adding asset classes to the asset mix may improve the entire set of portfolios and result in a more favorable efficient frontier. It is possible to determine whether there are benefits to including an additional asset class by first examining the efficient frontier of a basic set of asset classes and then observing how the additional asset class affects the frontier.

For this study, large-cap stocks, small-cap stocks, international stocks, U.S. long-term bonds, and U.S. Treasury bills were selected as the core set of asset classes. Portfolios developed with this core set of asset classes will henceforth be referred to as the *Base Case*. Efficient frontiers were constructed using historical data from 1970 through 2002. Once the Base Case efficient frontiers were developed, direct energy was added to the portfolio mix to determine if there was an improvement in the efficient frontier.

Historical Efficient Frontier Analysis

The Base Case efficient frontier portfolios were chosen based on their risk, and they have standard deviations of 8%, 12%, and 16%. These portfolios are labeled A, B, and C, and represent three distinct investment risk tolerances (low risk, medium risk, and high risk, respectively).

For comparison purposes, we selected six portfolios from the Base Case + Direct Energy frontier. Three of the portfolios, A-1, B-1, and C-1, have the same standard deviation, or equivalent risk, as the Base Case portfolios. The other three portfolios, A-2, B-2, and C-2, have the same expected return. Exhibit 8.6 lists the portfolios on the two frontiers.

Exhibit 8.7 displays the historical Base Case efficient frontier with the low-, medium-, and high-risk portfolios selected. Also plotted on the graph are Base Case + Direct Energy portfolios that have equivalent risk or return to the Base Case. Exhibit 8.8 is a tabular display of the characteristics of the portfolios from Exhibit 8.7.

Notice in Exhibit 8.7 that the Base Case + Direct Energy frontier lies above and to the left of the Base Case frontier. This position means that all the portfolios with direct energy offered more return for the same risk (A-1, B-1, and C-1) or the same return for less risk (A-2, B-2, and C-2). Exhibit 8.8 shows the details behind these relationships. Within the set of A portfolios the equivalent risk portfolios (A-1) allocated 28% to direct energy with a higher historical return (10.16% compared to 9.64%) for the same risk (standard deviation = 8%). The equivalent return portfolios (A-2) allocated 21% to direct energy and achieved a smaller standard deviation (5.92% compared to 8%) with the same historical return (9.64%). We obtained the same results for portfolios B and C. The

EXHIBIT 8.6

Base Case and Direct Energy portfolios

Base Case Portfolio	Direct Energy Portfolios with Equivalent Risk as Base Case	Direct Energy Portfolios with Equivalent Return as Base Case
A	A-1	A-2
B	B-1	B-2
C	C-1	C-2

portfolios with direct energy had a better return-per-unit-risk than the portfolios without it. This study used historical data, and while it may not work this way in the future, it is illustrative to see the diversification benefits that a satellite asset class like direct energy would have added to a core portfolio.

BENEFITS OF DIRECT ENERGY
IN DIVERSIFIED PORTFOLIOS

An additional display of the role that direct energy plays in improving portfolio risk and return characteristics can be

EXHIBIT 8.7

Base Case and Base Case + Direct Energy historical efficient frontiers

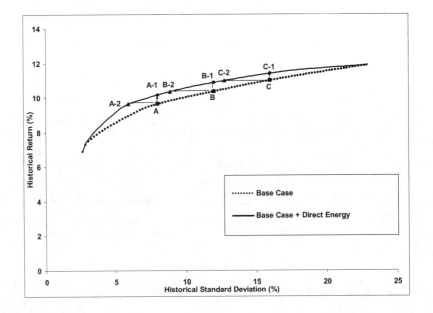

EXHIBIT 8.8

Base Case and Base Case + Direct Energy historical efficient portfolio allocations and statistics

Asset Class Allocation	Portfolio A			Portfolio B			Portfolio C		
	A-1 Base Case	Equivalent Risk	A-2 Equivalent Return	B-1 Base Case	Equivalent Risk	B-2 Equivalent Return	C-1 Base Case	Equivalent Risk	C-2 Equivalent Return
Large-Cap Stocks	4%	14%	8%	11%	19%	16%	9%	6%	20%
Small-Cap Stocks	22	8	3	39	29	10	60	57	33
International Stocks	4	9	9	0	2	8	0	0	0
Direct Energy	0	28	21	0	35	32	0	37	36
Long-term Bonds	0	21	0	20	15	33	31	0	11
Intermediate-term Bonds	70	20	59	30	0	1	0	0	0
Cash Equivalents	0	0	0	0	0	0	0	0	0
Expected Return	9.64	10.16	9.64	10.36	10.89	10.36	10.99	11.41	10.99
Standard Deviation	8.00	8.00	5.92	12.00	12.00	8.90	16.00	16.00	12.74
Sharpe Ratio	1.21	1.27	1.63	0.86	0.91	1.16	0.69	0.71	0.86

found in Exhibit 8.9, which shows the benefit of incremental-
ly adding small amounts of direct energy to a three-asset-class
portfolio (large-cap stocks, long-term bonds, and direct
energy). The first portfolio is made up of 60% large-cap stocks
and 40% long-term bonds. In each subsequent portfolio 1% is
subtracted from each asset class and added to direct energy.
The Sharpe Ratio suggests that adding a modest amount of
direct energy improves the return-per-unit-risk for the portfolio. Exhibit 8.10 plots two portfolios from Exhibit 8.9
constructed with and without direct energy. The first portfolio,
without direct energy, is made up of 60% large-cap stocks and
40% long-term bonds. The second portfolio, with direct
energy, contains a 10% allocation to direct energy, 55% to
large-cap stocks, and 35% to long-term bonds. As Exhibit 8.9
shows in detail, while the returns of the portfolios are similar,
including just a small allocation to direct energy reduces the
risk substantially.

EXHIBIT 8.9

Diversification benefits of Direct Energy using
1970–2002

Portfolio Allocations			Portfolio Statistics			
Large-Cap Stocks	Long-Term Bonds	Direct Energy	Arithmetic Mean	Geometric Mean	Standard Deviation	Sharpe Ratio
60%	40%	0%	11.33	10.60	12.83	0.88
59	39	2	11.37	10.69	12.41	0.92
58	38	4	11.40	10.76	12.08	0.94
57	37	6	11.43	10.82	11.76	0.97
56	36	8	11.46	10.88	11.47	1.00
55	35	10	11.50	10.94	11.19	1.03
50	30	20	11.66	11.20	10.13	1.15

EXHIBIT 8.10

Portfolios with and without Direct Energy

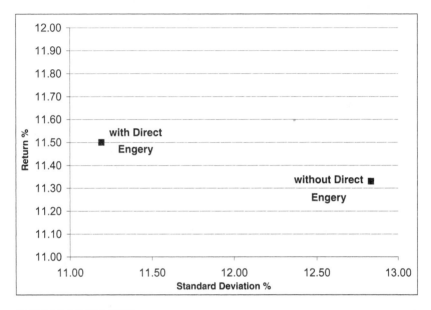

CONCLUSION

Direct energy offers investors an attractive option for portfolio diversification. Given the asset classes evaluated in this chapter, adding direct energy to a portfolio can potentially increase returns and/or reduce risk, Furthermore, satellite allocations to direct energy should help fiduciaries further diversify their core portfolios without impacting their expected return. Using Sharpe ratio analysis and historical data, our results suggest that portfolios including direct energy can offer better performance than those without direct energy. Direct energy alone has not presented an opportunity for extraordinary returns, nor does it eliminate portfolio risk. However, as part of a satellite allocation, its low correlation with other asset classes and positive correlation with inflation offer some protection against adverse market movements.

APPENDIX A

Direct Energy Total Return Series Construction Methodology

We created a synthetic direct energy total return series (defined for the purposes of this study as a portfolio comprised of 50% crude oil and 50% natural gas) based on the theoretical model, data, and assumptions outlined below.

The annual returns of a direct energy investment are derived from two components: income and capital gain (loss). The income portion is defined as the cash flow generated by the oil or natural gas production. It is simply the difference between the selling price of energy and the production cost. It can be calculated by equation (1):

$$I_{t,t+1} = PD_t \times (SP_t - C_t) \tag{1}$$

where PD_t = production in period t

SP_t = spot price of direct energy in period t

C_t = cost of production in period t

A production decline curve was derived from domestic crude oil production data (excluding Alaska) obtained from the February 2001 *Basic Petroleum Data Book* published by the American Petroleum Institute. The production decline curve experienced over the 1972–1986 time period was deemed typical and the relative production over this 15-year period was utilized in the above calculation.

Crude oil and natural gas spot prices are obtained from the Producer Price Index available from the Bureau of Labor Statistics. The per-unit cost of direct energy is assumed to be the average historical expense-to-revenue ratio of the major U.S. energy-producing companies.[6] Revenue and expense data for the major U.S. energy-producing companies are obtained from the Energy Information Administration's Financial Reporting System database. The calculated average is based on operating figures over the 1977–2000 time period; data prior to 1977 was not available because the FASB rules on oil and gas disclosures did not become effective until after 1977. The implicit assumption is that over a long period of time the average expense-to-revenue ratio will remain constant. That is, when energy prices are up, high-cost (less efficient) producers will enter the market, thereby driving the average expense ratio up. When energy prices are down, high-cost (less efficient) producers will exit the market, thereby driving the average expense ratio down. On the other hand, when energy production expenses (including costs of drilling, chemical materials, electricity, distribution, labor, etc.) increase, high-cost producers will exit the market, driving the average expense ratio down. When energy production expenses decline, high-cost producers will enter the market, driving the average expense ratio up. The historical average expense ratio is assumed to be the breakeven point, determining whether companies will remain in the market.

To calculate annual capital gain figures, market prices for direct energy properties must be estimated. The market price of direct energy properties can be proxied by the present value of the discounted cash flows generated from the investment properties. Equations (2) and (3) calculate the market price of direct energy properties in periods t and $t + 1$:

$$P_t = \sum_{i=t+1}^{T} \frac{PD_{i,t} \times (FP_{i,t} - FC_{i,t})}{(1 + r_{i,t+1})^{i-t}} + \frac{TV_t}{(1 + r_{T,t})^{T-t}} \qquad (2)$$

$$P_{t+1} = \sum_{i=t+1}^{T} \frac{PD_{i,t+1} \times (FP_{i,t+1} - FC_{i,t+1})}{(1 + r_{i,t+1})^{i-t-1}} + \frac{TV_{t+1}}{(1 + r_{T,t+1})^{T-t-1}} \qquad (3)$$

where $PD_{i,t}$ = projected production in period i, based on information at period t

   $FP_{i,t}$ = future price of direct energy in period i at period t

   $FC_{i,t}$ = cost of production in period i, based on information at period t

   $r_{i,t}$ = forward interest rate for period i at period t

   TV_t = estimated terminal value of the investment at period t

For every year from 1970 through 2002, equations (2) and (3) are employed to price an assumed 15-year income stream from producing wells. Due to the unavailability of historical energy futures price data over this entire period, spot prices are substituted as a proxy for futures prices. Also, for the sake of simplicity, the cost of production term (i.e., $FC_{i,t}$) is assumed to be the constant C_t described above. Rather than utilize forward interest rates as the discount factor for $r_{i,t}$, a constant 10.0% was utilized.[7] It is assumed that this is a viable standard cost of capital for the industry over sufficiently long time periods. An investment time horizon (i.e., holding period of a producing well) of 15 years is assumed. The terminal value of a well is assumed to be five times the final year's cash flow (i.e., revenues less expenses).

The total return of a direct energy investment is derived from equation (4):

$$TR_{t,t+1} = \frac{P_{t+1} - P_t + I_{t+1}}{P_t} \tag{4}$$

The aforementioned process was utilized to create a series of annual total returns over the 1970–2000 time period. The resultant series serves as the benchmark for direct energy used throughout this chapter.

A P P E N D I X   B

Historical Mean-Variance Analysis Benchmarks and Inputs Summary (1970–2002)

BENCHMARKS USED TO DERIVE EFFICIENT FRONTIERS	
Asset Class	Benchmark Used in Historical Analysis
Equity	
Large-Cap Stocks	S&P 500
Small-Cap Stocks	CRSP Deciles 6–8
International Stocks	MSCI EAFE
Direct Energy	Ibbotson Associates' Synthetic Series
Fixed Income	
U.S. Long-Term Bonds	Ibbotson Associates' U.S. Long-Term Government Bond
U.S. Intermediate-Term Bonds	Ibbotson Associates' U.S. Intermediate-Term Government Bond
Cash Equivalents	Salomon Brothers 3-Month Treasury bill

HISTORICAL AVERAGE RETURNS AND DESCRIPTIVE STATISTICS

Asset Class	Arithmetic Mean	Geometric Mean	Standard Deviation	Highest Return	Lowest Return	No. of Positive Years	No. of Negative Years	Sharpe Ratio
Large-Cap Stocks	12.23	10.81	17.52	37.43	−26.47	25	8	0.70
Small-Cap Stocks	14.24	11.86	22.88	61.67	−34.42	24	9	0.62
International Stocks	12.24	10.05	22.62	69.94	−23.19	23	10	0.54
Direct Energy	12.71	10.80	21.49	75.47	−26.39	24	9	0.59
U.S. Long-Term Bonds	9.99	9.39	11.85	40.36	−8.96	24	9	0.84
U.S. Intermediate-Term Bonds	9.08	8.89	6.69	29.10	−5.14	31	2	1.36
Cash Equivalents	6.74	6.71	2.77	15.05	1.70	33	0	2.43
Inflation	4.92	4.87	3.23	13.31	1.13	33	0	1.52

EXPECTED CORRELATION COEFFICIENTS

	Large-Cap Stocks	Small-Cap Stocks	International Stocks	Direct Energy	Long-Term Bonds	Intermediate-Term Bonds	Cash Equivalent
Large-Cap Stocks	1.00	0.79	0.58	−0.20	0.30	0.22	0.09
Small-Cap Stocks	0.79	1.00	0.46	0.02	0.16	0.11	0.07
International Stocks	0.58	0.46	1.00	−0.30	0.11	−0.01	−0.04
Direct Energy	−0.20	0.02	−0.30	1.00	−0.29	−0.24	0.39
Long-Term Bonds	0.30	0.16	0.11	−0.29	1.00	0.93	0.02
Intermediate-Term Bonds	0.22	0.11	−0.01	−0.24	0.93	1.00	0.21
Cash Equivalents	0.06	0.07	−0.04	0.39	0.02	0.21	1.00

N O T E S

1. This chapter is partly based on Chen and Pinsky (2003).
2. See Ankrim and Hensel (1993) and Kaplan and Lummer (1998).
3. Exhibit 8.1 assumes that all cash flows generated from each asset class are reinvested and that no taxes or transactions costs are paid.
4. Consult Appendix B for benchmarks used to represent these asset classes. Appendix B also contains historical and expected summary statistics expanding on the result presented in Exhibits 8.2–8.5.
5. Among the first empirical works in this area were Jaffe and Mandelker (1976), Bodie (1976), and Nelson (1976).
6. Major U.S. energy-producing companies are defined as "… any U.S.-based company (or its parent company) that is publicly-traded and accounts for 1% or more of U.S. production or reserves of crude oil (including natural gas liquids) or natural gas, or 1% or more of U.S. refining capacity." Source: *U.S. Department of Energy Financial Reporting System Form EIA-28.*
7. We also used U.S. forward interest rate as the discount rate; there was no material difference between the results from using a 10% discount rate.

B I B L I O G R A P H Y

Ankrim, E., and C. Hensel (1993 May/June). "Commodities in Asset Allocation: A Real-Asset Alternative to Real Estate," *Financial Analysts Journal*, pp. 20–29.

Basic Petroleum Data Book (2001 February). Washington, DC: American Petroleum Institute.

Bodie, Zvi (1976 May). "Common Stocks as a Hedge Against Inflation," *Journal of Finance.*

Chen, Peng, and Joseph Pinsky (2003 Summer). "Invest in Direct Energy," *Journal of Investing*, Vol. 12, no. 2, pp. 64–71.

Georgiev, Georgi (2001 Summer). "Benefits of Commodity Investment," *The Journal of Alternative Investments*, pp. 40–47.

Jaffe, Jeffrey F. and Gershon Mandelker (1976 May). "The 'Fisher Effect' for Risky Assets: An Empirical Investigation," *Journal of Finance*, pp. 459–470.

Kaplan, Paul D., and Scott L. Lummer (1998 Winter). "Update: GSCI Collateralized Futures as a Hedging and Diversification Tool for Institutional Portfolios," *The Journal of Investing*, pp. 11–17.

Markowitz, Harry M. (1952 March). "Portfolio Selection," *Journal of Finance*, pp. 447–458.

Nelson, Charles (1976 May). "Inflation and Rates of Return on Common Stocks," *Journal of Finance*, pp. 471–483.

CHAPTER 9

Finding Value in Small Stocks

Gary G. Schlarbaum

Bradley S. Daniels
Schlarbaum Capital Management, L.P.

OVERVIEW

Small stocks are distinct enough in their return pattern to be a separate satellite asset class. Investors have many tools at their disposal for selecting small stocks that they believe will lead to superior performance. Two categories of tools often used by professional managers are value and business momentum. The basic idea is to own the inexpensive stocks of companies with improving business fundamentals. While there are many measures of value, such as price/earnings ratios, price/book value, enterprise value/sales, and price/net asset value, we have chosen to focus on the price/earnings (P/E) ratio.

We believe that the P/E ratio is the best indicator of value across the market. While other measures of value are important in certain sectors, such as price/book value in financials, we do not believe that they are applicable in all sectors. Thus, we identify value based on P/E ratios. Sales growth, long-term earnings growth, near-term earnings estimate revision, and

cash-flow growth can all measure improving business fundamentals. We focus on analysts' earnings estimate revisions
over the past 3-month periods, as we believe they are the
timeliest of these measures. The study described in this chapter is a continuation of research that was conducted at Miller,
Anderson & Sherrerd in the 1980s and 1990s by Gary
Schlarbaum. That research focused on the performance of
these factors in the large-market-capitalization universe (see
Schlarbaum 1999). The present research focuses on the small-
cap universe, and looks at performance during and after the
stock market "bubble period" from the late 1990s through
2003. In this chapter we will look at the performance of P/E
and estimate revision factors, and how those two factors can be
used together by small-stock managers to add return in the
context of a core-satellite portfolio.

OUR DEFINITION OF SMALL-CAP STOCKS

Our research was conducted over the period from September
1990 to December 2003. At the beginning of each calendar
quarter, we calculated the equity market capitalization of all
the stocks in the U.S. stock market, and ranked them largest to
smallest, with the largest market capitalization stock getting a
rank of 1. The smallest of these stocks can have very small
market capitalizations, $1 million or less. Generally, these
smallest stocks are too small to be of interest to institutional
investors. Thus, for the purpose of this research, we limited our
universe each quarter to the largest 3,000 stocks in the stock
market. Like many other investors, we define large-cap stocks
as being the largest 1,000 stocks in the market. Small-cap
stocks are then the next largest 2,000 stocks in the market, or
those ranked 1,001 to 3,000 by market capitalization. Our
research focuses on those small-cap stocks.

SMALL-CAP STOCKS, LOW P/E TO HIGH P/E

Valuation often plays an important part in the professional managers' stock selection methodology. We calculated value based on the *price/earnings ratio* using the consensus forecasted earnings for the next 12 months. We believe that market participants generally value companies on future earnings, and so these forecasts are more meaningful than looking at trailing earnings. Forward earnings estimates generally do not include one-time charges or extraordinary items. Investors must understand the nature, magnitude, and frequency of one-time charges because they radically change the stock's valuation. If the one-time charges raise concerns among analysts regarding a company's current earnings or future growth prospects, those concerns are generally reflected in reduced earnings estimates, which would impact on the analysts' earnings estimate revision factor.

We took our small-cap stocks and grouped them by 12 economic sectors. Then within each economic sector, we ranked the stocks on P/E ratio from low to high, placing the stocks into quintiles. Thus, within each economic sector, the 20% of the stocks with the lowest P/E ratios went into quintile 1, the 20% of the stocks with the next highest P/E ratios went into quintile 2, etc. The highest P/E stocks within each sector went into quintile 5. (For a technical discussion of how to rank stocks by P/E ratios, please read the last section of this chapter "Details, Details, Details.")

When evaluating the usefulness of a stock selection factor, we believe it is important to group stocks by their economic sector before ranking the stocks by a factor such as P/E. This step allows for a better understanding of the usefulness of the ranking method in each sector. If instead all stocks were ranked by a factor, such as P/E, without regard to the economic sector, the result would be that most stocks in one or two sectors would end up at the low end of the ranking, while most stocks of some other sectors would be at the high end of the ranking. Any test of the performance of such a ranking then becomes a comparison of the performance of one economic sector versus another. Because financials and utilities generally have lower P/E ratios than technology and health care companies, sorting all stocks by P/E ratios would show the financial and utility sectors as low P/E and the technology and health care sectors as high P/E by default. Grouping by economic sectors before sorting by the factor eliminates this distortion.

With the stocks grouped by economic sector and sorted into quintiles of P/E ratio, we calculated the total return of the stocks over the subsequent 3 months, and then calculated the market capitalization weighted total return for the 5 quintiles. We repeated this process for the 53 quarters from September 1990 through December 2003. We then compared the average annual total return for each quintile to the average annual total return for all the stocks in our study. The results are shown in Exhibit 9.1.

The companies with the lowest P/Es in each economic sector outperformed the universe of small stocks by 7.23%, while the stocks with the highest P/Es underperformed, returning -7.64% below the average. On average over the $13\frac{1}{4}$-year study, low P/E stocks outperformed high P/E stocks.

LOOKING FOR A CATALYST

Another characteristic that managers often look for is a catalyst. Typically, the catalyst is improving fundamental performance of the company, perhaps through faster sales growth, higher gross or operating margins, lower debt levels, or share

EXHIBIT 9.1

P/E ratio quintiles: small-cap companies average
annual total return by P/E quintile versus the overall
small-stock average.

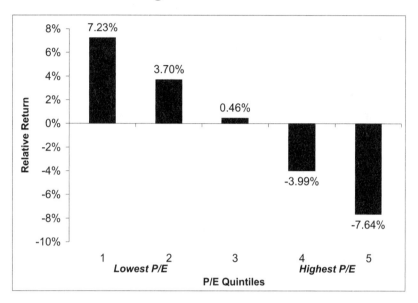

buybacks. These improving fundamental characteristics usually result in higher earnings and rising earnings estimates from
Wall Street.

We calculated an *earnings revision score* based on
changes in analysts' earnings estimates over the prior 3-month
periods, with a heavier weighting on the change in estimates
over the most recent month.

As with the P/E ratios, we took all the stocks in our small-
capitalization universe and grouped them by economic sector.
Then within each economic sector, we ranked the stocks from
the highest earnings estimate revision to the lowest estimate
revision and put the stocks into quintiles. Thus, quintile 1 had

the stocks with the best estimate revisions while quintile 5 had the worst estimate revision.

Again, we calculated the total return over the subsequent 3 months, calculated the market capitalization weighted total return for each quintile, repeated the process for 53 quarters, and compared that average to the average return for all our small stocks. The results are shown in Exhibit 9.2.

Stocks with the best estimate revisions had an average total return that was 5.18% above average, while the worst estimate revision stocks had a return 4.60% below the average. Without looking at valuations, it clearly paid to own stocks where the analysts' estimates had been rising the fastest over the prior 3 months.

EXHIBIT 9.2

Earnings estimate revision quintiles: small-cap companies' average annual total return by revision score quintile versus the overall small-stock average

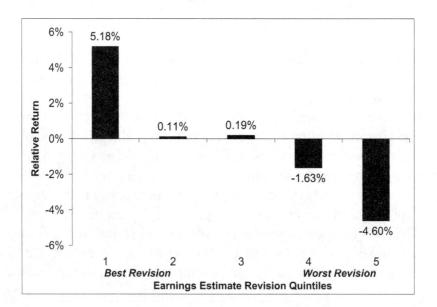

VALUE WITH A CATALYST

Over the period of time covered by this study, it helped to own the cheapest stocks. It was also smart to own stocks with improving fundamentals. How about owning stocks with both characteristics at the same time, that is, owning cheap stocks with rising earnings estimates? To determine which stocks had both characteristics, we calculated a *Value with a Catalyst* score, or VC score. Within each economic sector, we calculated the percentile rank of each stock by P/E ratio. The lowest P/E stocks got a percentile rank of 1, and the highest P/E stocks got a percentile rank of 100. Putting that aside, we calculated the percentile rank of each stock by estimate revision within each economic sector. The highest estimate revision stocks got a percentile rank of 1, while the lowest estimate revision stocks got a rank of 100. We then added the ranks together, giving a heavier weight to valuation than to estimate revision. We then reranked the result, giving us our VC scores.

To test the VC scores, we again grouped the stocks by quintile. Quintile 1 contained stocks that were low P/E with the best estimate revisions. Quintile 5 had high P/E stocks with the worst estimate revisions.

As before, we calculated the subsequent 3-month total return for the stocks, calculated the market capitalization, weighted average return for each quintile, repeated the process for 53 quarters, and compared the average to the average return for small stocks. The results are presented in Exhibit 9.3.

Small-cap, low P/E stocks with rising estimates had an average annual return of 8.13% higher than our average small-cap stock. This group of stocks also outperformed just the low P/E stocks, and just the high estimate revision stocks. Likewise, the high P/E, negative estimate revision stocks underperformed by 9.46% per year, worse than simply high P/E stocks or those with negative estimate revisions. Exhibit

EXHIBIT 9.3

Value with Catalyst quintiles: small-cap companies' average annual total return by VC Score quintile versus the overall small-stock average.

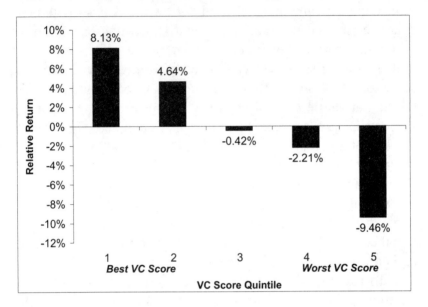

9.4 summarizes the performance of the highest and lowest quintiles for P/E (Exhibit 9.1), earnings estimate revisions (Exhibit 9.2), and VC (Exhibit 9.3).

COMPARING THE RESULTS SECTOR BY SECTOR

While the results are very good across the entire small-cap universe, how do they stack up when we look at individual sectors? It turns out that the VC score works best in 6 of the 12 sectors and is second best in 5 of the remaining 6 sectors. The only sector in which the VC score did not work well was tele-

EXHIBIT 9.4

P/E earnings estimate revision and Value with Catalyst quintiles: small-cap companies' average annual total return by quintile versus the overall small-stock average.

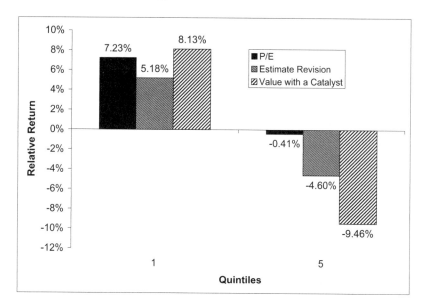

com services. P/E ratios worked best in 4 of the 12 sectors, second best in 3 sectors, and were third in 5 sectors. Estimate revision topped the charts in 2 sectors, came in second in 4 sectors, and third in 6 sectors.

While no stock ranking system can be expected to outperform in all sectors all the time, it is encouraging that the VC score is either the best or second-best measure in all but one economic sector. The detailed results are shown, sector by sector, in Exhibits 9.5A through 9.5L. Each of these graphs illustrates small-cap companies' average annual total return versus the overall small-stock average for each factor for the period of September 1990 to December 2003.

If you calculate the difference in total return between quintile 1 and quintile 5, and use that criterion to determine the effectiveness of a factor, you see the following:

- The VC score was the best in 8 of 12 sectors, and second best in the other 4.
- P/E was the best factor in only 2 sectors, consumer durables and utilities, while it was second best in 7 sectors, and the least effective factor in 3 sectors.
- Estimate revision was the best in 2 sectors, consumer services and retail, second best in 1 sector, telecom services, and the lagging factor in the remaining 9 sectors.

PATIENCE REQUIREMENTS

All of the exhibits thus far have shown the average annual results over the $13\frac{1}{4}$-year study; however, we know that there is no such thing as an "average year." The stunning returns in the stock market from 1995 through 1999, with the S&P 500 up 34%, 20%, 31%, 27%, and 19%, respectively, followed by the years 2000 through 2002, with returns of -10%, -13%, and -23% were far from average. The period of high returns from 1995 through 1999 is, of course, now called *the bubble period*. In 1998, the P/E ratios for technology stocks were high. Over the next 2 years, they went higher. At the same time, the P/E ratios for bank stocks were low, and they went lower.

How did the P/E ratio, earnings estimate revision factor, and the VC scores perform during the bubble period? Was the patient investor rewarded?

To answer these questions, we can look at two types of charts. The first one, Exhibit 9.6, is a bar graph that shows the

EXHIBIT 9.5A

Consumer nondurables sector

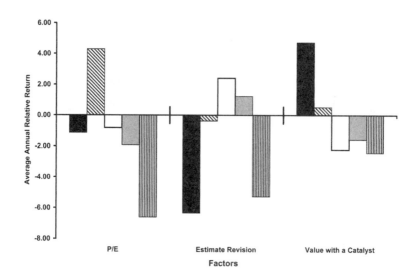

EXHIBIT 9.5B

Consumer durables sector

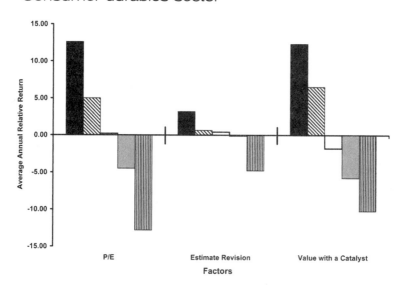

EXHIBIT 9.5C

EXHIBIT 9.5C

Consumer nondurables sector

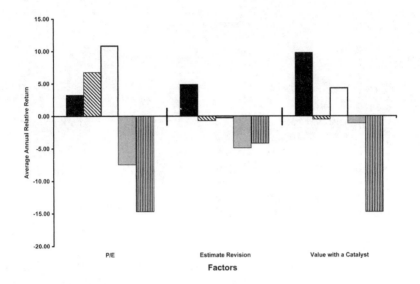

EXHIBIT 9.5D

EXHIBIT 9.5D

Consumer services sector

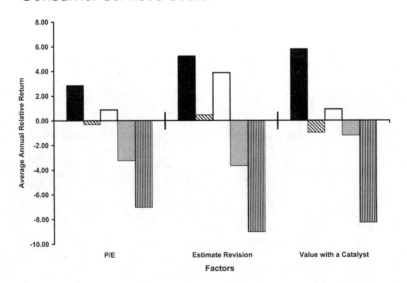

EXHIBIT 9.5E

Energy sector

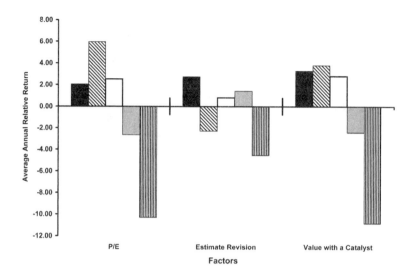

EXHIBIT 9.5F

Financials sector

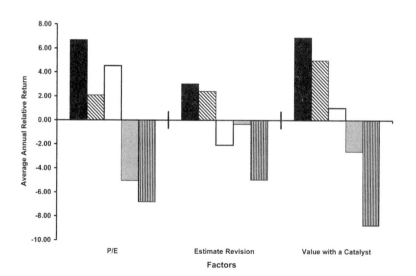

EXHIBIT 9.5G

Health care sector

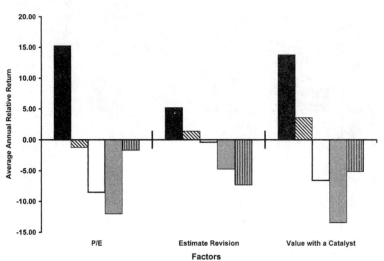

EXHIBIT 9.5H

Industrials sector

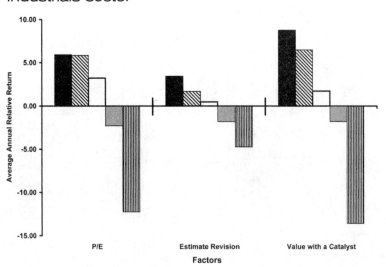

EXHIBIT 9.5I

Retail sector

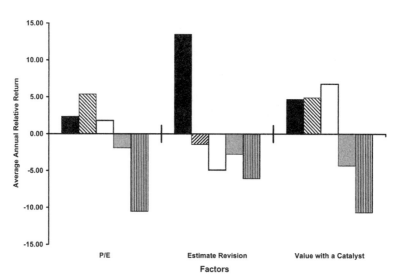

EXHIBIT 9.5J

Technology sector

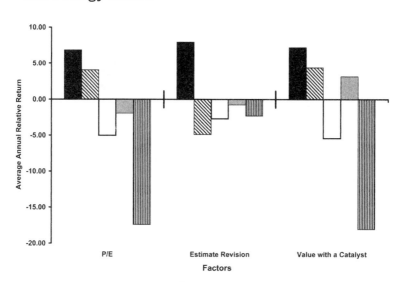

EXHIBIT 9.5K

Telecom services sector

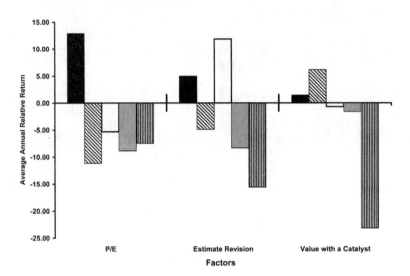

EXHIBIT 9.5L

Utilities sector

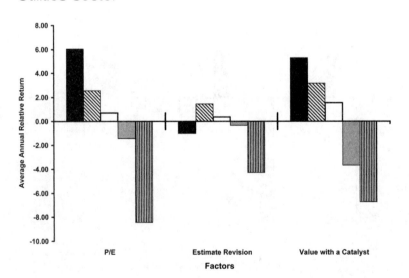

quarterly total return of low P/E stocks relative to the small-stock universe.

When the bar is above the zero line, the lowest P/E quintile is outperforming the small-stock universe in that quarter. When the bar is below the zero line, the lowest P/E quintile is underperforming the small-stock universe.

The strategy of using low P/E stocks worked well from September 1990 through September 1997. The lowest P/E quintile outperformed in 21 out of 28 quarters. However, from the fourth quarter of 1997 though the first quarter of 2000, this quintile underperformed the market, winning in only 1 of the 10 quarters. Starting in the second quarter of 2000, the pattern again reversed, with the lowest P/E quintile outperforming in 11 of 15 quarters through the fourth quarter of 2003. Low P/E investing went through a difficult $2\frac{1}{2}$-year period in the run-up

EXHIBIT 9.6

Lowest P/E quintile versus small stocks

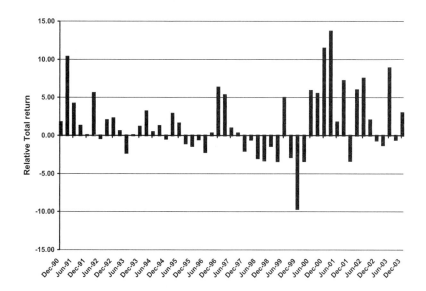

to the bubble period. Was the investor who remained committed to a low P/E investment philosophy through that period
rewarded with extraordinary relative returns in the subsequent
3 years? Was the investor ahead or behind after the entire
episode? To answer that question, we can look at a relative
wealth index chart. Exhibit 9.7 shows the wealth generated by
investing in low P/E stocks relative to the wealth generated by
investing in all small-cap stocks.

When the line is rising, low P/E stocks are outperforming
the small-stock universe. Conversely, when the line is falling,
low P/E stocks are underperforming. The scale on the left
shows the ratio of the wealth generated by low P/E stocks versus the small-stock universe. The line starts at a value of 1.00
at September 1990, representing an equal amount of wealth in
low P/E stocks and all small stocks. When the line reaches the

EXHIBIT 9.7

Low P/E relative wealth index

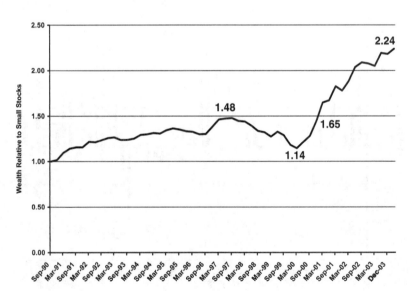

value of 2.00, there is twice as much wealth in the low P/E portfolio as there is in a portfolio of all small stocks.

The relative wealth index line generally rises from September 1990 through September 1997, matching up with the data shown in the previous bar chart. In fact, the relative wealth line peaks at 1.48, indicating that the low P/E portfolio had generated 148% of the wealth generated by investing in the entire small-stock universe. Then, the line falls until March 2000, showing the relative return lost through the peak of the bubble period. The relative wealth hits a low of 1.14 in March 2000. The professional investors and fiduciaries that stayed with this strategy were handsomely rewarded over the next 3 years. As you can see in the graph, the relative wealth index for low P/E investors increases again. By March 2001, the relative wealth index hits 1.65, surpassing the previous peak set in September 1997. In other words, in just 12 months, the lowest P/E quintile made up all the ground it lost in the prior $2\frac{1}{2}$ years. The lowest P/E quintile continued to outperform the average small cap stock over the next $2\frac{3}{4}$ years. At the end of the study in December 2003, the relative wealth stood at 2.24.

The estimate revision factor also had a very interesting return pattern over the time period of this study. Exhibit 9.8 shows the quarterly returns of the high estimate revision factor versus all small stocks.

From the fourth quarter of 1990 though the third quarter of 1997, the returns were generally positive, with the most positive estimate revision stocks outperforming in 23 of 28 quarters, similar to the pattern of the low P/E stocks. At this point, the performance of the two factors diverges. In the run-up during the bubble period, the most positive estimate revision stocks outperformed. From the fourth quarter of 1997 through the first quarter 2000, these stocks outperformed in 8 of 10 quarters. Recall that the low P/E stocks generally underper-

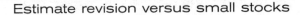

EXHIBIT 9.8

Estimate revision versus small stocks

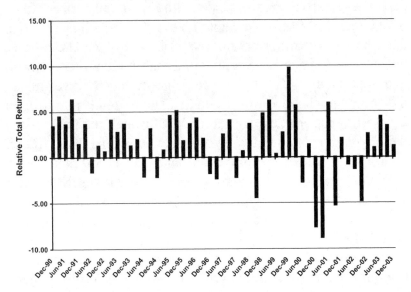

formed at this time. During the decline in the market after the bubble, from the second quarter 2000 through the third quarter of 2002, the highest estimate revision stocks only outperformed in 3 of 10 quarters, whereas the low P/E stocks generally outperformed. In the last 5 quarters of the study, the highest estimate revision stocks outperformed in all quarters.

The relative wealth index chart in Exhibit 9.9 shows that the returns to the estimate revision factor were quite strong from the inception of the study through September 2000, and particularly during the run-up in the bubble period from September 1998 through September 2000. In September 1998, the relative wealth index stood at 1.65; then rose to a peak of 2.15 at March 2000. The next $2\frac{1}{2}$ years were difficult, as the relative wealth index fell down to a level of 1.61 in September

EXHIBIT 9.9

Estimate revision relative wealth index

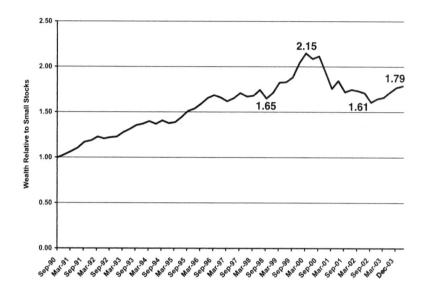

2002, a level approximately equal to that before the bubble period started. From that point to the end of the study, the relative wealth index slowly rises, and it finishes the study at a level of 1.79.

Now let's turn to the Value with a Catalyst factor. How did it perform over these various time periods? As you might expect, it generally outperformed both the low P/E factor and the high-estimate revision factor. Since the VC has a larger weighting toward the low P/E factor, there is a closer correlation with it, but it outperforms in most time periods.

Exhibit 9.10 shows that Value with a Catalyst performed very well from the fourth quarter of 1990 through the third quarter of 1997, when it outperformed in 23 of the 28 quarters. When the bubble period began, the VC factor started to under-

EXHIBIT 9.10

Value with a Catalyst versus small stocks

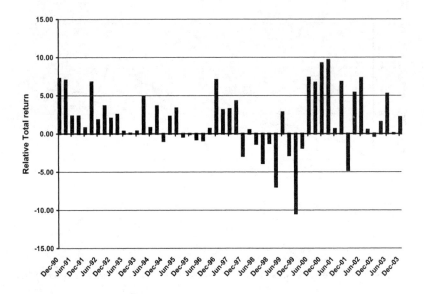

perform, as did the low P/E stocks. For the next $2\frac{1}{2}$ years, the VC factor only outperformed in 2 of the 10 quarters. Starting with the second quarter of 2000, however, the VC factor again outperformed through the end of the study, winning in 13 of 15 quarters.

The relative wealth index for the VC factor shows a return pattern similar to that of the low P/E factor. The relative wealth increases from the inception through the third quarter of 1997, reaching a level of 1.84, or 184% of the wealth generated by investing in all small-cap stocks. The relative wealth index line then falls through the second quarter of 2000, when the relative wealth falls to 1.4, a level not seen since December 1993. But then, as value investing returned to the market, the VC factor's relative performance also increased, and the relative

EXHIBIT 9.11

Value with a Catalyst relative wealth index

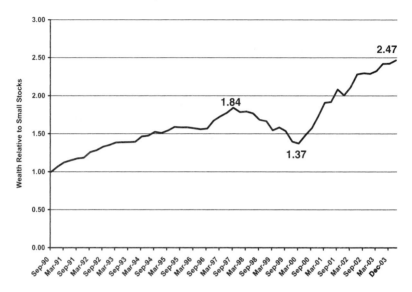

wealth index started to climb quickly. As with the low P/E stocks, the VC factor's returns over the four quarters ending March 2001 more than made up for the underperformance of the prior $2\frac{1}{2}$ years. The performance continued to be strong, and the VC factor ended the study with a relative wealth of 2.47, or 247% of the wealth generated by all small stocks.

The most interesting aspect of this study can be seen by putting the three relative wealth indices on the same graph as shown in Exhibit 9.12.

Notice that from the inception of the study through the third quarter of 1997, when both low P/E investing and high estimate revision investing were working, the Value with a Catalyst factor was usually outperforming both of them, as it had the highest relative wealth index in most time periods. As the stock market entered the bubble period, the VC factor

EXHIBIT 9.12

Relative wealth indices

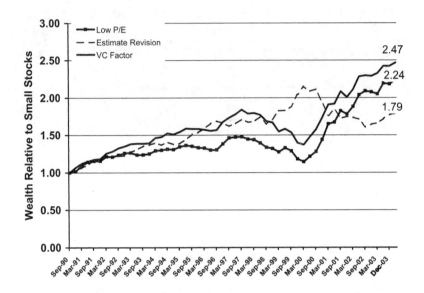

lagged the overall small-cap market, as did the P/E factor. With the larger weighting toward P/E within the VC factor, that correlation of returns should be expected. But as low P/E investing started to work again in the second quarter of 2000, the VC factor kept up with the P/E factor. Thus, the VC factor outperformed both low P/E and high estimate revision during a period of time when both factors were working fairly well, and it was able to match the strong performance of the low P/E from the peak of the bubble period to the end of the study.

CONCLUSION

Clearly, valuation matters. The VC scores and P/Es dominated the back test in terms of the ability to differentiate between attractive and unattractive small stocks across the entire small-cap universe and in most economic sectors. At the same time, we would recommend that fiduciaries make sure their managers look at the broad range of valuation metrics that would be appropriate for a given sector or stock. For example, price/book value is important within financials and price/net asset value is important for real estate. For companies with very low net margins relative to their history and potential future, earnings estimates are perhaps too low, resulting in a P/E ratio that is too high. A better measure of value for that type of company might be the price/book value, or price/sales. What is important is to buy inexpensive small stocks, whether that is measured by P/E or some other appropriate valuation metric.

Estimate revision is an important overlay. It helps identify those cheap stocks where the companies' fundamentals are improving. If investors continue to pay the same multiple of earnings for a stock where earnings are rising, then the return to the stock should equal the percentage increase in earnings. But, if investors value the company more highly because of the increased earnings growth rate, then the P/E multiple will also increase, and the return to the stock will equal the percentage increase in earnings times the percentage increase in the P/E ratio. This impact of higher earnings and a higher valuation is what leads to the superior return to the Value with a Catalyst score.

Small stocks can be a valuable addition to the satellite ring of a core-satellite portfolio. As this chapter has suggested professional small-cap managers may be able to add considerable return by carefully selecting small stocks based on value and business momentum. The potential increase in return and the diversification benefit described in Chapter 1 make small stocks worthy of serious consideration.

DETAILS, DETAILS, DETAILS

Here is a discussion of the finer details of the research described in this chapter for those readers who are interested.

One question that generally arises when discussing P/E ratios is how to handle those stocks with negative earnings. We view those stocks as high P/E stocks. Take, for example, a stock with a $20 price and $2.00 in earnings. The P/E ratio for the stock is 10x. Say the company falls on hard times, and earnings fall to $1.00. Assuming a constant $20 price, the P/E rises to 20x. If earnings fall to $0.50, the P/E rises to 40x. As the earnings continue to fall, the P/E ratio rises to infinity when earnings are zero; and when earnings become negative, the P/E ratio becomes negative. If we sorted on the P/E ratio, stocks with negative earnings would be right next to stocks with true low, but positive, P/E ratios. This is clearly not what we want to happen.

The way to handle this when sorting companies by P/E ratio is to flip the ratio and sort by E/P, or the earnings yield. Low P/E companies are now high earnings yield companies. High P/E companies are now low earnings yield companies. In the prior example, the company with a $20 stock price, $2.00 in earnings, and a 10x P/E ratio has an earnings yield of 10%. As earnings fall, the earnings yield also falls. With $1.00 in earnings, the P/E ratio is 20x and the earnings yield is 5%. With earnings of $0.50, the earnings yield is 2.5%. Zero earnings give zero earnings yield, and negative earnings give negative earnings yield. Now if we rank on earnings yield, we get the desired effect of stocks with negative earnings being ranked as high P/E stocks.

Thus, all of the work done in this chapter on P/E ratios is really done on earnings yield, or E/P ratios. When discussing the results, we flip the description of the analysis back to the more familiar P/E ratios.

B I B L I O G R A P H Y

Schlarbaun, Gary G. (1979). "Value-based Equity Strategies" in *Applied Equity Valuation*, T. Daniel Cogan and Frank J. Fabozzi, eds. New York: Wiley, pp. 123–140.

PART III

Practical Advice

Risk Measurement of Investments in the Satellite Ring of a Core-Satellite Portfolio

Traditional versus Alternative Approaches

Hilary Till
Premia Capital Management

INTRODUCTION

The issues covered in this chapter apply to those satellite investments in a core-satellite portfolio that have default, devaluation, and liquidity risk associated with them, as well as to risk measurement issues for hedge funds. This chapter will help fiduciaries understand the return-to-risk trade-offs that may be present in the satellite ring.

It would be ideal if the return-to-risk trade-off could be summarized with a single metric such as the Sharpe ratio (average returns – T-bill returns/standard deviation of returns). The higher the Sharpe ratio, the better is the reward per unit of risk. Unfortunately, as Nobel Laureate William Sharpe himself has noted, "The Sharpe ratio is oversold."

This chapter will discuss the following topics:

- Why the Sharpe ratio has become the main performance evaluation metric for investments

- A number of shortcomings with the Sharpe ratio
- Several alternative metrics
- The need to understand the source of returns for a satellite investment strategy rather than solely relying on summary performance numbers

THE SHARPE RATIO

William Sharpe introduced the *reward-to-variability ratio* in 1966 to evaluate the performance of mutual funds. Other authors later referred to this ratio as the *Sharpe ratio*. Sharpe came up with this ratio to provide a way for investors to take into consideration the risk they were incurring to earn an investment's return. He believed that the use of such a ratio was far better than solely evaluating an investment's return.

Until recently it was fine to use the Sharpe ratio to summarize the attractiveness of an investment. The measure was accepted because the predominant investment was portfolios of large-cap equities. And by and large, the statistical properties of diversified portfolios of equities have met the restrictive assumptions that should be met before using the Sharpe ratio.

The Sharpe ratio has also been widely used by the alternative investment industry to evaluate their strategies. Because the hallmark of such strategies is the use of leverage, a strategy's returns can be arbitrarily restated, according to the amount of leverage allowed. Exhibit 10.1 shows how returns can differ solely as a function of leverage (e.g., event-driven and merger arbitrage styles have the same levered return but, because of differences in leverage, different delevered returns). These alternative strategies depend on leverage for their double-digit returns.

Therefore, to get a clearer picture of the trade-off between return and risk in a leveraged investment, many investors have

EXHIBIT 10.1

Levered and delevered returns by hedge fund strategy, 1997–2001 (Source: Rahl, 2002)

Style	Average Levered Return (%)*	Average Delevered Return (%)*
Short Biased	13.7	9.3
Global Macro	16.8	8.9
Emerging Markets	16.9	8.8
Event Driven	14.7	8.3
Merger Arbitrage	14.7	7.0
Long/Short Equity	14.0	6.3
Fixed Income	9.6	4.8
Convertible Arbitrage	10.6	4.2
Managed Futures	10.5	4.2
Distressed Securities	n/a	n/a

* Leverage was computed for funds with 5-year historical leverage and performance data.

turned to the Sharpe ratio. One has to make a number of restrictive assumptions when using the Sharpe ratio to compare investments. Drawing from a 1992 article in the *Journal of Portfolio Management* by Sharpe himself (Sharpe 1992), these assumptions are as follows:

- Historical results have at least some predictive ability.
- The mean and standard deviation of the investment's returns are sufficient statistics for evaluating a portfolio.
- The investment's returns are not serially correlated; that is, they do not trend.
- The candidate investments have similar correlations with the investor's other assets.

Sharpe cautions that the use of historical Sharpe ratios as the basis for making predictions "is subject to serious question."

SHORTCOMINGS OF THE SHARPE RATIO

The key problem with the Sharpe ratio is that an investment has to meet these very restrictive assumptions before its use is appropriate. Some authors even advocate that if the Sharpe ratio is used as the evaluation metric for a portfolio's investments, then certain strategies should be disallowed. In other words, only those investments that meet the restrictive assumptions underlying the Sharpe ratio should be included in a portfolio. This chapter takes the opposite point of view: Fiduciaries should have complete freedom in deciding among investments in their satellite ring, but they should make sure that their evaluation metric is appropriate for their chosen investments.

Predictive Ability in Question

Does a Sharpe ratio calculated from historical data provide any meaningful information for expected future results? Exhibit 10.2 indicates that the answer may be no, especially if one were evaluating investments at the beginning of 2000.

In Exhibit 10.2, for example, Fidelity Growth and Income starts out at the end of 1999 with a relatively high Sharpe ratio. Note, though, that it suffers serious losses in 2000, 2001, and through the summer of 2002, at which point it has a negative Sharpe ratio. The other funds chosen to illustrate this point demonstrate that Sharpe ratios have not been predictive of future results.

EXHIBIT 10.2

Historical risk-adjusted returns are not predictive of future results (Source: Lux 2002, p. 32)

Mutual Fund	Sharpe Ratio 12/30/99	2000 Return	2001 Return	2002 Return*	Sharpe Ratio 6/30/02
American Century Ultra Fund	1.25	−19.91	−14.61	−12.45	−0.20
American Funds New Perspectives	0.33	−7.24	−8.30	−0.22	−0.11
Fidelity Contrafund	0.26	−6.80	−12.59	8.27	−0.14
Fidelity Growth & Income	1.39	−1.98	−9.35	−10.42	−0.14
Fidelity Magellan	0.30	−9.29	−11.65	−18.24	−0.18
Janus	0.29	−14.91	−26.10	−17.02	−0.21
Janus Worldwide	1.49	−16.87	−22.88	−16.19	−0.24

* Through August.

In viewing Exhibit 10.2, fiduciaries should note that a high Sharpe ratio might indicate that an investment is nearing the end of a successful momentum-based strategy. Further, most asset allocation strategies rely on the principle of mean reversion and rebalance a portfolio whenever investments attain extremely attractive returns. In this context a high Sharpe ratio may be a warning signal to consider allocating away from a manager or fund.

Another example concerns the prominent hedge fund Long Term Capital Management (LTCM). In September 1996, after 31 months of operation, LTCM reportedly had a Sharpe ratio of 4.35 (*after* fees). Subsequently LTCM nearly went broke, helping to deepen an international financial crisis. With the benefit of hindsight, we can say that LTCM's realized

Sharpe ratio after $2\frac{1}{2}$ years of operation did not give a meaningful indication of how to evaluate its investments.

Another problem with assuming that the Sharpe ratio has predictive ability is that one is assuming that the investment manager's style will not change going forward. Dr. David Harding of Winton Capital Management (Harding 2003) warns that among hedge fund managers: "It is common for a manager's early track record to differ significantly from later performance, due to his [or her] ability ... to exploit a particularly good anomaly with a small amount of money, or because when ... [the manager] had little to lose ... [the manager] could afford [to engage in risky investment practices]."

Harding notes that given how dynamic markets are it is probably unreasonable to expect managers to be consistently successful with one investment approach.

Insufficiency of Mean and Standard Deviation Measures

Should one evaluate an investment solely by examining the mean and standard deviation of its returns? The short answer is no, especially if one's investments have highly *asymmetric outcomes* or contain *illiquid securities* as with a number of hedge fund strategies.

Asymmetric Outcomes

The Sharpe ratio defines risk as the standard deviation of returns around the investment's mean. This approach is appropriate only if the investment's return distribution is symmetric. Because empirical studies from the 1970s showed that diversified large-cap equity portfolios had returns that appeared to be distributed in a symmetric fashion, the Sharpe ratio became widespread in investment evaluation.

Negatively Skewed Outcomes

But if an investment's returns are highly *skewed*, as with highly leveraged or optionlike strategies, the Sharpe ratio is inappropriate. As Hayne Leland of University of California–Berkeley has pointed out (Leland 1998), one can increase the Sharpe ratio of an investment by selling fairly valued options: In this case, an investor is accepting the possibility of negatively skewed outcomes in exchange for improving the investment's average return.

Exhibit 10.3 provides an example of an investment return distribution that is symmetrically distributed; that is, it is not skewed. This exhibit shows the frequency of S&P 500 Index (large-cap stocks) total returns from 1926 to 2003.

Exhibit 10.4 illustrates a portfolio whose return distribu-

EXHIBIT 10.3

Histogram of U.S. large-cap stock returns, 1926–2003

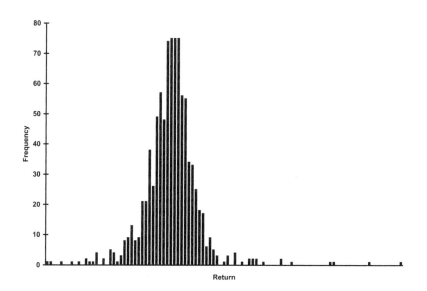

tion is negatively skewed (labeled as *Maximal Sharpe*). You can see this skewness by reference to the symmetric distribution labeled "Basis." This portfolio's return distribution maximizes the Sharpe ratio and is discussed further below.

The fact that investors have a preference for positively skewed outcomes and an aversion to negatively skewed outcomes is not captured by any variance-based risk measure because they all weight the two types of outcomes equally.

Four Yale professors have pursued this argument to its logical conclusion in a working paper entitled, "Sharpening Sharpe Ratios" (Goetzmann 2002). They mathematically derive a strategy for maximizing the Sharpe ratio. The resulting strategy has limited upside returns and the possibility of very large losses, as illustrated in Exhibit 10.4. By undertaking a maximum Sharpe ratio strategy, an investor may be accept-

EXHIBIT 10.4

The distribution of the Sharpe ratio—maximizing portfolio

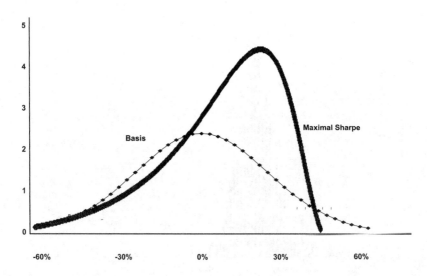

ing negatively skewed returns in exchange for improving the mean or standard deviation of the investment.

The Yale professors show that one can achieve a maximum Sharpe ratio portfolio by selling certain ratios of calls and puts against a core equity market holding. The authors conclude: "Expected returns being held constant, high Sharpe ratio strategies are, by definition, strategies that generate modest profits punctuated by occasional crashes." (Goetzmann 2002, p. 26)

The experience of the Art Institute of Chicago's endowment supports the Yale professors' concern. One of the endowment's hedge fund managers noted in their marketing material that their fund had "the highest Sharpe ratio in the industry," according to the *Wall Street Journal* (Dugan 2002). The hedge fund was quoted as saying it would combine "cash holdings with stocks and riskier index options" in such a way that they "could guarantee profits of 1% to 2% a month in flat or rising markets. The fund ... could lose money only if the stocks to which the options were tied dropped more than 30%." This fund reportedly had large losses in late 2001.

An informative, hypothetical example has been provided by Dr. Mark Anson, chief investment officer of the California Public Employees' Retirement System, in a *Journal of Alternative Investments* article (Anson 2002). Anson illustrates the problem of using symmetric performance measures like the Sharpe ratio for evaluating trading strategies with asymmetric outcomes. In Anson's hypothetical example, an investment manager leverages his or her initial investment capital by selling out-of-the-money puts and calls on the S&P 500 to achieve a certain performance objective above Treasury bills.

Exhibit 10.5 illustrates the superior performance of this strategy until a "volatility event" or large move occurs in the stock market. What is striking about Anson's simulated

EXHIBIT 10.5

Simulated short-volatility investment strategy
(Source: Anson 2002, Exhibit 1)

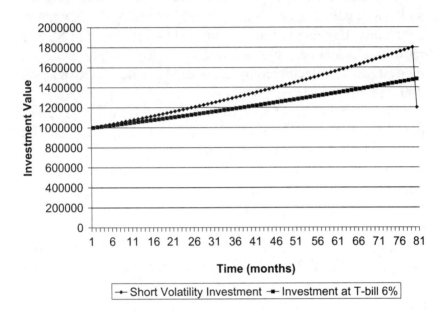

examples is that on average, it takes about 7 years for the
volatility event to occur and leave the investor with sub-
Treasury bill returns. This event could occur in 1 month, or it
could take as long as 20 years.

Exhibit 10.6 shows statistics from Anson's example
where the strategy will have high returns (9% on average and
3% above Treasury bills), minimal standard deviation (0.42%),
and a superior Sharpe ratio (7.14) until the volatility event
occurs and reveals the underlying riskiness of the strategy.
Fiduciaries with long time horizons should not be mislead by
short-term (prevolatility event) performance.

After reviewing the examples above, one can understand

EXHIBIT 10.6

Performance *statistics* for short-volatility investment strategy *(Source: Anson 2002, Exhibit 2)*

	Prevolatility Event	**Postvolatility Event**
Average Annual Return	9.00%	2.85%
Excess Return	3.00%	−3.15%
Standard Deviation	0.42%	3.71%
Sharpe Ratio	7.14	−0.85

the statement of City University (London) Professor Harry Kat: "I would probably only trust … [Sharpe ratios] for large diversified portfolios investing in large [equity] names."[1]

Positively Skewed Outcomes

Even though it is intuitively obvious that, all things being equal, investors would prefer investments that have the possibility of large gains, this feature of an investment is not rewarded by the Sharpe ratio.

An extreme example of this is given in an article in the *Journal of Political Economy* by Professor Antonio Bernardo of the University of California–Los Angeles and Dr. Olivier Ledoit of Credit Suisse First Boston (Bernardo 2000). The authors provide an extreme example of how a superior investment can have a low Sharpe ratio. They note that a lottery where a ticket costs 1 cent today, and where winners pocket $50 billion next year with a probability of 10%, and nothing otherwise, has a Sharpe ratio of 0.33.

Questioning the Mean-Variance Paradigm

As Sharpe notes in his 1994 article, the Sharpe ratio builds on the Markowitz mean-variance paradigm, which assumes that the mean and standard deviation are sufficient for evaluating an investment. Other authors have noted that only taking into consideration the first and second moments of a distribution may not be enough to characterize the attractiveness of an investment. The first moment of a distribution is the *mean*; the second moment is its *variance*. The *standard deviation* is the square root of the variance.

A number of researchers have suggested that one should also take into consideration the skewness and kurtosis of an investment's distribution. *Skewness* is the third moment, which describes how asymmetric a distribution is; and *kurtosis* is the fourth moment, which is linked to the existence of extreme returns. Further, one should also consider how the addition of a candidate investment to a portfolio will impact the overall portfolio's skewness and kurtosis.

In financial applications, *negative skewness* refers to an investment having a higher probability of a very large loss and a lower probability of a high positive return than one with equally balanced (symmetric) probabilities of gains and losses. The higher the kurtosis is, the more likely extreme observations are. For given levels of mean return and variance, one would expect most investors to like positive skewness and dislike high kurtosis.

In a *Journal of Alternative Investments* article, Professor Chris Brooks of the University of Reading (UK) and Professor Harry Kat of City University (London) (Brooks 2002) report to have found among individual hedge fund indices a strong relationship between their Sharpe ratio and their skewness and kurtosis properties. In their empirical study, they find: "High Sharpe ratios tend to go together with negative skewness and high kurtosis. This means that the relatively high mean and low standard deviation offered by hedge fund indices is no free lunch."

In a *Journal of Portfolio Management* article, Professor Harry Kat and Dr. Gurav Amin of Schroder Hedge Funds (Kat 2003) find further evidence that when one uses mean-variance optimization to construct portfolios that include a sufficiently large number of hedge funds, one ends up with portfolios that have lower skewness as well as higher kurtosis in the overall portfolio's return distribution. In other words, they find that there is a trade-off between improving a portfolio's mean-variance characteristics and taking on more risk of rare, but large losses.

For many investment practitioners, it is no a surprise that improving a portfolio's mean-variance ratio may come at the cost of taking on the possibility of extreme loss. Anecdotally, one manager of a fund of hedge funds has stated to the author that he will not invest in a manager with a Sharpe ratio of over 1.5, figuring that such a ratio is unsustainable in competitive markets. Instead, it may be the result of earning risk premiums for a catastrophic event that has not occurred yet.

Illiquid Holdings

Fiduciaries should use performance measures that indicate a manager's skill in providing superior returns per unit of risk. If a manager can adopt a passive strategy that inflates the performance measure, then that performance metric is flawed. Our earlier discussion noted how a skewness-inducing strategy that requires no manager skill (e.g., by selling options) could produce a superior Sharpe ratio. Unfortunately, there is another popular way to increase a Sharpe ratio, which also does not require skilled management: illiquid holdings.

Required Return Premium
One way to produce a higher average return is to invest in equity proxies that are illiquid. Naturally the market will demand a

liquidity premium when pricing such investments. The Sharpe ratio, however, does not penalize illiquidity. But investors do value flexibility; this is the basis of *real options* theory. In real options theory, one explicitly values the optionality associated with decision-making flexibility. In essence, with illiquidity, the portfolio is short real options, and investors give up the flexibility to readily liquidate their investments.

In an article in *Risk* magazine, Dr. Hari Krishnan of Morgan Stanley and Dr. Izzy Nelken of Super Computer Consulting (Krishnan 2003) argue that the illiquidity associated with hedge fund investments should be explicitly priced. Frequently hedge fund investors must agree to have their investment "locked-up" for lengthy periods of time. Krishnan and Nelken solve for what this illiquidity premium should be using the following framework.

The typical incentive clause in hedge fund contracts gives managers a call-option–type structure. Managers collect a performance fee if their fund is profitable (or above a high-water mark) and they are not penalized monetarily if the fund loses money.

Krishnan and Nelken extend previous work by noting that a manager's incentive clause is most like a convertible bond. As long as a hedge fund firm stays in business, the firm collects a management fee or a "coupon." If the firm does well, it collects an incentive fee, which is an ever-increasing payment linearly related to the performance of the fund. If the fund does poorly, investors will liquidate the fund, resulting in a "default," in which the managers lose all future coupon payments.

The authors hypothesize that a hedge fund will alter its leverage level according to what would optimize the value of the manager's incentive contract, which, as discussed, can be modeled as a kind of convertible bond.

On the other hand, investors would prefer to rebalance their hedge fund investments according to the likelihood of a fund doing very poorly. Because investors cannot rebalance, they need to be paid a premium for this lack of flexibility. Their specific, hypothetical example implies an investor should reduce an illiquid investment's return by 10% so that the investment will have an equivalent *utility* with a liquid investment. The authors define "utility" as the investment's return-to-risk ratio. The message for fiduciaries is that illiquid investments may be appropriate but Sharpe ratios that are not adjusted for the added risk will give an upwardly biased view of their value.

Artificially Stable Returns

A portfolio's investments may contain illiquid securities for which one may have trouble obtaining current prices, so there may be a lag in investments being revalued. This would give the false impression of stable returns and, therefore, would result in an artificially low standard deviation. This factor would then tend to inflate the investment's Sharpe ratio. Hedge funds are typical targets of empirical studies because they tend to have illiquid investments. Other assets like high-yield bonds, venture capital, and small-cap stocks also can be quite illiquid.

The principals of AQR Capital Management, LLC, address a related issue in a *Journal of Portfolio Management* article (Asness 2001). They question the reported lack of relationship between hedge fund indices and the S&P 500. When they regressed a hedge fund index's returns versus lagged returns of the equity market, they found a strong relationship between the hedge fund index and the S&P using data from January 1994 to September 2000. Because there was such a strong relationship once they compared the hedge fund index's returns to dated returns in the stock market, they inferred that hedge funds making up the index have been using stale pricing in evaluating their holdings.

Fiduciaries might consider hedge funds for their satellite portfolios because they would like to diversify away some of their equity market exposure. If this were one's investment rationale, then the AQR procedure would be useful in evaluating potential hedge fund strategies. The AQR researchers recalculated the Sharpe ratio of a number of hedge fund styles as if each style's true equity market exposure had been hedged away. Their measure of true equity market exposure takes into consideration the probable stale pricing of hedge funds.

Exhibit 10.7 shows an excerpt from the authors' results. "Monthly Unhedged Sharpe Ratio" is the unadjusted Sharpe ratio of the hedge fund style. "Monthly Beta Hedged Sharpe Ratio" is the Sharpe ratio of the hedge fund style if it were hedged according to its relationship with the stock market based on regressing contemporaneous returns. "Summed Beta Hedged Sharpe Ratio" is the Sharpe ratio of the hedge fund style if it were hedged according to its relationship with the stock market plus an adjustment for the stale-pricing effect.

With several noteworthy exceptions, Exhibit 10.7 illustrates that once market exposure is taken into consideration, the attractiveness of a number of hedge fund strategies declines fairly dramatically. Further, the adjusted Sharpe ratios shown in the last column of Exhibit 10.7 (Summed Beta Hedged Sharpe Ratio) are mostly negative; indicating that at least over the period, January 1994 to September 2000, there is no evidence that most categories of hedge funds were able to add value after taking into consideration their actual equity market exposure.

One caveat to AQR's empirical findings is that these results are valid only for indices of hedge fund manager results. They do not provide us with information on the expo-

EXHIBIT 10.7

Annual Sharpe ratios of unhedged and hedged hedge fund returns, January 1984 to September 2000 (Source: Asnes 2001, Table 6)

Portfolio	Monthly Unhedged Sharpe Ratio	Monthly Beta Hedged Sharpe Ratio	Summed Beta Hedged Sharpe Ratio
Aggregate Hedge Fund Index	0.80	0.31	−0.40
Convertible Arbitrage	1.07	0.95	−0.11
Event Driven	1.05	0.55	−0.27
Equity Market Neutral	1.85	1.55	1.06
Fixed Income Arbitrage	0.35	0.28	−0.56
Long/Short Equity	0.94	0.39	−0.23
Emerging Markets	0.11	−0.47	−0.82
Global Macro	0.54	0.18	−0.40
Managed Futures	−0.10	−0.12	0.14
Dedicated Short Bias	−0.38	0.61	0.89

sures of individual managers, which can vary widely, even within categories, as noted by Leola Ross and George Oberhofer of the Frank Russell Company (Ross 2002).

The third section of this chapter will provide performance metrics that other researchers have proposed as alternatives to the Sharpe ratio.

As Andrew Weisman of Strativarius Capital Management and Jerome Abernathy of Stonebrook Structured Products note in *Risk Budgeting* (Weisman 2000), if one uses the Sharpe ratio for evaluating hedge fund investments, one may be inadvertently maximizing risk (due to taking on negatively skewed investments) and illiquidity (due to these investments giving the appearance of stable, superior returns).

Some Investments' Returns Do Trend

Sharpe notes in his 1994 article that the returns of an investment strategy should not be serially correlated if one is going to use simple adjustments to "annualize" the Sharpe ratio. It is common practice to calculate an investment strategy's standard deviation based on monthly data and then annualize the statistic by multiplying by the square root of 12.

Professors Brooks and Kat (Brooks 2002) report that the monthly returns of hedge fund indices show significant serial correlation. *Serial correlation* is the correlation of something with itself over time and indicates a trend in the underlying data. Specifically, these researchers found: "All of the Convertible Arbitrage [hedge fund] indices have a first order serial correlation of at least 0.4, which are also statistically significant at the 1% level. A similar feature is observed for Distressed Securities and some of the Risk Arbitrage, Emerging Markets and Equity Market Neutral [hedge fund] series. It is also reflected in the Fund of Funds results."

Finding serial correlation is not surprising in investments that suffer from stale pricing. Other investments that exhibit stale pricing, like high-yield bonds, venture capital, real estate, and small-cap stocks, also exhibit serial correlation in their returns

Similarly, when Professor Andrew Lo of the Massachusetts Institute of Technology examined 12 hedge funds in a paper published in the *Financial Analysts Journal* (Lo 2002), he found that most of the funds exhibit meaningful serial correlation. Lo found: "The annual Sharpe ratio can be overstated by as much as 65% due to the presence of serial correlation in monthly returns, and once this serial correlation is properly taken into account, the rankings of hedge funds based on Sharpe ratios change dramatically."

Fiduciaries should not naively compare investments using Sharpe ratios that do not consider the appropriate statistical adjustment for each return history.

The Candidate Investments May Not Have Similar Correlations with the Investor's Other Assets

Sharpe writes in his 1994 article (Sharpe 1994) that the Sharpe ratio does not take into consideration an investment's correlation with other investments. Therefore, the ratio "will not by itself provide sufficient information to determine a set of decisions that will produce an optimal combination of asset risk and return, given an investor's tolerance for risk."

This issue is particularly relevant for alternative investments because, for some fiduciaries, their attractiveness relies on these investments being satellite diversifiers for existing core equity portfolios. One would prefer a performance metric that would incorporate the degree of diversification that the investment could provide.

Researchers at Kenmar Global Investment found that diversified portfolios of hedge funds are highly correlated to the equity market, mirroring the concerns of the AQR researchers. In an article for *Risk* magazine (Goodman 2002), they note that the Sharpe ratio "does not differentiate between risk that is correlated with the equity market—to which most investors have significant exposure via traditional investments—and risks that are not correlated with the equity market."

As a result, the Kenmar researchers devised a new risk-adjusted return measure, which adjusts returns for correlation to the equity market. This measure will be discussed in the next section of this chapter, "Alternative Metrics."

Business Risks Are Not Taken into Consideration

An article in the *Singapore Economic Review* by Professor Francis Koh of Singapore Management University and two researchers from Ferrell Asset Management (Koh 2002) recommends including a penalty function to adjust returns downward to account for additional business risks associated with hedge fund investing. The authors recommend including the following sources of risk in computing the penalty function: style purity, asset growth, leverage, liquidity, and asset concentration. By extension this advice would apply to other satellite investments that have some or all of these characteristics. The details are beyond the scope of this chapter but the point is that researchers advise against taking most satellite investments' historical returns at face value. The next section introduces some alternatives.

ALTERNATIVE METRICS

During the discussion of the shortcomings of the Sharpe ratio, the previous section touched upon enhanced risk-adjusted return methodologies that have been published in the *Journal of Portfolio Management*, the *Financial Analysts Journal*, the *Singapore Economic Review*, and *Risk* magazine. This section will discuss several additional approaches. Basically there are two fundamentally different ways to address the shortcomings of the Sharpe ratio. One way is to come up with a better summary risk-adjusted return number, given the demand for having one number with which to compare all kinds of diverse investments. The second way is to summarize an investment by deriving its primary asset-based style factors. If one is allowed more than one number to summarize an investment, this is the preferred approach.

Summary Risk-Adjusted Return Metrics

A number of researchers have advocated improvements in risk-adjusted return metrics and risk measures.

Stutzer Index

One alternative measure is the Stutzer index (Stutzer 2000). For Professor Michael Stutzer of the University of Colorado–Boulder the main concern for investors is the probability of underperforming a benchmark on average. Stutzer's performance measure, therefore, rewards those portfolios that have a lower likelihood of underperforming a specified benchmark on average. This measure penalizes negative skewness and high kurtosis (for given levels of mean returns and variance).

Bernardo-Ledoit Gain-Loss Ratio

Another performance measure is the Bernardo-Ledoit Gain-Loss Ratio (Bernardo 2000). This measure is the ratio of the expectation of the positive part of the returns divided by the expectation of the negative part. If an investment's expected returns are large, and the potential loss is low, then this measure would reward such an investment in a way that the Sharpe ratio would not. So, for example, this ratio would very much reward the lottery mentioned previously.

Excess Downside Deviation as an Adjustment to the Sharpe Ratio

In the *Alternative Investment Management Association Newsletter*, researchers from Financial Risk Management (Johnson 2002) note that many hedge fund strategies appear to be in effect "short option" strategies that bear risks associated with rare events. This brings up the problem of using the Sharpe ratio when there are asymmetric outcomes, as noted in the previous section.

The authors advocate examining the downside deviation of an investment strategy's return distribution. The downside deviation measures the degree to which the overall return distribution is due to returns below a threshold level.

Given that the Sharpe ratio is so prevalent as a performance measure, the authors propose making an adjustment to this ratio to incorporate the extra information from the downside deviation calculation. Their *adjusted Sharpe ratio* is defined as "the Sharpe ratio that would be implied by the fund's observed downside deviation if returns were distributed normally." The authors show one example of a hedge fund strategy where this adjustment would be quite dramatic: "a Sharpe ratio of over 2.50 is reduced to 0.79 [for one particular fund]."

The researchers conclude that their framework has the benefit of being sensitive to rare events that might otherwise go undetected when using standard measures.

BAVAR (Beta and Volatility Adjusted Returns) Ratio

The previous section of this chapter noted that researchers at Kenmar had devised a performance metric to explicitly take into consideration an investment's correlation with the stock market (Goodman 2002). Their metric shares the spirit of the AQR authors' adjustments shown in the second column of Exhibit 10.7.

The Kenmar researchers propose that investors use the BAVAR (Beta and Volatility Adjusted Returns) ratio. This ratio "adjusts the beta of various investments to be equivalent, so that a fund that has a lower return but is uncorrelated to the market can be appropriately compared with a fund that achieves a higher return but is highly correlated with the market."

The authors note that investing in hedge funds that are not market neutral is acceptable as long as the higher correlation to the stock market is sufficiently compensated with higher returns.

Risk Metrics

Conditional Value-at-Risk

Professor Vikas Agarwal of Georgia State University and Professor Narayan Naik of the London Business School (Agarwal 2003) recommend applying the Conditional Value-at-Risk (CVaR) framework to satellite asset classes like hedge funds. They advocate replacing Value-at-Risk (VaR), which has been popular among traditional asset managers. The authors explain: "[Whereas] VaR measures the maximum loss for a given confidence interval,... CVaR corresponds to the expected loss conditional on the loss being greater than or equal to the VaR."

By using CVaR, the authors are able to capture the left-tail risk of those hedge fund strategies that have short put option-like exposures. (Exhibit 10.4 above shows an example of a return distribution that has noteworthy *left-tail risk*.) They additionally show that the application of the mean-variance framework for some hedge fund strategies can underestimate tail risk by as much as 50%.

The authors conclude that if a fiduciary's goal is to create portfolios for which the magnitude of extreme losses can be kept under control, then that fiduciary should consider using CVaR as their risk constraint during portfolio construction.

Modified Value-at-Risk

When one cannot assume that an investment's returns are distributed normally (or at least symmetrically distributed), Andreas Signer of Morgan Stanley and Laurent Favre of UBS (Signer 2002) propose a risk measure that also incorporates the third and fourth moments of an investment's distribution. They describe a statistical method for adjusting VaR to incorporate skewness and kurtosis—they refer to this new measure as *modified VaR*.

The authors advocate using modified VaR as the risk constraint for portfolios that include hedge funds because "Nearly all hedge fund strategies show negatively skewed return distributions with positive excess kurtosis."

The authors provide an example that shows how the efficient frontier is affected when using modified VaR rather than VaR as the risk constraint. Exhibit 10.8 "shows the degree to which [a] ... sample portfolio with a hedge fund portion of maximum 10% is represented too positively (in the sense of returns being too favorably risk-adjusted) by not taking account of the skewness and kurtosis of the return distributions."

The authors conclude that an evaluation of the benefits of hedge funds needs to incorporate the higher moments of the investment strategies' return distributions.

Not all hedge fund strategies can be characterized as exhibiting negative skewness. It is mainly the event-driven and fixed-income arbitrage strategies that have been characterized as having disadvantageous skewness and kurtosis properties (for given levels of average returns and variance).

One should also add that the cautionary note on taking into consideration an investment strategy's skewness and kurtosis properties do not only pertain to hedge funds. It also applies to investments with default risk (like high-yield bonds)

EXHIBIT 10.8

Sample portfolio with a maximum investment in hedge funds of 10%. *(Source: Signer 2002, Exhibit 6)*

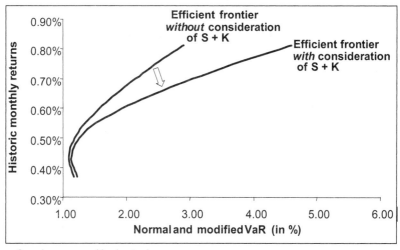

S = skewness   K = kurtosis

and investments with potential liquidity problems (like small-cap stocks).

For example, the four Yale professors in their "Sharpening Sharpe Ratios" article (Goetzmann 2002) note: "... some assets in the U.S. market, primarily small cap stocks, behave as if they are short a [out-of-the-money] put [on the overall stock market.]"

This latter point will be revisited in the fourth section of this chapter, "The Need for Understanding the Source of Returns of an Investment Strategy."

A last qualifying remark is that, to be more precise, in contemporary capital asset pricing theory the important statistical characteristics are coskewness and cokurtosis rather than skewness and kurtosis per se. *Coskewness* refers to the component of an asset's skewness related to the market portfolio's skewness, and *cokurtosis* refers to the component of an asset's kurtosis related to the market portfolio's kurtosis.

Coskewness and cokurtosis provide an investor with information on how an investment will perform during times of overall market stress. Negative skewness, as with a hurricane bond, which results from factors unrelated to market stress, is not as undesirable an investment as one that does very poorly during times of equity market stress and so has negative coskewness. This is because it is during times of market stress that one is particularly worried about having a portfolio of seemingly diversified investments that all perform poorly at the same time.

Professors Brooks and Kat's empirical study (Brooks 2002) suggests how this qualification matters in portfolio construction. They note:

> ...in most cases where the skewness of the hedge fund index is lower (higher) than that of the portfolio to which it is added ..., the skewness of the new portfolio tends to be less (more) attractive than that of the original portfolio comprising only stocks and bonds. The Equity Market Neutral [hedge fund] indices are an exception, though. Although the latter do not exhibit much skewness themselves, adding them still causes portfolio skewness to deteriorate. This strongly suggests that the correlation between the Equity Market Neutral indices and the S&P 500 is higher in down markets than in up markets.

Asset-Based Style Factors

The current academic thinking on how to evaluate alternative investment strategies, which may have short option-like risk and brief track records, is to use asset-based style factors to characterize an investment.

Ideally, financial economists would prefer to come up with the universe of fundamental risk factors that can explain the time-series behavior of an investment's returns rather than just explain an investment's return based on other assets' returns. In other words, if an investment's return cannot be entirely explained by its exposure to the market, what are the additional underlying risk factors of special concern to investors (that give rise to the investment's excess return)? But that effort has not been fruitful as yet. Instead, linking a portfolio, whether it is a fiduciary account, mutual fund, or a hedge fund, to a limited set of investment styles has been a lot more successful empirically.

William Sharpe originally used this approach in a *Journal of Portfolio Management* article (Sharpe 1992) to model mutual fund risk. A current effort by academics is to extend this approach to hedge funds. This effort has been spearheaded by William Fung of the Center for Hedge Research and Education, London Business School, and David Hsieh of Duke University (Fung 2002) and also by Professors Agarwal and Naik (Agarwal 2003). In addition to including various asset classes and rule-based investment styles, they also explicitly include options as explanatory factors of a hedge fund's returns.

The idea is if researchers can link a hedge fund's returns to its underlying "style factors," then they could use the style factor's longer history of returns to evaluate the specific hedge fund. Presumably the return history of the style factor would be long enough so that if the hedge fund incorporates a short event-risk–type strategy, the magnitude of the losses that have occurred (and perhaps could occur) would be apparent from the long-term data.

The asset-based style factor approach provides more useful information about alternative investments and their unique risk exposures than purely relying on the summary metrics covered above. The following section provides examples of the asset-based style factor approach.

Example: Equity Arbitrage Strategies

A number of arbitrage strategies have been characterized as implicitly including short put options.

For example, in the merger arbitrage strategy, a merger candidate is bought by a hedge fund at a discount to what its intended buyer has announced it will pay for the company. These investors assume the risk that a merger deal will fail. This strategy tends to earn consistent returns but sustains very large losses in the event that a deal is not consummated.

A historical analysis of merger arbitrage deals conducted by Professor Mark Mitchell of Harvard University and Todd Pulvino of Northwestern University (Mitchell 2001) shows that this strategy's return is correlated to the overall market during severe market downturns, giving a return profile similar to short index put options.

Professors Agarwal and Naik (2003) take into consideration the optionlike features inherent in a number of arbitrage strategies. The authors found that the following risk factors are significant in explaining the returns of the hedge fund research (HFR) event arbitrage strategy: a short out-of-the-money put on the S&P 500 along with two equity-style factors: size and value.

These researchers found that in addition to event arbitrage, the payoffs of the restructuring, event driven, relative value arbitrage, and convertible arbitrage hedge fund strategies resemble those from selling a put option on the market index. The authors created replicating portfolios for each hedge fund strategy based on their respective significant risk factors. They did so using out-of-sample data. The authors wanted to make sure that their results were not mere statistical artifacts of the data. If the replicating portfolios resemble their hedge fund index's results using out-of-sample data, this is highly suggestive evidence that the risk factors represent the true financial risks of the particular hedge fund strategy.

With only one exception, the replicating portfolios and their respective indices are statistically indistinguishable. Exhibit 10.9 illustrates the out-of-sample results for the event-driven index. (EDRP is the event-driven replicating portfolio, and ED is the actual event-driven index results.)

The authors go one step further. They looked into whether the superior performance of arbitrage strategies is unique to

EXHIBIT 10.9

Out-of-sample performance of a replicating portfolio versus the event-driven hedge fund strategy (*Source: Agarwal 2003, Figure 1*)

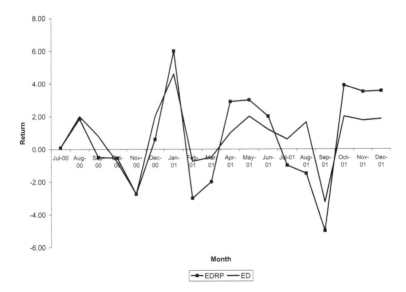

the decade of the 1990s. There has not been an obvious way to determine this because the return history of hedge funds only goes back to 1990.

If the authors' replicating portfolios, which are constructed using buy-and-hold and option-based risk factors, are accurate models for describing the returns of arbitrage strategies, one can use the replicating portfolios as proxies for the strategies and therefore look into the past to see how these strategies would have performed.

The authors examine the period from 1927 to 1989 to find the long-run returns and volatility of the hedge funds' replicating portfolios. In the main, they found that hedge funds' returns are smaller, and the long-run volatilities are higher compared to their performance in the 1990s. Their conclusion is that the performance of the arbitrage strategies "during the recent period appears significantly better compared with their potential long-run performance."

Example: Fixed-Income Arbitrage Strategies

Professors Fung and Hsieh (Fung 2002) advocate extracting common risk factors from groups of fixed-income funds. Their procedure then links the extracted factors to market observable prices, which have longer price histories.

The authors found that fixed-income hedge funds primarily have exposure to fixed-income related spreads, including the convertible/Treasury spread, the high yield/Treasury spread, the mortgage/Treasury spread, and the emerging market bond/Treasury spread.

The authors also constructed a one-factor model with a corporate credit spread as the factor. Their goal was to examine how sensitive a particular fixed-income hedge fund strategy is to changes in credit spreads. They found a strong correlation using recent data. They showed that if one extrapolates this relationship using a longer price history, one would find losses that are double the worst loss experienced in the brief history of this category of hedge fund.

The researchers conclude that the returns for bearing the added sources of risk identified in their study need to be balanced against the additional tools needed to manage the attendant left-tail risk of the strategies.

Example: Generic Model Decomposition

Weisman and Abernathy (in *Risk Budgeting* 2000) suggest a practical application of the asset-based–style factor approach.

Based on a qualitative review of an individual hedge fund, the authors classified the fund's exposure to different asset classes and option types. They then use an optimization technique that fits the hedge fund's returns to these exposures. The particular nonparametric, nonlinear optimization technique they chose is based on their experience with which characteristics are most important in evaluating a manager. They try to capture the manager's large winning and losing months, the manager's use of leverage, and the inflection points of the manager's returns.

One of their examples emphasizes why such an approach is needed. The authors reference a mortgage-backed securities manager who had a historical Sharpe ratio of 4.99 using performance data from July 1995 to August 1998. A Sharpe ratio of greater than 1.0 is considered quite good. A decomposition of the exposures in this portfolio revealed that the pattern of reported returns could have been achieved with substantial leverage and short option exposure. After August 1998, this manager reported a very large loss during a time of large dislocations in the fixed-income markets.

The authors took the investment performance produced by the likely exposures driving a portfolio's return and compared it with the manager's reported performance. They noticed a tendency for hedge fund manager performance to be less volatile than the performance produced by their optimization. They hypothesize that because certain over-the-counter securities are illiquid and difficult to value, their owners may underestimate the periodic changes in the value of these holdings. With their derived performance figures, the authors are in a position to evaluate the real underlying volatility of a portfolio and adjust the risk measure used in evaluating a manager.

This approach is helpful as a forensic tool in determining the implicit short options risk of any manager or investment style, especially if one only has a short track record to analyze.

Example: Systematic Style Biases

Besides determining a hedge fund's exposure to the equity market, researchers at Kenmar have advocated in a *Risk* magazine article (Goodman 2002) that one should also determine the other structural or systematic risks undertaken by the hedge fund allocation in a fiduciary's overall portfolio. These systematic or factor risks could include "... sector exposures (e.g., technology, banking), style exposures in equities (e.g., small/large cap, growth/value, and financial leverage), and style exposures in fixed income (e.g., credit, yield curve, and prepayment)."

That way when an investor is creating a portfolio with a number of hedge funds, he or she can ensure that the overall portfolio will not be inadvertently exposed to too much of any one risk factor.

The researchers note that diversified portfolios of hedge funds currently have a structural bias to the small-capitalization and value equity styles. Fiduciaries who are considering adding these asset classes to the satellite ring of their portfolio should consider the possibility they would be double counting existing asset class exposures.

THE NEED FOR UNDERSTANDING THE SOURCE OF AN INVESTMENT STRATEGY'S RETURNS

Bismarck's Advice

When hedge funds were solely of interest to high net worth individuals, the need to understand the types of exposures taken on by these investment vehicles was practically nonexistent.

A hedge fund manager who now has over a billion dollars under management once told the author of this chapter that his prospective investors were only interested in receiving a one-page summary of performance numbers. The ensuing discussions would then focus on the nuances of how the performance numbers were calculated. There was no interest in discussing the underpinnings of the investment process, he said. It was as if hedge fund investors were applying Baron von Bismarck's advice on sausages and legislation to their investments. ("Anyone who likes legislation or sausage should watch neither one being made," Bismarck was quoted as saying.)

But now that U.S. and European fiduciaries are actively adding alternative investments to their satellite rings, there is tremendous academic and practitioner interest in accurately characterizing the risk exposures of these investments. The following section will briefly discuss the risk exposures of a number of investment strategies that provide superior returns (whether these returns are due to manager skill or not).

St. Petersburg Paradox

Andrew Weisman warns in a *Journal of Portfolio Management* article (Weisman 2002) to be careful of investment strategies that require no investment skill and yet for long periods of time seem to provide superior returns. The key point is that these strategies have large occasional losses, much like hedge funds and other more traditional asset classes. Mark Anson provided one example of such a strategy, which was cited earlier in this chapter. Weisman provides a further example.

Weisman simulates an investment strategy that requires no skill where one makes a bet on a single coin toss. If the bet is successful, one bets again with the bet size being the same size as before. If one loses, one doubles up, increasing the bet size by a factor of two in the next trial. This strategy is named after the paradoxical St. Petersburg coin toss game that was originally solved by Bernoulli in 1738. Exhibit 10.10 illustrates the monthly performance of a hypothetical manager who elects to follow this strategy.

EXHIBIT 10.10

Performance of St. Petersburg–like investment strategy

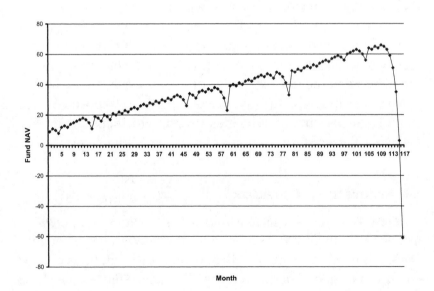

In this hypothetical example, the expected time until a month-end loss of 50% of capital is over 9 years. In Weisman's particular simulation, he found:

> *Monthly reporting tends to obscure much of the fund's volatility, the "draw-downs" (losses of capital) have a very limited duration, and the returns are consistently positive. In fact, right up until [the strategy fails] ..., such a fund would generate approximately a 15% annualized rate of return with about a 12% annualized standard deviation and would be profitable approximately 78% of all months.*

Weisman's example illustrates the importance of understanding whether the underlying return-generating process of a manager's strategy comes from luck or skill.

Risk Premia Strategies

Another way of earning superior returns besides Weisman's "informationless" approach is to implement risk premia strategies. A number of diverse traditional *and* alternative investment strategies appear to earn their returns from assuming risk positions in a risk-averse financial world. The investors in these strategies are in effect taking on risks that others would prefer not to hold.

In some cases, one can see a direct analogy between particular risk premia strategies and the provision of insurance. Selling insurance is the essence of a short put position. While insurance is socially useful, insurance companies are widely diversified to spread the risk of any one local disaster. Investment managers who follow short put strategies, either explicitly or implicitly, are typically not diversified enough to avoid catastrophic losses. Prudent fiduciaries who invest with these managers should do so knowingly and with sufficient diversification in other asset classes to withstand the occasional disaster. One benefit of the core-satellite approach is that it potentially allows fiduciaries to invest in these satellite higher-return short-option–like strategies without taking extraordinary portfolio risk.

The following section gives examples of investment strategies where it appears that the investor earns a risk premium. Most of these examples are drawn from two NBER articles by Professor John Cochrane of the University of Chicago (Cochrane 1999a and 1999b).

Relative-Value Bond Funds

A relative-value bond fund earns its returns by taking on the illiquid assets that international banks desire to sell when they need to reduce risk. The fund hedges this risk by shorting liquid assets. A relative-value bond fund thereby provides a reinsurance function for financial institutions, but it also exposes the fund to liquidity crises. As a result, an examination of empirical data shows that relative-value bond funds have short-put-option–like returns. An investor in such funds assumes the risk of infrequent systemic financial distress and provides other investors with the flexibility of being able to readily liquidate their investments. A relative-value bond fund is in essence providing real options to financial institutions.

Value versus Growth Equity Strategy

One market anomaly identified by Barr Rosenberg (Rosenberg 1985) and others in the 1980s was that an investor could earn returns beyond that predicted by the Capital Asset Pricing Model by investing in *value stocks*, those with low price-to-book-value ratios. This value-based strategy has historically had twice the Sharpe ratio of the overall market.

Professor Cochrane notes that value stocks may earn premium returns because of the risk associated with distressed stocks all going bankrupt during a financial panic. This is precisely the time that investors would not like to find their equity portfolio doing poorly. Therefore, investors pursuing a value-based equity strategy may be in effect earning a risk premium for assuming the risk of a "credit crunch, liquidity crunch, flight-to-quality or similar financial event" that other investors would prefer not to take on. By assuming these risks, the value investor may be in effect providing financial-distress insurance to other investors.

To further understand why value investing may require excess returns, we need to emphasize that most individual investors have larger economic worries than just the performance of their investment portfolios. The main source of income is from their jobs. In the event of systemic financial distress, individuals whose jobs are tenuous would not want their portfolios to be particularly at risk. This means avoiding stocks of companies that could be threatened with bankruptcy. One indication of a weak company is one in which its price-to-book ratio is low—the same metric that traditionally signals a value stock.

An investor who systematically buys stocks based on "value" considerations such as a low price-to-book ratio and sells stocks based on "growth" considerations maybe taking on risks that most individual investors desire to avoid.

Small-Capitalization Stocks

Cochrane notes that small-capitalization stocks seem to have abnormally high returns, even after accounting for this style's market Beta. (*Beta* provides a measure of how much a portfolio's performance varies with respect to the overall stock market).

In two studies (Harvey 2003 and Low 2000), which will

be discussed below, researchers have found that small-capitalization stocks do particularly poorly when the stock market does poorly. Investors may require a return premium for taking on this risk. This premium may be a contributing explanation for why, over very long periods of time, small-cap stocks have historically had superior returns.

In an *Institutional Investor* article, Hal Lux (Lux 2002), now with Paloma Partners, discusses one of the risks associated with small capitalization stocks: "Illiquidity is one of the biggest hazards with investments that are outside the mainstream, such as small capitalization stocks ... small-cap fund managers are betting that liquidity won't dry up in thinly traded stocks, causing their prices to plunge."

Lux notes that "taking such a gamble to earn excess returns is not unreasonable," but fiduciaries should take this risk into consideration when investing.

Negative Coskewness

Professor Campbell Harvey of Duke University and Professor Akhtar Siddique of Georgetown University (Harvey 2000) note that the smallest market capitalization stocks are among the assets with the most negatively skewed return profiles.

As noted in the Alternative Metrics section of this chapter, one would expect negative skewness to be an undesirable investment property, especially negative coskewness. Therefore, one might expect that an investor would need to be compensated to take on investments with these properties. In confirmation of this expectation, Harvey and Siddique find that a portfolio that is long equities with undesirable coskewness properties and short equities with desirable coskewness properties on average made an excess return of 3.6% per year from July 1963 to December 1993.

Harvey and Siddique's article was the first empirical research to suggest that skewness is priced; in other words, that investors are compensated for taking on this undesirable distributional property. As the authors note, if investors did not need a return premium for skewness, then it would be acceptable to continue to represent investors' preferences in terms of mean/variance trade-offs—even when an investment's distribution is highly skewed.

Fiduciaries who do not consider the systematic skewness properties of a portfolio of investments might be misled into thinking they have discovered a "free lunch" by incorporating certain types of negatively skewed investments in their portfolio, as discussed by Kat and Amin in their *Journal of Portfolio Management* article (Kat 2003).

Beta-Gap

Professor Cheekiat Low of the National University of Singapore (Low 2000) finds that small-capitalization stocks have a different response to bullish and bearish equity market conditions when compared to large-capitalization stocks. He captures this differential response through a measure called *Beta-gap*, as follows. Low calculates an investment's Beta during bearish market conditions, a measure he refers to as *Beta-negative*, and a Beta during bullish market conditions, a measure which he refers to as *Beta-positive*. He then constructs the composite risk measure Beta-gap, which is defined as Beta-positive minus Beta-negative. Beta-gap is positive when an investment's relationship to the overall market is stronger during bullish times than bearish times. Low characterizes a portfolio with a positive Beta-gap measure as convex with respect to the overall equity market. Conversely, Beta-gap is negative when an investment's relationship to the overall market is stronger during bearish times than bullish times. He defines a portfolio with a negative Beta-gap measure as concave.

Using data from 1963 to 1998, Low found a positive correlation between Beta-gap and the size of a portfolio's equity capitalization; the return profiles of small-capitalization stocks tend to be more concave than those of large stocks.

One might expect low Beta-gap portfolios to be regarded as undesirable and investors would require a return premium to hold such a portfolio. In fact Low found that a low Beta-gap portfolio outperformed a high Beta-gap portfolio by 6.1% per year over the time period 1967 to 1998.

A concluding remark on Beta-gap is similar to the concluding remark on coskewness: Unless one takes into consideration the asymmetric response of an investment to bullish and bearish market conditions, one may again believe that they have found a free lunch by investing in assets or strategies that have undesirable (but as yet unrealized) responses to market conditions.

High-Yield Currency Investing

Another strategy that seems to have the hallmarks of a risk premia strategy is high-yield currency investing. In this strategy, one invests in currencies with relatively high interest rates and funds this purchase in a currency with relatively low interest rates. On average this kind of strategy has proved profitable; the forward rate of currencies is not predictive of where future currency spot rates will be. Particularly in cases where a currency pair has an extreme interest-rate differential one could argue that this devaluation risk increases with global financial panics and, therefore, that this strategy has a short-option–type payoff profile.

One example was investing in the Thai Baht. The Sharpe ratio for investing in Thai Baht deposits that were funded by U.S. dollar–denominated loans was 2.55 over the period 1980 to 1996, according to data in a *Risk* magazine article by David Shimko of Risk Capital Management Partners and Robert Reider of Millennium Partners (Shimko 1997). Given the unexpected, dramatic devaluation of the Baht in 1997, it appears that an investment in Baht carried a well-deserved risk premium over this period.

CONCLUSION

One purpose of this chapter is to suggest that a number of the candidate investments in a fiduciary's satellite ring may have asymmetric return distributions. Investments will have these return features when they are earning returns because they are, in effect, selling insurance or providing liquidity to other investors. One result is that a fiduciary should not exclusively rely on traditional risk-adjusted return measures like the Sharpe ratio for evaluating investments. Also, because a number of alternative investment strategy managers provide minimal transparency to their investors, the burden is on the fiduciary to understand the economic basis of their manager's returns.

This chapter has focused on quantitative solutions to the risk measurement of satellite ring investments. An emerging alternative view is that investors, and for that matter regulators, should not press for more transparency of hedge fund investments or require more elaborate summaries of an investment's significant risk factors. Instead, this view advocates regulators and investors should focus on verifying the quality and independence of an alternative investment firm's risk management function.

This author's view is that this solution is not sufficient for fiduciaries. The fiduciary must receive enough information about a manager's strategies and key risk factors so that the fiduciary is in a position to properly understand how the satellite ring's investments interact with the risks of their core portfolio. This article provides some examples of alternative performance and risk measures that a fiduciary might take into consideration when investing in the satellite ring.

N O T E

1. Quoted in Lux (2002), p. 32.

B I B L I O G R A P H Y

Agarwal, Vikas, and Narayan Naik (2003 October). "Risks and Portfolio Decisions Involving Hedge Funds," *Review of Financial Studies*, pp. 63–98.

Anson, Mark (2002 Summer). "Symmetrical Performance Measures and Asymmetrical Trading Strategies: A Cautionary Example," *Journal of Alternative Investments*, pp. 81–85.

Asness, Clifford, John Liew, and Robert Krail (2001 Fall). "Do Hedge Funds Hedge?" *Journal of Portfolio Management*, pp. 6–19.

Bernardo, Antonio, and Olivier Ledoit (2000 February). "Gain, Loss and Asset Pricing," *Journal of Political Economy*, pp. 144–172.

Brooks, Chris, and Harry Kat (2002 Fall). "The Statistical Properties of Hedge Fund Index Returns and Their Implications for Investors," *Journal of Alternative Investments*, pp. 26–44.

Cochrane, John (1999a). "New Facts in Finance," NBER Working Paper 7169.

Cochrane, John (1999b). "Portfolio Advice for a Multifactor World," NBER Working Paper 7170.

Dugan, Ianthe, Thomas Burton, and Carrick Mollenkamp (2002 February 1). "Chicago Art Institute's Hedge-Fund Loss Paints Cautionary Portrait for Investors," *Wall Street Journal*.

Fung, William, and David Hsieh (2002 September). "Risk in Fixed-Income Hedge Fund Styles," *Journal of Fixed Income*, pp. 6–27.

Goetzmann, William, Jonathan Ingersoll, Matthew Spiegel, and Ivo Welch (2002 February). "Sharpening Sharpe Ratios," Yale School of Management, Working Paper.

Goodman, Marc, Kenneth Shewer, and Richard Horwitz, Kenmar Global Investment (2002 June). "Integrating Market Correlation Into Risk-Adjusted Return," *Risk*, Risk Management for Investors section.

Goodman, Marc, Kenneth Shewer, and Richard Horwitz, Kenmar Global Investment (2002 December). "Beware of Systematic Style Biases," *Risk*, pp. S17–S19.

Harding, David (2003 July). "Sharpe Justification?" *Hedge Funds Review*, p. 37.

Harvey, Campbell, and Akhtar Siddique (2000 June). "Conditional Skewness in Asset Pricing Tests," *Journal of Finance*, pp. 1263–1296.

Johnson, Damian, Nick Macleod, and Chris Thomas, Financial Risk Management Ltd. (2002 September). "A Framework for the Interpretation of Excess Downside Deviation," *AIMA Newsletter*, pp. 14–16.

Kat, Harry, and Gaurav Amin (2003 Summer). "Stocks, Bonds and Hedge Funds," *Journal of Portfolio Management*, pp. 113–120.

Koh, Francis, David Lee, and Phoon Kok Fai (2002 April). "An Evaluation of Hedge Funds: Risk, Return, and Pitfalls, *Singapore Economic Review*, pp. 153–171.

Krishnan, Hari, and Izzy Nelken (2003 April). "A Liquidity Haircut for Hedge Funds," *Risk*, pp. S18–S21.

Leland, Hayne (1998 October). "Beyond Mean-Variance: Performance Measurement of Portfolios Using Options or Dynamic Strategies," University of California–Berkeley, Research Program in Finance Working Papers.

Lo, Andrew (2002 July/August). "The Statistics of the Sharpe Ratio," *Financial Analysts Journal*, pp. 36–52.

Low, Cheekiat (2000 August). "Asymmetric Returns and Semidimensional Risks: Security Valuation with a New Volatility Metric," Working Paper, National University of Singapore and Yale University.

Lux, Hal (2002 October). "Risk Gets Riskier," *Institutional Investor*, pp. 28–36.

Mitchell, Mark, and Todd Pulvino (2001 December). "Characteristics of Risk and Return in Risk Arbitrage," *Journal of Finance*, pp. 2135–2175.

Rahl, Leslie (2002 December 10). "Hedge Fund Transparency: Unraveling the Complex and Controversial Debate," Slide 52, RiskInvest 2002, Boston.

Rosenberg, Barr, Kenneth Reid, and Ronald Lanstein (1985 Spring). "Persuasive Evidence of Market Inefficiency," *Journal of Portfolio Management*, pp. 48–55.

Ross, Leola, and George Oberhofer (2002 May). "What the 'Indexes' Don't Tell You about Hedge Funds," Russell Research Commentary.

Sharpe, William (1992 Winter). "Asset Allocation: Measurement Style and Performance Measurement," *Journal of Portfolio Management*, pp.7–19.

Sharpe, William (1994 Fall). "The Sharpe Ratio," *Journal of Portfolio Management*, pp. 49–58.

Shimko, David, and Robert Reider (1997 January). "Many Happy Returns," *Risk*.

Signer, Andreas, and Laurent Favre (2002 Summer). "The Difficulties of Measuring the Benefits of Hedge Funds," *Journal of Alternative Investments*, pp. 31–41.

Stutzer, Michael (2000 May/June). "A Portfolio Performance Index," *Financial Analysts Journal*, pp. 52–61.

Weisman, Andrew (2002 Summer). "Informationless Investing and Hedge Fund Performance Measurement Bias," *Journal of Portfolio Management*, pp. 80–91.

Weisman, Andrew, and Jerome Abernathy (2000). "The Dangers of Historical Hedge Fund Data," in *Risk Budgeting* (Edited by Leslie Rahl), Risk Books, London, pp. 65–81.

Author's Note: Some of the ideas presented in this chapter were drawn from articles by Hilary Till previously published in *Quantitative Finance, Risk & Reward, Derivatives Week*, and *GARP Risk Review* (the Journal of the Global Association of Risk Professionals).

Identifying and Adopting Best Practices for Institutional Investors

Samuel W. Halpern, Executive Vice President
Independent Fiduciary Services, Inc.

Andrew Irving, Senior Vice President and General Counsel
Independent Fiduciary Services, Inc.

INTRODUCTION

In recent years, institutional investors of various types and the government agencies that regulate them have devoted considerable energy and resources to identifying and implementing "best practices" for the design and operation of their investment programs. A remarkable feature of this development has been the cross-fertilization of ideas developed across different institutional settings and by different "players," including public and private pension fund trustees, endowment officials, investment consultants, mutual fund complexes, and various federal and state regulatory agencies. That work has brought about a growing consensus about many elements of best practices for effective and efficient institutional investment organizations. Accordingly, the fiduciaries ultimately responsible for the structure and results of their investment programs— the "governing fiduciaries"—should draw upon this body of experience-tested standards and processes for structuring and operating their respective programs.

SOURCES OF BEST PRACTICES IN INSTITUTIONAL INVESTMENT

The body of best practices has emerged from several distinct but interrelated sources:

- Various legal standards (enacted or proposed)
- Professional organizations
- Practitioners and commentators
- Special evaluative studies of best and common practices (so-called *fiduciary audits* or *operational reviews*)

Law

Various existing and proposed statutes impose general duties and criteria on fiduciaries. From these have emerged many concrete policies and procedures concerning specific aspects of governance and investing. For example, by imposing the core duties of prudence and loyalty, the federal pension law regulating private sector pension funds in the United States—the Employee Retirement Income Security Act of 1974 (ERISA)—has encouraged development of many specific policies and procedures (some discussed below) involving risk control, selection of service providers, ethics and conflicts of interest, cost controls, and other essentials. (Links to important documents like ERISA are listed in the bibliography on page 337–338. They are marked in the text with an asterisk.)

ERISA does not apply to state and local government employee retirement systems, university and church endowments, or private trusts. Rather, state and local laws create the fiduciary standards applicable to those entrusted with the management of such funds, and they rarely match either ERISA or each other in all respects. The pension funds and other pools of assets for collective investment in foreign countries are, of course, regulated by the laws of their respective jurisdictions.

Although a single, universally binding articulation of legal standards has yet to emerge, and likely never will, a consensus is emerging about elements of governance and accountability suitable for any prudently run investment program. In the past many state and local laws prescribed a "legal list" of permissible investments, thus restricting fiduciaries' investment discretion, but that is far less prevalent today. Some 40 states have adopted a version of the Uniform Prudent Investor Act (UPIA),* published by the National Conference of Commissioners on Uniform State Laws (the National Conference) as a model statute governing the investment of private trusts. UPIA sets forth standards of prudence and diversification similar to ERISA standards, eliminates the legal list concept, and enumerates specific issues a governing fiduciary must consider in making investments and processes to use when delegating investment authority. For example, UPIA directs the governing fiduciary to consider both macroeconomic issues, such as inflation, and matters specific to the particular trust, such as tax consequences and the purpose of the trust. When authority is delegated, the scope and terms of the delegation must be established prudently.

The National Conference has also issued a draft Uniform Management of Public Employee Retirement Systems Act (UMPERSA).* Although thus far adopted in only one state, UMPERSA has advanced the development of standards of conduct for public sector pension funds, with rules similar to those stated in UPIA. On the international front, in 2002 the Organisation for Economic Cooperation and Development adopted Guidelines for Pension Fund Governance,* with eight standards for governance structure and four more for governance mechanisms.

Courts and regulators have also issued directives or guidance regarding specific processes to promote effective, prudent investing. The U.S. Department of Labor has promulgated regulations, advisory opinions, class exemptions from ERISA's prohibited transaction rules and other guidance on subjects such as investment guidelines, proxy voting, "economically targeted investments," securities lending and "soft dollar" arrangements.[1] These rulings have set a floor for evaluating the conduct of fiduciaries subject to ERISA. The federal courts interpreting the statute have ruled on the processes fiduciaries have used to consider and make particular types of investments (from private equity to real estate to publicly traded securities), select service providers (like investment managers), install risk controls (such as diversification standards), and manage costs (such as brokerage and service provider fees). Most recently, the Securities and Exchange Commission has proposed new regulations requiring that mutual funds be governed by boards of directors with increased independence and resources, as well as mandating disclosure of the process for selecting and retaining their advisers.

Professional Organizations

Professional organizations and investors have also helped articulate and refine best practices for investing institutional assets. The Foundation for Fiduciary Studies and the American Institute of Certified Public Accountants collaborated on the publication of *Prudent Investment Practices: A Handbook for Investment Fiduciaries (Prudent Practices)*,* published by the foundation in 2003. The Association of Public Pension Fund Auditors (APPFA), the National Council of Teachers' Retirement Systems, and the National Association of Public Pension Attorneys have all sponsored conferences and publications devoted to the development of standards of fiduciary conduct.

Among these, for instance, are the APPFA's *Public Pension Systems Operational Risks of Defined Benefit and Related Plans and Controls to Mitigate those Risks,** issued in July 2003.

The Association for Investment Management and Research—an organization of investment professionals—has also promulgated voluntary standards for reporting investment performance. Their Performance Presentation Standards (periodically revised) are designed to help investment managers create "performance presentations that ensure fair representation and full disclosure."[2] The organization also supports a global standard to "allow investors to compare investment managers and ... allow managers to compete for new business in foreign markets."[3] Governing fiduciaries should inquire whether their managers comply with these standards and, if not, why not.

Practitioners and Commentators

In 1996 a voluntary group of leading, active institutional investors from various organizations developed and promulgated a compendium of 20 *Risk Standards for Institutional Investment Managers and Institutional Investors,** which encouraged debate over best practices in identifying and managing investment risk. In July 2000, a group of practitioners in the world of public pension funds issued *Public Pension Systems Statements of Key Investment Risks and Common Practices to Address those Risks.** Similarly, individual practitioners who have successfully managed institutional investment operations have published widely influential treatises and articles explaining the processes and structures they have used to achieve superior results (e.g., Swensen 2000). More broadly, innovative ideas come from the ongoing stream of confer-

ences and literature. Debate and, often, consensus on what
constitutes best practices comes from industry commentators
and practitioners.[4]

Operational Reviews/Fiduciary Audits

An additional source of best practices has emerged from
implementing one of the practices themselves, the periodic
"fiduciary audit" or "operational review." At least since a 1993
evaluation of the Virginia Retirement System, commissioned
by that state's Joint Legislative Audit and Review Commission, dozens of the largest state and local retirement systems in
the United States—or the agencies that oversee them—as well
as many jointly trusteed benefit funds in unionized private sector industries, have commissioned independent firms to conduct sweeping and in-depth analyses of their governance and
investment program. As explained more fully below, these
studies analyze current practices against both the systems' stated guidelines and the practices of similar funds in other jurisdictions.

Numerous commentators have praised such studies,
and a 2003 paper presented to the World Bank specifically
recommends that public pension funds subject themselves to
"periodic review of the governance procedures and their effectiveness within the agency" (Carmichael and Palacios 2003,
p. 16). Similarly, the Association of Public Pension Fund
Auditors specifically recommended periodic fiduciary audits
to mitigate risk (APPF 2003). In June 2004, the Ohio legisla-
ture passed and the governor signed a bill requiring regular
outside "fiduciary" performance audits of each of that state's
public pension funds. Pennsylvania's state auditor and the
boards of trustees of two large state funds are currently in litigation regarding who is authorized to undertake and guide
such a review.

The findings and recommendations emerging from such studies provide an important source of best practices tested by real-world experience. And the dissemination of these studies—and ensuing debate about them—helps refine and promote best practices, industrywide.

WHAT MAKES A PRACTICE A BEST PRACTICE?

Examining the experiences of successful institutional investors provides important guidance in identifying structures and controls that enhance fiduciary performance. But mere common practices may not constitute best practices. Widespread judgments in the 1990s about proper metrics for evaluating Internet and telecommunications stocks led many institutional investors to significant losses. In the investment environment of 2004 and beyond, observers predict investors will increasingly turn their attention to new asset classes.[5] But fiduciaries should not allow the novelty, popularity, or short-term success of an investment idea to obscure the costs or risks associated with it, or the possibility that it is not suitable for a particular fund.

True best practices evolve out of a focus on fiduciary responsibility. But the test is based not only on principle—what is prudent and in the interest of beneficiaries—but also on pragmatism—what works effectively, based on experience. Moreover, the test is not only what works in general, but rather, what works for the particular investor group, given its particular circumstances. For example, delegation of authority from the governing fiduciaries to competent staff and external investment managers is commonly considered a best practice. However, in any given case, whether, in what form, and to what extent to delegate depends on a host of particulars, including, for example, the qualifications of the staff, the adequacy of their resources, checks and balances on their activities, the level and structure of their compensation, and the mechanisms for monitoring them. In a word, what is "best" partly depends on the circumstances.

Finally, best practices also may evolve over time. What was deemed optimal yesterday may be overtaken by new insights or methods.

EXAMPLES OF EVOLVING BEST PRACTICES

An exhaustive explanation of the aspects of fiduciary investing as to which scholars, regulators, and working fiduciaries have developed best practices would constitute a book in itself. Operational reviews and fiduciary audits of substantial state and local government retirement systems run to hundreds of pages, not including substantial exhibits. What we present here is, first, an extensive inventory of distinct aspects of institutional investments programs as to which standards of best practice have developed, and second, a brief discussion of a few select topics from the longer list. The "long list" is designed to help governing fiduciaries identify the many aspects of their investment program that they should address, matters for which they should make decisions and install effective policies and practices. Brief discussion of the select, few topics should introduce governing fiduciaries to current thinking on those topics and help them apply that thinking to those aspects of their investment programs. These concrete examples should also help fiduciaries understand how best practices evolve from useful theory into practical strategies for improving investment programs.

Inventory of Topics with Best Practice Standards

The following is a list of topics where—based on our experience—standards of best practices have emerged. Many or all of these are also commonly included in a broad scope operational review or fiduciary audit, although some pertain only or primarily to specific types of investment organizations (e.g., public pension funds). Some of the topics overlap, so a comprehensive evaluation might not itemize each and every one of the following points:

Organizational Structure and Resources

- Board composition and status
- Functions of board and committees
- Staff resources and duties
- Consultant's duties
- The "middle office" (This term is explained in the next section.)
- Lines of authority and separation of functions
- Internal audit and audit committee issues
- Conflicts of interest and ethics policies

Governance

- Board composition
- Powers and role of trustees
- Powers and roles of committees
- Rules of order
- Relationship to the plan sponsor
- Lines of reporting and authority relative to staff
- Lines of reporting and authority relative to external providers
- Education and training

Legal Matters

- Statutory fiduciary standards
- Legal or statutory provisions that constrain performance

- Securities class action litigation policy
- Use of legal counsel

Fiduciary Liability Insurance

- Self-insurance versus third-party coverage
- Cost/benefit
- Statutory requirements/restrictions

Personnel Practices

- Staffing
- Size of staff
- Staff skill set
- Adequacy of job descriptions
- Compensation
- Adequacy of compensation
- Use of incentive compensation
- Ability to attract and retain
- Competitiveness
- Turnover rate
- Adequacy of personnel evaluation process
- Adequacy of training

Investment Policy Statement

- Suitability for board's objectives and risk tolerance
- Suitability for financial and actuarial conditions
- Clarity
- Completeness

Asset Allocation

- Methodologies
- Rationale behind the current allocation
- Capital markets assumptions and other inputs for risk/return analysis
- Asset-liability modeling
- Rebalancing process
- Review of consultant's study

Retainer Consultant's Responsibilities

- Fiduciary status
- Conflicts of interest
- Scope of services
- Actual performance versus contractual requirements
- Reasonableness of fees

Investment Management Structure

- Use of internal versus external management
- Use of active versus passive management
- Number of managers
- Manager selection
- Manager guidelines
- Suitability in light of investment policy and asset allocation
- Adequacy and sufficiency of investment manager guidelines

Investment Performance

- Total portfolio performance
- Performance of individual components

- Absolute performance
- Risk-adjusted performance
- Peer rankings

Investment Performance Reporting

- To governing fiduciary
- To all stakeholders
- Adequacy of content and frequency

Performance Benchmarks

- Strategic level
- Policy level
- Appropriateness

Due Diligence Procedures

- Process for selecting external managers
- Monitoring external and internal accounts, including compliance with guidelines
- Clarity and thoroughness, by asset class and strategy

Costs and Fees

- Reasonableness and consistency of asset management fees
- Reasonableness of other fees, e.g., consulting and custody

Brokerage and Trading

- Trade order management systems
- Procedures for evaluating trade execution
- Use of minority-owned firms

- Directed brokerage
- Commission recapture
- Soft dollar practices

Controversial Investment Practices

- Derivatives strategies
- Hedge funds
- Appraised assets
- Real estate
- Private equity
- Economically targeted investments

Trust and Custody Arrangements

- Costs and fees
- Cash management
- Securities lending—risk, return, monitoring
- Securities class action claims process
- Ancillary services
- Accounting
- Performance reporting
- Compliance
- Service capability versus needs of fund

Investment Accounting and Operations

- Investment accounting system and "book of record" issues
- Internal control framework
- Trade order entry management systems
- Preparedness for straight through processing
- Clearance/settlement/reconciliation processes

Other

- Operational Reviews
- Fiduciary Audits

SELECTED BEST PRACTICE STANDARDS

Organizational Structure and Resources

Board Composition and Status– Constituency Representation

Even as institutional investors have become leaders in the movement to use the courts to hold companies responsible for losses suffered by investors as a result of corporate scandals, leaders in the institutional investment community have recognized that funds have a corresponding need to examine and improve their internal governance. "If we expect corporate America to do better, it seems reasonable for others to expect us to do better as well," wrote Gary Findlay, the executive director of the Missouri State Employees' Retirement System and the chair of the Council of Institutional Investors (Findlay 2003).

What constitutes best practices regarding many aspects of governance of an institutional investment organization continues to evolve. One example concerns constituency representation. Many laws governing public sector pension funds explicitly require including representatives of the covered workforce on the fund's board of trustees. Taft-Hartley funds, the collectively bargained private sector employee benefit funds in many unionized industries, are required to have joint boards of trustees with equal representation of the union and contributing employers. For most such funds, the union trustees are the union's officers or members appointed by the officers (though elected trustees are not unheard of).

Participant representation in the governance of corporate plans is rare, and legislative proposals to require such representation have foundered. Outside the benefit plan sector, at college endowment funds, for example, concerns arising out of political "hot buttons" such as investing in companies in disfavored industries (firearms, tobacco, and oil) or other issues may be susceptible to resolution by including students and faculty in a decision-making role regarding fund investments.

Having a "representative" body govern the asset investment process has advantages in terms of promoting broad acceptance of the investment program, enhancing accountability, and assuring that decisions are made in the interests of the ultimate beneficiaries of the fund (OECD 2002). But because the law imposes the same obligations on fiduciaries regardless of their backgrounds, a regular program of fiduciary education becomes essential to protect the fund from the consequences of ill-informed decisions (Carmichael and Palacios 2003).

Staff Resources and Duties

Providing adequate staff and professional advice to the governing fiduciaries is increasingly recognized as a key feature of effective institutional investment. One recent perspective on this subject comes from the rules proposed in early 2004 by the SEC for mutual funds, which, if adopted, specifically authorize providing independent directors resources to hire their own staff, separate from the staff of the advisory firm. Mutual fund directors would thus be catching up with their counterparts in other institutional investment settings. Case law under ERISA has long recognized that fiduciary decision makers should seek expert advice before making decisions in areas where their own education and experience is inadequate to the task.[6]

The Middle Office

Large public funds and some other institutional investors with substantial staffs are beginning to implement a "middle office" concept designed to enhance separation of functions and thus improve risk management, compliance, and oversight. The *middle office* is a distinct internal operational unit between the "front office" functions of portfolio management, manager selection, and (where assets are managed internally) trading and the "back office" functions of accounting, reporting, and internal audit. The middle office may also implement fund policies in areas such as securities lending, proxy voting, brokerage commission management, and securities class action litigation claim filing and monitor compliance with internal guidelines as a support function for the overall investment management function. As this practice matures and its functions become better defined, it will likely spread to other institutional settings. Examples of large public pension funds that have instituted a middle office are the New York State Common Retirement Fund, the Texas Teacher Retirement System, and the Ohio Public Employees Retirement System.

Internal Audit and Audit Committee Issues

Institutional investors have also been developing more sophisticated internal audit functions. An internal auditor acts as the governing fiduciaries' "eyes and ears." The internal audit staff can perform compliance tests, verify the sufficiency of records maintenance, monitor the implementation of policy decisions, and verify compliance with legal requirements. For the internal auditor to function with the requisite independence, the office should report directly to the fund's governing body such as the board of trustees, rather than to an executive director or other staff person. This serves to separate the internal audit function from other staff, an appropriate control because most of the functions the internal auditor reviews are performed by staff.[7]

Conflicts of Interest and Ethics Policies

The wave of corporate and mutual fund scandals has also brought to the fore the need for clear and rigorous conflict of interest and ethics policies—as well as effective enforcement of such policies—regarding governing fiduciaries, key staff, and external service providers. ERISA has always contained prohibited transaction provisions which bar fiduciaries from self-dealing and "serving two masters." While UMPERSA's text does not contain a similar catalog, the Official Comments indicate that the drafters expected that the general conflict of interest and ethics rules virtually every state has enacted will apply generally to public officials and employees. The Official Comments to the UPIA confirm that the duty of loyalty articulated in its Section 5 also includes a bar against self-dealing and conflicts of interest.

The mutual fund regulations that the SEC proposed in early 2004 would require registered investment advisers to adopt and enforce codes of ethics establishing standards of conduct for their key personnel, including a duty to report personal securities and mutual fund holdings and transactions, and a duty to report ethics violations by others to a compliance officer.

Even with these sorts of general standards regarding conflicts and ethics, leading institutional investors have increasingly imposed customized provisions, specifically addressing their specific activities as an investment organization. Increasingly common are detailed and specific guidelines that

- Articulate the situations in which an individual fiduciary should be disqualified from acting
- Require disclosure of the fiduciary's material personal business interests that could affect his or her fiduciary investment responsibilities
- Limit and require documentation for reimbursement of fund-related expenses
- Require certifications and disclosures from existing and prospective service providers, regarding payments

of money or bestowing of benefits (free travel, accommodations, etc.) on fiduciary decision makers or (in the case of public funds) influential political figures

Investment Policy Statements

A now standard practice for institutional investors is to adopt a written investment policy statement (IPS). The Department of Labor has defined this as a "written statement that provides the fiduciaries who are responsible for plan investments with guidelines or general instructions concerning various types or categories of investment management decisions," and stated that maintaining such a statement is consistent with the fiduciary obligations in ERISA.[8] Because the prudence of investment decisions is evaluated in a "whole portfolio" context,[9] an IPS should articulate an investment policy for the entire portfolio, with appropriate subdivisions for the different asset classes approved for inclusion in the portfolio. The *Prudent Practices* include the preparation of an IPS as one of seven fundamental Uniform Fiduciary Standards of Care.

The IPS should be an integral part of the fiduciary decision-making process, and not just a record of it. Preparation of an IPS requires fiduciaries to focus on the fund's objectives and tolerance for various types of risk, because suitable asset classes cannot be identified in a vacuum. An IPS will also reflect consideration of the anticipated financial demands on the fund in terms of cash flow and, in the pension context, actuarial considerations such as the assumed long-term rate of return used to set funding rates and benefit levels. Periodic review of the IPS is essential in order to confirm that the investment program matches the fund's needs as they evolve over time.

While there is no such thing as a "generic" IPS, the governing fiduciaries of every institutional investment program should address certain fundamentals and document them in the IPS:

- *Purpose:* the overall purpose of the fund and the identity of its participants and beneficiaries.

- *Objectives:* the fund's investment goals over the near and long term, e.g., earning a particular average expected return, reserving capital and avoiding even a single year of negative returns, generating a specified level of income (as distinct from total rate of return), maintaining a certain funded ratio, ranking in the top quartile of a peer group, etc.

- *Governance:* who is responsible for each function regarding the investment program and how they interrelate, including who reports what to whom, how often, based on what information, and subject to what standards.

- *Risk:* types and degrees of risk that are acceptable and unacceptable, in terms of operations, asset classes, and individual instruments.

- *Asset classes:* which asset classes are suitable for investment as well as target, minimum, and maximum ranges of the portion of the overall fund's assets to be allocated to each. The IPS should also state a policy and procedure for rebalancing when the fund's actual allocation falls outside the articulated limits.

- *Ancillary policies:* the fund's policies and procedures regarding such matters as proxy voting, securities lending, brokerage (including soft dollars and commission recapture), and securities class action litigation.

- *Periodic review:* who is responsible for periodically reviewing the policy.

Asset Allocation

ERISA, UPIA, and UMPERSA all direct fiduciaries to diversify investments unless, in ERISA's words, "under the circumstances it is clearly prudent not to do so."[10] The importance of the asset allocation decision simply cannot be overstated. The *Prudent Practices* document states the point succinctly: "The fiduciary's choice of asset classes and their subsequent allocation will have more impact on the long-term performance of the investment strategy than all other decisions." Accordingly, identifying and applying best practices to the asset allocation process should be a priority for investment fiduciaries. You will find an extended discussion of asset allocation in Chapters 1 and 2.

Capital Markets Assumptions and Other Inputs for Risk/Return Analysis

One increasingly recognized best practice in asset allocation is for the governing fiduciaries—not just staff and external investment consultants—to critically evaluate the capital market assumptions (expected investment return, risk, and correlation of returns among the asset classes) used in the asset allocation modeling. Careful scrutiny by the top investment policy makers is crucial because such modeling is ultimately a "garbage in/garbage out" exercise; blind reliance on the model's results can have unintended consequences. Governing fiduciaries may gain a better sense of the reasonableness of the capital markets assumptions if the consultant or staff provides some scenario testing to demonstrate the impact on the output of varying the return, risk, and correlation assumptions for the different asset classes. Another way is for the governing fiduciaries to learn the range of capital markets assumptions other consultants and other investors employ.

Asset Liability Modeling

Another emerging best practice is to model not only the expected performance of assets in isolation but in relationship to the liabilities the fund is expected to satisfy. This type of asset liability modeling can illustrate the impact of changing capital markets on subjects critical to most institutional investment programs including, for example, a pension plan's funded ratio (value of assets relative to value of liabilities) and required annual contributions, as well as (for corporate pension funds) the "spill over" effect of the fund's actuarial condition on the sponsor's balance sheet.

In coming years, we anticipate that a best practice for many institutional investors obligated to cover retirement liabilities will be to structure portfolios that are designed primarily to maintain or increase funded status and/or stabilize the level of annual employer contributions, rather than earning high risk-adjusted (or absolute) returns in isolation. A recent example along these lines is the January 2004 announcement by the Pension Benefit Guaranty Corporation, the insurer of private sector defined-benefit pension plans, that it intended to increase its allocation to duration-matched fixed-income securities and reduce its allocation to equities from 37% to between 15% and 25%. The PBGC's announced reasoning was that it views itself as akin to an insurer providing annuities—liabilities which should be defeased without exposing the agency to radical shifts in its own funding—rather than as an extension of the underfunded pension plans whose assets were transferred to the PBGC on termination.

Rebalancing Process

A third aspect of asset allocation policy is how and when the assets should be rebalanced as actual investment results or cash flows cause the portfolio to deviate from the stated targets and limits. The rebalancing issue raises several interrelated problems. While frequent rebalancing can minimize the duration and extent of deviations from the established policy, transaction costs associated with rebalancing render frequent rebalancing expensive. In addition, when an asset allocation policy sets ranges of permissible concentration around a target, rebalancing can mean returning the asset class to the target or just to the nearest "edge" of the range. Again, transaction costs and related efficiencies inform the results of this analysis. Also, fiduciaries must assign to a specific decision maker and service provider responsibility for implementing the rebalancing strategy and identify the circumstances, if any, in which rebalancing transactions otherwise dictated by the policy should not be made.

Retainer Consultant's Responsibilities

Using an ongoing investment consultant to help design and oversee the investment program has become widespread. Whether to engage such a consultant and the scope of the consultant's services will often be a function of the expertise and resources of the board of trustees or other governing fiduciary body. Consultants are prevalent in the Taft-Hartley fund arena (where large pension plans are governed by boards of trustees consisting of union officers and the executives of contributing employers who are not themselves investment professionals), in the corporate pension arena (where company officials are typically not skilled pension investment professionals and, with other company duties, have little time to spend on the pension fund), and among public funds (where, again, few board members have institutional investment expertise). Likewise, foundations run by boards focused on the organization's charitable purposes often require the expertise of an investment professional to provide oversight of the investment operation. Maximizing the benefits a retainer consultant can provide requires careful attention to structuring the relationship.

Fiduciary Status

The governing fiduciaries should insist that the retainer consultant accept fiduciary responsibility for its advice and recommendations. When this concept was first proposed in the late 1980s, the investment consultant that contractually accepted fiduciary responsibility was called an *advising fiduciary* (Halpern 1987). Given the liabilities associated with fiduciary status, the retainer consultant who accepts fiduciary status will necessarily have to provide oversight and advice geared to the specifics of each of its client funds, rather than generic "one size fits all" advice. Accepting fiduciary responsibility also precludes the consultant from self-dealing—an important constraint, given the many forms of "pay to play" monies from investment managers that may compromise the consultant's loyalty to the client fund. In addition, the consultant's status as a fiduciary may reduce the litigation risk faced by the fiduciary body that appoints the consultant, and it can be taken into account by a fund's insurers to offer more favorable premium and coverage levels. This is not to say, however, that if the consultant accepts fiduciary responsibility, the governing fiduciaries can shed all responsibilities themselves. Based on general principles of fiduciary responsibility, and in all likelihood, in nearly any contract with a consultant, the governing fiduciaries remain obliged to act prudently in selecting, monitoring, and determining whether to continue utilizing the consultant. The governing fiduciaries also retain responsibility for deciding whether to accept, revise, or reject the consultant's advice, as well as the steps they take to implement the advice they choose to accept.

Conflicts of Interest

Governing fiduciaries should obtain from the consultant disclosure of all potential conflicts of interest that may compromise the consultant's advice before the relationship begins, and that information should be updated periodically thereafter. The potential for conflicts can arise when the consultant is a large financial services firm which provides brokerage, investment management, custody, or other services of the type which the consultant is supposed to monitor. More generally, a consultant's business relationships with other service providers may include "pay to play" moneys that sometimes compromise the consultant's judgments and advice to the client fund. The Securities and Exchange Commission's Office of Compliance Inspections and Examinations takes the problem seriously enough to have launched, in late 2003, a nationwide investigation of leading consulting firms seeking a broad range of information about services the consultants furnish to plan sponsors, investment managers, and other service providers. For example, the SEC's 12-page information request demands details of all "direct and indirect, hard-dollar and soft-dollar type of compensation arrangement the consultant and its affiliates/related entities had in effect ... that was in any way related to the [benefit] plan sponsor marketplace" (*Pensions & Investments,* January 12, 2004). Governing fiduciaries need to know whether and how these key professionals may be influenced by their proprietary concerns when called upon to give advice and make recommendations at the heart of their clients' investment processes.

Scope of Services

The governing fiduciaries are responsible for identifying all functions that *someone* should perform on behalf of the investment program and assuring that all such functions are indeed reasonably performed. Governing fiduciaries should never have to say, after an investment mishap, "I thought the *consultant* was handling that." Best practices call for preparing and executing a contract with the consulting firm which clearly states the scope of the consultant's duties and limits on its discretion. For example, the contract may provide that upon commencement of the engagement the consultant will complete a thorough review of the existing IPS, asset allocation, roster of outside investment managers, and other aspects of the investment function and report findings and recommendations to the governing body. The contract may also require the consultant to assist in implementing policy changes. The frequency and content of the consultant's reports should also be spelled out. If the consultant has responsibilities associated with the solicitation and review of proposals from prospective investment managers, the contract should specify the consultant's role in preparing requests for proposals, reviewing proposed contracts, and other matters. If the consultant is to have authority to take action on behalf of the fund by, for example, voting the fund's proxies or executing the rebalancing policy, the contract should say so.

Investment Management Structure

With an IPS and asset allocation policy in place and, perhaps, a retainer investment consultant engaged to assist in oversight, the governing fiduciaries should decide upon and implement an investment management structure to carry out the investment policy through prudent portfolio management. There is no "best practice" in manager structure per se, although there are recognized criteria to consider in properly deciding on an appropriate structure. Institutional investors have different internal resources and invest in different asset classes, and those differences require tailoring the structure to fit the particular fund's needs. But best practice in tailoring the structure requires careful choices in at least four key areas.

Use of External versus Internal Management

A threshold issue for large funds is whether to manage assets through internal staff rather than external money management firms and, if so, which asset classes should be managed internally and which externally. The law does not compel any particular formula. But ERISA's elaborate provisions concerning the delegation of investment responsibility to investment managers who are either registered investment advisers, banks, or insurance companies creates incentives for external management in the form of relief to the appointing fiduciaries from fiduciary responsibility for the managers' investment decisions (but not from responsibility for prudently selecting and monitoring the managers).[11] And as the "prudent expert" standard becomes the norm across a variety of institutional investment settings, fiduciaries may be well advised to engage experts to make investment decisions if they lack the expertise courts will expect.

The out-of-pocket costs for internal management, particularly at public pension funds, may be far lower than the costs of external management, insofar as the compensation structures of state and local governments are far less generous than the compensation paid to "Wall Street" investment professionals. Internal management may also provide greater control of and responsiveness from the people responsible for the portfolio-level decisions. These advantages may render prudent internal management of certain core asset classes, especially where expertise of individual managers is less likely to add long-term value. However, enthusiasm for internal management should be tempered by the fact that modest compensation to internal staff may render it difficult to attract and retain talented investment professionals. When assets are internally managed, the scope of the internal audit function, and the expense associated with that function, will significantly increase.

Emphasizing internal management may mean forgoing investments in asset classes for which in-house expertise does not exist or is difficult to install. A 2003 Operational Review of the New Jersey Division of Investments conducted by Independent Fiduciary Services, Inc., examined these and other impacts of the exclusive use of internal management at a $72 billion public fund (*Pensions & Investments* November 10, 2003). The New Jersey experience presents an extreme case because that retirement fund is alone among statewide public funds in its combination of exclusively active, internal asset management, without any exposure to real estate, equity, or alternative assets (such as private equity).

Use of Active versus Passive Management

Aspects of the debate regarding internal versus external management also arise in the decision whether to use active or passive management. Passive managers construct portfolios designed to track a particular benchmark and do not make investment decisions concerning individual securities. Accordingly, passive management is available at significantly lower cost than active management. The choice between active and passive management turns on a judgment as to whether active management is likely to produce returns, after fees, which outperform the benchmark, a judgment which depends largely on one's view of the competitiveness of the markets in various asset classes. Greenwich Associates reports that funds with more than $10 billion in assets passively manage 44% of their total domestic stock assets. The core-satellite approach discussed in the rest of this volume contemplates a mix of core asset classes where active investing is unlikely to achieve that goal (such as large-capitalization U.S. stocks) and other satellite asset classes (like venture capital, microcap stocks, and commodities) where either active management can add value because the particular market lacks competitiveness or passive management is impractical because a reliable benchmark does not exist.

Manager Selection

The selection of the managers to implement the fund's policies could be the subject of a separate chapter, if not an entire volume. Due diligence in selecting managers begins with clarity in the criteria for evaluating candidates. Using a formal request-for-proposal process in the selection of managers necessarily requires that the governing fiduciaries decide what they seek in terms of the particular investment mandate to be filled and the qualities of the firm that are most desirable.

Organizational structure and stability, amount of assets under management, and variety of investment styles the manager pursues are all relevant criteria for evaluating whether the manager is competent and will align its interests with its clients' interests. For example, the advantages of a large multistrategy firm in terms of research resources and depth of analysis may be of little value to the client if the firm places limited emphasis on the particular strategy under consideration. Firms with the most assets under management enjoy economies of scale and may enjoy good reputations, but the size of their portfolios or their organization may impair their ability to react or adapt to certain changes in market conditions. Intangibles regarding the firm's investment process, including the focus, nature, and consistency of its discipline and risk controls as well as its internal governance, including how its personnel are compensated and whether their motivations are well-aligned with the client's interest, also are essential.

Manager Guidelines

Building an effective investment management structure requires providing active managers, whether external or internal, with guidelines that reflect the manager's expected investment strategy, limits on the manager's discretion, criteria over risk and expense, plus benchmarks for evaluating performance. These guidelines should be customized for the particular manager involved and thus are distinct from the IPS, which articulates strategy at the level of the entire portfolio. So, for example, the IPS should include a "policy index" used to evaluate the performance of the entire portfolio, and to isolate factors such as "style drift" that contribute to under- or over-performance. By contrast, individual manager guidelines govern the components of the portfolio on a manager-by-manager basis and therefore contain benchmarks appropriate to the manager's particular investment style, such as the S&P 500 or style-related indices like the S&P/BARRA 500 Value or S&P/BARRA 500 Growth Style Indices. The guidelines should, however, be consistent with (even if more detailed than) related aspects of the IPS, including, for example, limits on particular types of instruments, strategies, and risks. Benchmarks for performance should also include the applicable time horizon over which performance will be evaluated and a suitable "peer group" of comparable managers.

Reasonableness of Fees

Although it is not one of the four key areas of investment management structure, the reasonableness of the consultant's fees can be gauged by using a competitive process to select the consultant. Once the consultant is retained, the contract should contain a detailed fee schedule which describes the services included in a flat retainer and any separate fees (if not included in the retainer) for discrete services such as proxy voting, manager searches, executing rebalancing transactions, and managing transitions when investment managers are terminated or added or assets are reallocated. The contract should also specify whether the consultant may receive brokerage commissions in connection with its services to the client fund and any limitations or conditions (including disclosures) regarding such amounts.

Operational Reviews/Fiduciary Audits

Institutional investors—particularly public and private pension funds—are increasingly engaging objective, outside consultants to evaluate their investment organizations and operations in light of their own stated policies as well as industry best practices (Halpern and Henderson 1994).[12] These operational reviews or fiduciary audits have themselves emerged as a best practice. The editors of *Pensions & Investments* recognized the value of the operational reviews performed in 2003 for the New Jersey Division of Investment and the New York City Retirement Systems, stating, "Both studies should have been done long ago. Without doubt other pension funds need to conduct similar reviews" (*Pensions & Investments* 2003).[13] Four years earlier, the auditor of the state of Washington wrote, "The time has come for performance audits to be established a standard operating procedure ..." (Sonntag 1999). Investment boards, which initially resisted such reviews as outside interference or motivated by inappropriate considerations, have come to appreciate that such reviews could be helpful tools for diagnosing the fund and upgrading it (Lindahl 1998).

Conducting an operational review begins with a decision as to the scope of functions to be evaluated. The scope can be limited to purely investment-related subjects such as the IPS, asset allocation, manager structure, manager selection, performance monitoring, and investment management costs and fees. Or it can cover broader governance and administration issues as well. A well-crafted request for proposals will focus the scope of work so that both the board and the firms solicited clearly understand the project and the form of the desired end product.

Among the key criteria for selecting a suitable firm to conduct the review are experience, work plan, and objectivity. Experience performing similar evaluations is an important factor because firms that have conducted such reviews in the past have accumulated a rich knowledge of practices in the industry that can inform the analysis of a particular fund and improve the value of the recommendations. Each respondent's suggested approach to the project, consisting of interviews, surveys, site visits, and other data gathering, should be compared for appropriateness with the subjects being considered and the budget for the project. The firm's independence can be gauged not only by its institutional and business affiliations with current and prospective service providers, but also by whether the firm actively competes with those service providers in the relevant market. A review of a fund's retainer consultant is of questionable value if conducted by a firm that had unsuccessfully bid for the assignment against the consultant being reviewed, as happened with an operational review conducted for the State of Hawaii Retirement System.

The contract with the firm conducting the operational review should delineate the scope of work by cataloging the subjects the firm is expected to examine and listing significant issues excluded from the scope of work. The project's "deliverables" and a timetable for their delivery should also be clearly described. The contract should also describe the stages in the work. In this regard, allowing the firm to circulate a draft report so staff, fiduciaries, and service providers can check it for accuracy will assure that the report is solidly grounded in the facts. Nevertheless, the contract can and should specifically recite that the firm retains full and final responsibility for the report, notwithstanding the comments received on the draft.

SPECIAL PROBLEMS OF PARTICULAR FUNDS

Different categories of institutional investors face issues unique to their respective environments. These require special attention from governing fiduciaries as they structure and implement their investment programs. We review some of those issues for public retirement funds, jointly trusteed labor-management ("Taft-Hartley") benefit funds, and corporate pension plans to illustrate how best practices should be tailored to meet those special needs.

Public Funds

Relationship of the Board to the Sponsoring Government

Retirement systems sponsored by state and local governments often occupy an ambiguous position within the governmental structure. In some jurisdictions, such as the New Jersey Division of Investment, the investment function is housed within a larger governmental agency (the Office of the Treasurer, in the New Jersey example). In other jurisdictions, however, such as California and the City of New York, the retirement systems are separate entities governed by autonomous boards with a mix of public officials serving *ex officio* and union officials or other representatives of the covered employees. In each case, however, the board's autonomy is diminished to the extent that the retirement system depends on the sponsoring government for staff and budget support or is required to comply with civil service and procurement regulations of general application. These links to the general processes of government may affect the investment function by limiting the resources available to the investment process and the flexibility to respond nimbly to market or industry developments.

UMPERSA addresses this issue by providing that the body with authority to manage the system and invest its assets also is empowered to establish the system's administrative budget, fund that budget from the system's assets, and contract for investment, legal, actuarial, auditing, and custodial services, all without being bound by procurement or other laws of general application relevant to those functions.[14] Of course, the governing body is subject to fiduciary liability in exercising those functions. Establishing such a structure can often become politically contentious. Employee representatives and civil service officials may resist outsourcing of certain functions, while legislators want some control over a retirement system that creates significant liabilities that ultimately are funded by the government (to the extent investment returns do not cover all liabilities).

Pay-to-Play Problems
Another source of stress on public retirement systems is the "pay to play" problem. Elected officials serve as public fund fiduciaries, either as members of a board of trustees or, as is the case with some retirement systems (e.g., New York State, Michigan, New Jersey, and Connecticut, among others) as sole trustee. Campaign contributions by financial institutions to those officials can have the real or perceived effect of improperly influencing the hiring, monitoring, and firing of investment managers, custodians, brokerage firms, and other service providers. Ultimately, this problem can be best addressed in the context of the broader societal debate over campaign finance reform. In the shorter run, a combination of features (which some progressive state funds have adopted) may curb

abuse, such as requiring competitors who propose to provide money management, custody, or other services to disclose relevant political contributions and requiring comparable, periodic disclosure of campaign contributions from firms already working for the retirement fund. In addition, the consistent use of a disciplined, objective process for selecting and monitoring service providers, combined with public disclosure of those decisions and the reasons for them, can mitigate, if not eliminate, the appearance and the reality of improper influencing of these critical decisions.

Taft-Hartley Funds

Trustee Education

As explained above, half of the trustees of every jointly trusteed Taft-Hartley fund are appointed by the union representing the workers covered by the fund, and half are appointed by the contributing employers. Frequently, service on the board is the only institutional investment experience for most if not all of the trustees. As with many public and corporate funds, education of Taft-Hartley trustees is essential to enhancing the quality of decision making and assuring compliance with legal requirements. Thus, many funds (especially Taft-Hartley and public funds) adopt policies and procedures on trustee education, such as:

- Presentations by the fund's regular professional advisers, such as the investment consultant and legal counsel
- A list of particular, suitable outside conferences and educational programs
- An annual budget for attending such sessions
- Procedures for trustees who attend such programs to report back to the full board

Economically Targeted Investments

Taft-Hartley trustees, like their public fund counterparts, also can be tempted to select investments based on collateral benefits such as creating jobs and providing capital for contributing employers—so-called economically targeted or social investments. ERISA's prohibited transaction provisions bar many such programs by limiting investments in employer securities and real estate. But pooled funds providing construction and permanent financing for real estate development conditioned on the use of unionized labor, or venture capital funds focusing on "labor friendly" companies and other investment vehicles with various "social" screens, are not inherently unlawful. Fund trustees are often asked to support union campaigns and other social action by refusing to invest in particular companies or industries, transferring accounts from financial institutions viewed as hostile to organized labor's interests, and supporting through their proxy votes shareholder propositions addressing broad social issues.

ERISA's rigorous standards of prudence and loyalty impose significant limits on trustee discretion in these areas. But they do not ban the consideration of such collateral benefits. Rather, such investments and decisions must satisfy ERISA's requirements on their own merits. As the Department of Labor explained in the context of "economically targeted investments," ERISA prohibits subordinating the interests of participants and beneficiaries to accomplish unrelated objectives. But an investment that accomplishes such objectives without sacrificing the interests that fiduciaries are legally obligated to serve will not violate the statute. What renders an investment imprudent is not necessarily its collateral effects but, rather, "if it [i.e., the investments] would be expected to provide a plan with a lower rate of return than available alternative investments with commensurate degrees of risk or is riskier than alternative available investments with commensurate rates of return."[15] Similarly, when voting proxies, trustees must "consider those factors that may affect the value of the plan's investment and not subordinate the interests of the participants and beneficiaries."[16]

Accordingly, investment opportunities presented with collateral benefits as attractive features need to be reviewed with the same, if not more, rigor as other investment opportunities. An increasing number of Taft-Hartley funds seek to meet this standard by utilizing a special purpose, independent fiduciary to evaluate the transaction. The independent fiduciary may either render advice (as a fiduciary) to the board of trustees, with the board deciding whether and on what terms to proceed, or the independent fiduciary may itself assume decision-making authority and liability.

Corporate Pension Funds
Conflicted Fiduciaries
Most companies sponsoring their own, single-employer pension or 401(k) plans appoint as the plan's investing fiduciaries senior executives and staff with a combination of human resources and financial responsibilities. Those executives face potential conflicts of interest between their duties as members of a plan committee (with a fiduciary duty to act solely in the interest of plan participants) and their "day jobs" in which they put the interests of the business first. This conflict manifests itself in several types of investment situations.

In-Kind Contributions
To meet or exceed minimum funding standards applicable to a defined-benefit pension plan, numerous companies over the years have proposed contributing employer-owned real estate or employer securities in lieu of—or in addition to—regular

cash contributions to the plan. However, the plan's trust agreement may entitle it to cash contributions, and accepting an asset other than cash may be less attractive from the plan's perspective, even if advantageous to the company. Deciding whether to accept such a contribution requires the exercise of fiduciary judgment.[17] Moreover, an in-kind contribution will be an ERISA-prohibited transaction unless the plan's holdings of employer securities or real property are limited to 10% of the fund's assets and compliant with several other criteria as well.[18] The U.S. Department of Labor may individually exempt such a transaction if, among other things, an independent fiduciary negotiates its terms and determines that it is prudent and solely in the plan's interest to proceed. If the decision maker is demonstrably independent and expert, and structures a transaction that genuinely works to the plan's benefit, an in-kind contribution may be not only acceptable but even advantageous to the plan and its participants and beneficiaries. That would be the case, for example, if the independent fiduciary succeeds in obtaining for the plan an excess contribution (enhancing its actuarial condition) of a marketable asset, at a reasonable price (i.e., constituting no more than a reasonable credit against the company's funding obligation), and remains in place objectively to decide in the future whether, when, and under what circumstances to sell it.

Employer Stock

Employer stock creates special challenges to the fiduciaries of a corporate plan. With 401(k) plans, employer stock may be offered as an investment option for participants' own accounts and employers may make matching contributions using employer stock rather than cash. Although certain technical prohibited transaction rules of ERISA don't apply to 401(k) plans, the plan's governing fiduciaries must nonetheless monitor whether offering employer stock remains a suitable investment option. When business reverses or corporate scandals diminish (or, as in the Enron and WorldCom situations, destroy) the value of the stock, those fiduciaries will be answerable for their decision to continue to allow investments in the stock. Courts have held, in the Enron and other cases, that if the plan owns company stock, corporate executives who sit on the plan committee or appoint its members cannot keep secret from plan participants any adverse information or material about the company, and they must act upon that information to protect the participants. While the case law is still developing and the extent of these duties is far from certain, courts have rejected the notion that corporate officials can hide behind the securities laws to justify their silence or inaction as plan fiduciaries.

In terms of best practices, this means that as a starting point, plan committees should monitor plan investment in company stock with a discipline and objectivity at least equal to what they apply to other plan assets. Investment performance reports should describe the performance of the stock over various relevant time periods, on both absolute terms and relative to appropriate benchmarks. Independent analyses of the company from reputable sources should be available for review. Many companies have begun engaging an external, independent fiduciary to take responsibility for these duties as they relate to company stock.

In the event of shareholder class action litigation against the company, fiduciaries must recognize that the plan is likely a member of the plaintiff class and adverse to the company and perhaps even themselves. The Department of Labor has directed plan fiduciaries not to settle such cases, even as passive class members, unless the settlement has been approved by a fiduciary independent of the company and any other defendants who are being released from liability as part of the settlement.[19] Over recent years, when faced with securities class action litigation against the company, many corporate plans invested in company stock have transferred responsibility for managing the plan's role in that litigation to an independent fiduciary. Carrying out that task can involve deciding whether the plan should remain in the plaintiff class or opt out and file its own claims against the company, and choosing whether to accept or oppose a class action settlement. The independent fiduciary should also identify potential ERISA claims the plan may have against the plan's governing fiduciaries and the company in addition to the securities law claims alleged in the class action and related matters.

CONCLUSION

Regardless of whether they are in charge of public or private pension funds, endowments, or other types of institutional investment programs, the governing fiduciaries should seek to identify industry best practices suitable for their particular type of program. Armed with that knowledge, they can then seek to upgrade their respective policies and procedures. The result should be better management of risk, better control of expenses, enhanced governance, and, ultimately, a program better designed to achieve attractive net long-term returns consistent with a suitable set of objectives, in the interest of the plan's participants and beneficiaries.

N O T E S

1. See http://www.dol.gov/ebsa/compliance_assistance.html
2. See http://www.aimr.org/standards/pps/pps.html
3. See http://www.aimr.org/standards/pps/gips.html

4. See, e.g., Peter Bernstein interview, welling@weeden (28 February 2003) and Kneafsey (2003).

5. "Tradition Is Dead," *Pensions & Investments* (12 January 2004) at 1.

6. *Donovan v. Bierwirth*, 680 F.2d 263 (2d Cir.), cert. denied, 459 U.S. 1069 (1982).

7. A 2001 survey revealed that 26 public pension funds had implemented internal audit functions with direct reporting to the board or the board's audit committee. Survey of Internal Audit Staff Size, Summary of Member Questionnaires 2001, Association of Public Pension Fund Auditors, Inc.

8. ERISA Interpretive Bulletin 94-2, "Interpretive bulletin relating to written statements of investment policy, including proxy voting policy or guidelines," 59 Fed. Reg. 38860 (29 July 1994), codified at 29 CFR § 2509.94-2.

9. D. Levin, T. Ferrera, *ERISA Fiduciary Answer Book* at 4–37 (Panel Publishers, 2001); UPIA §2(b); UMPERSA § 8(a)(1)(C).

10. ERISA § 404(a)(1)(C). See, also, UMPERSA § 8(a)(2); UPIA §3.

11. ERISA Sections 403, 404, and 405. UMPERSA Section 6 and UPIA Section 9 also relieve trustees from responsibility for properly delegated investment decisions.

12. Over the past 10 years, IFS alone has completed over 40 operational reviews of public and private funds, with a marked increase in demand over the past 5 years.

13. Independent Fiduciary Services performed both reviews.

14. UMPERSA § 5.

15. ERISA Interpretive Bulletin 94-1, "Interpretive bulletin relating to the fiduciary standard under ERISA in considering economically targeted investments," 59 Fed. Reg. 32606 (23 June 1994), codified at 29 CFR § 2509.94-1.

16. ERISA Interpretive Bulletin 94-2, *op cit.*

17. ERISA Interpretive Bulletin 94-3, "Interpretive bulletin relating to in-kind contributions to employee benefit plans," 59 Fed. Reg. 66736 (28 December 1994), codified at 29 CFR §2509.94-3.

18. See ERISA Sections 406 and 407.

19. Prohibited Transaction Exemption 2003–39, "Class Exemption for Release of Claims and Extensions of Credit in Connection with Litigation," 68 Fed. Reg. 75632 (31 December 2003).

B I B L I O G R A P H Y

Carmichael, Jeffrey, and Robert Palacios (2003). "A Framework for Public Pension Fund Management," paper presented to the 2nd Public Pension Fund Management Conference, World Bank, Washington, D.C., May 5–7. This document can be viewed at: http://www1.worldbank.org/finance/assets/images/Carmichael_Palacios-pension_frmwrk-doc.pdf

Employee Retirement Income Security Act of 1974. http://www.dol.gov/dol/ topic/health-plans/erisa.htm.

Findlay, Gary. (2003 September). "Voice: Glass Houses," *Plan Sponsor*.

Halpern, Samuel (1987 June). "Why Hire an Advising Fiduciary?" *Pension World*.

Halpern, Samuel, and E. Henderson (1994 June). "A Physical Check-up of a Retirement System's Investment Program," *Government Finance Review*, p. 48.

Kneafsey, Kevin (2003 August). "Solving the Investor's Problem," *Investment Insights: The Investment Research Journal from Barclays Global Investors*, pp. 1–8.

Lindahl, K. (1998 March). "Performance Audits of Public Funds," *NASACT News*, National Association of State Auditors, Comptrollers and Treasurers, pp. 5ff.

OECD Secretariat (2002 July). *Guidelines for Pension Fund Governance*.

Pensions & Investments (2003 November 10). "Pension Funds in Need of Reform," p. 12.

Pensions & Investments (2004 January 12). "Consultants under the Gun with SEC Probe," p. 1.

Prudent Investment Practices: A Handbook for Investment Fiduciaries (2003). Foundation for Fiduciary Studies. http://www.aicpa.org/fiduciary/introduction.asp.

Public Pension Systems: Operational Risks of Defined Benefit and Related Plans and Controls to Mitigate those Risks (2003), The Association of Public Pension Fund Auditors. http://www.gfoa.org/services/dfl/bulletin/CORBA-RiskDocApprd-FINAL-8-03.pdf.

Sonntag, Brian. (1999 February 22). "Public Fund Accountability," *Pensions & Investments*, p. 12.

Swensen, David. (2000). *Pioneering Portfolio Management* (New York: Free Press).

20 Risk Standards for Institutional Investment Managers and Institutional Investors (1996). Risk Standards Working Group. http://www.cmra.com/risk.pdf.

Uniform Management of Public Employee Retirement Systems Act. http:// www.law.upenn.edu/bll/ulc/mopepf/retirsy2.pdf.

Uniform Prudent Investor Act (1994). http://www.law.upenn.edu/bll/ulc/fnact99/1990s/upia94.pdf.

INDEX

I N D E X

Abernathy, Jerome, 269–270, 283
Accounting
    fraudulent, 133
    investment, 309, 312
Active risk (alpha risk), 52–58, 82
Active v. passive investment approaches,
    51–64, 66, 68, 82–84
    best practices regarding, 307, 323–325
    with currency fluctuations, 150–165
Adelphia high-yield bonds, 133
ADRs, market indices excluded from,
    69, 71
Agarwal, Vikas, 275, 279
Airline stocks, 38
*Alternative Investment Management
    Association Newsletter*, 273–274
AMEX, 18–19, 22–3, 69
Amin, Gurav, 265, 291
Analyses, 15, 59, 64, 150. *See also* Mean-
    variance analysis
    high-yield/distressed debt and, 140–141
    of inflation-indexed bonds, 171, 182–189
Anson, Mark, 261–263, 286
AQR Capital Management, LLC, 267–269,
    271
Arbitrage strategies, 123, 166, 167, 192
    risk measurement and, 254–255, 269–270,
    276, 280–283
ASA/NBER Economic Outlook Survey. *See*
    Survey of Professional Forecasters
Asset allocation, 3, 5–6, 7–10, 21, 52
    best practices regarding, 307, 315–318,
    321, 326
    core, 4–5, 12–13, 21, 47–48, 57–63
    core-satellite, 12–16
    diversification in, 9, 13, 15, 20, 27–28, 32,
    44, 287–288

with fixed-income management, 93–94
risks and, 33–40
strategies, 52, 82–84
Asset classes, 9, 10–13, 64, 66. *See also
    specific classes*
    best practices and, 303, 308, 314, 315,
    316, 318, 321, 322–324
    core, 6, 21
    efficient portfolios in, 35–36
    pricing of, 4–5
    style drift between, 44–47
Assets, 33. *See also* Risk-free asset; *specific
    assets*
    asymmetric returns, 23–24, 31–32, 48
    correlations of, 26–28, 33, 271–272, 275,
    278
The Association of Public Pension Fund
    Auditors (APPFA), 300–301, 302
Audits, 300, 329
    fiduciary, 298, 302–303, 304–305, 310,
    326–327
    internal, 305, 312, 323, 336–8
Australia
    currency, 164
    inflation-indexed bonds, 170
Automated order systems, 12

Bankruptcy, 116, 132, 133, 136, 141, 289
Banks, 232, 288
    loans, 117–118, 126, 132, 135–137, 140
BARRA Indices, 39, 325
Basic Petroleum Data Book (American
    Petroleum Institute), 214
Bavar (Beta and Volatility Adjusted Returns)
    Ratio, 274–275
Bell-shaped curves (normal probability
    distribution), 23–24, 31–32, 36

341

Benchmarks, 59
  best practices and, 308, 323–324, 325–326,
    334
  for direct energy, 217
  global investment-grade, 99
  historical mean-variance analysis, 218–220
  indices and, 13, 18–20, 52, 57–73, 82–84,
    88–99, 102, 104, 106–107, 110, 325
  for management programs, 162–164, 165
  weightings and, 53, 97
Bernardo, Antonio, 263, 273
Bernardo-Ledoit Gain-Loss Ratio, 273
Bernoulli, Daniel, 286
Best practices, 7, 21, 297–338
Beta
  coefficient, 31
  market, 289
  risk. See market risk
Beta-gap, 291–292
Bid-to-cover ratio, at auctions, 178, 196–4
Bismarck, Baron von, 285
Bodie, Zvi, 171
Bonds, 46, 278. See also specific bonds
  call exposure for, 105–108
  contractual obligations for, 10
  convertible, 116, 266
  core asset allocation and, 47–48
  coupons, 106, 107, 117
  fixed-income management and, 88–111
  indices as rules-based, 94
  interest rates and, 47–48, 88–91, 95,
    100–101, 126
  issues, 94, 107–111, 117
  management spectrum, 89
  market weights of, 13–14, 20
  maturity, 8, 20, 22–1, 47–48, 94, 98, 107,
    117–118, 125, 126
  nominal, 174–194, 196–6
  quality, 89–91, 94, 96, 106
  ratings for, 20, 94–96, 115–116, 121–125,
    127–128, 130–133
  satellite, 115–144
  sectors, 89–91, 97, 103, 106–107
  stocks and, 5, 7–9, 10, 20–21, 126–130,
    187, 199–200, 202–212, 218–220
  subordinated/junior subordinated, 116, 117
Book entry form, securities held in, 78

Broad markets
  indices, 4–5, 12–13, 21, 52, 64–73, 83, 207
  selection criteria, 64–73, 83
Brokerage, 116, 137
  best practices regarding, 300, 308–309,
    315, 320, 322, 329
Broker-dealers, 78, 84
Brooks, Chris, 270, 278
Bubble
  corporate debt, 121, 134
  period, 224, 232, 240–243, 245, 246
Budget, active management risk, 52–57, 63,
    83–84
Bureau of Labor Statistics, 215

Cable sector, 120
Call
  exposure, 105–108
  protection, 118, 126
Callable securities, 89–90, 101, 106
Campaign contributions and finance reform,
    329–330
Campbell, John Y., 196–6
Capital gains
  income and, 214–216
  mutual funds/ETFs and, 79
  on passive investments, 63
Capital markets, 6, 55, 316
Capitalization. See also Market capitalization
  computation of, 18, 22–2, 43, 45
  float-adjusted, 71
  free-float, 70
  large-cap U.S. stocks/government bonds
    and, 13
  rankings and price fluctuations, 67
CAPM (Capital Asset Pricing model), 196–,
    288
Carried interest, 142
Cash, 332
  direct energy and, 201–207, 211, 214–216,
    218–220, 221–3
  diversification with, 189
  drag, 80, 82
  efficient portfolios in, 34–35
  flows, 89–91, 101–102, 224
  redemptions for mutual funds/ETFs, 79
  TIPS and, 185, 187

Catalysts, investment, 226–231, 243–247
CDSC. *See* Contingent-deferred sales charge
Charitable trusts, 4
Charities, income for, 55
Chen, Peng, 172, 196–7
Citigroup Indices, 94, 172
Closed-end funds, 22–3, 69, 71
Cochrane, John, 288–289
Collateralized debt obligations (CDOs),
    123–125, 138
Collateralized loan obligations (CLOs), 123,
    125
Commingled accounts, 138, 143–7. *See also*
    Mutual funds
Commodities, 38–39, 199–200, 207
Communications sector, 125
Compound interest, Manhattan Island sale
    and, 7
Conditional Value-at-Risk (CVaR), 275
Conflicts of interest, 307, 320, 332
    ethics and, 298, 305, 312–314
Consultants, 45, 59, 83
    best practices for, 297, 305, 307, 316,
        318–322, 327, 330
Consumer price index (CPI-U), 173–174,
    176, 180, 191
Consumer nondurables sector, 234
Consumer services sector, 232–234
Contingent-deferred sales charge (CDSC), 76
Core
    asset allocations, 4–5, 12–13, 21, 47–48,
        57–63
    asset classes, 6, 21
    direct energy in, 207–210
    equity, 51–85
    fixed-income management, 87–112
    large company stocks in, 20
    market weights in, 12–15
    performance of, 20–21
    risk in, 36–40
    U.S. government bonds in, 12, 13–15
    value/growth in, 16–17
Core-satellite approach, 52, 83
    asset allocations, 12–16
    with broad/large-cap equity index, 61–63
    importance for fiduciaries, 6–7, 10
    inflation-indexed bonds in, 182–190

portfolio measurement, 63–64
    strategies of, 3–22
Corporate bonds, 13, 94, 95
    comparisons to, 46
    high-yield, 116, 119, 120
    high-yield bonds *v.*, 130–133
    risks of, 20, 88, 99–100
Corporate debt bubble, 121, 134
Correlations
    of assets, 26–28, 33, 271–272, 275, 278
    coefficients, 203–207, 213, 220
    risks and returns, 41–43
    serial, 255, 270–271
Costs
    -benefit analysis on small-cap allocation,
        15
    mutual fund marketing and, 77
    for rebalancing, 318
    reducing, 51, 63
CPI-U. *See* Consumer price index
Credit ratings, 20, 95, 131, 136
    for bonds, 20, 94–96, 115–116, 121–125,
        127–128, 130–133
    for CDOs, 123–125
    for distressed debt, 133–135, 140–141,
        143
    downgrades/upgrades, 122, 125, 130–133,
        134–135
Credit risks, 88, 91–92, 94–95, 99, 105–106
Credits (marginal credit issuers), 119–120
Currencies, 98, 145–167. *See also* Foreign
    currencies

Debt, 116, 121, 123, 134. *See also*
    Collateralized debt obligations;
    Distressed debt
Defaults
    distressed debt and, 135–137, 139
    event risks and, 108
    for high-yield bonds, 115–117, 119–122,
        124–125, 126, 276
    recovery rate on, 135–137
Deflation, 121, 173
Depository Trust Company, 78
Deviation. *See* Downside deviation; Standard
    deviations
Direct Energy. *See* Energy

Distressed debt, 115, 133–143
    bankruptcy and, 133, 136, 141, 289
    investment-grade bonds and, 135, 143
    management of, 137–141, 143
    ratings for, 133–135, 140–141, 143
    returns for, 134–135
Diversification, 51
    in asset allocations, 9, 13, 15, 20, 27–28,
        32, 44, 287–288
    with cash, 189
    CDOs and, 124
    with fixed-income management, 88, 90,
        91–92, 99, 110
    with hard assets, 199–201, 207, 210–213
    with hedge funds, 284
    with high-yield bonds, 119, 124, 129,
        132–133, 142
    with inflation-indexed bonds, 172, 174,
        183, 189, 190
    among managers, 162
    through mutual fund/ETFs, 62, 74, 83
    with stocks, 189
    styles and, 41–44
Dividends, 68, 70, 82
DJJ. See Dow Jones Japan Index
DJU. See Dow Jones UK Index
Domestic Fisher Relation, 191–194
Dow, Charles Henry, 63–64
Dow Jones Industrial Average, 4, 63–64, 70
Dow Jones Japan Index (DJJ), 146–149,
        153–154, 158–161, 164
Dow Jones UK Index (DJU), 146–149,
        153–154, 158–161, 164
Dow Jones U.S. Total Market, 68, 70, 72–73
Downside deviation, 273–274
Drexel Burnham Lambert, 120
Duff and Phelps Credit Rating Company, 95
Duration
    bond risk as, 48
    convexity value and, 105–107
    issuer exposure v., 111
    mismatches around, 89–91
    modified adjusted, 100–101
    option-adjusted, 107–108
    percent of credit quality and, 103–105
    sector/subsector percent and, 103–105

Earnings growth, 39, 223–224
Economy, 38–39, 71, 108. See also
        Deflation; Inflation; Recession
    defaults and, 120–122
    high-yield bonds/distressed debt and,
        120–123, 131, 143
    macroeconomic conditions/issues, 126,
        201, 299
EDRP (event-driven replicating portfolio),
        281
Efficient frontiers, 28–30, 37
    Base Case, 208–211
    benchmarks for, 218
    with direct energy, 208–210
    with hedge funds, 276–277
    with inflation-indexed bonds, 184–189
Efficient set, 29
Elsasser, Robert, 172
Emerging-markets bonds, 88, 91, 95, 119
Employee Retirement Income Security Act
        (ERISA), 298–300, 311, 313–314, 316,
        322, 331, 333, 335
Enderle, Pope, and Siegel, 65
Endowments, 4, 51, 55, 261
    best practices with, 297, 298, 311, 335
    inflation and, 40, 171, 172, 173
Energy, 200–221
    correlation coefficients, 203–207, 213
    Information Administration's Financial
        Reporting system database, 215
    prices, 180
    returns for, 214–217, 235
Enron, 133, 333–334
Enterprise value/sales, 223
E/P (earnings yield), sorting by, 248
ERISA. See Employee Retirement Income
        Security Act
ETFs. See Exchange-traded funds
Ethics, conflicts of interest and, 298, 305,
        312–314
Eurodollar bonds, 95, 98
Exchange rates, 21, 39
    currency fluctuations and, 145, 147–151,
        156, 158, 165–167
Exchange-traded funds (ETFs), 12. See also
        Mutual funds

creation/redemption of, 77, 78, 79
diversification through, 62, 83
dividends for, 82
investing in, 65, 66, 67, 71, 74–84
stop/limit orders for, 79
trading, 79–82

Favre, Laurent, 276
Fees. *See also* Costs
  best practices and, 300, 307, 308, 309,
    324, 325, 326
  for ETFs, 82
  for hedge funds, 142, 266
  for high-yield/distressed debt, 141–142
  indices and, 12, 82
  for mutual funds, 74, 77, 82, 141–142
  one-time charges, 225
  and transaction costs for benchmark
    indexes, 68
  and transaction costs with fixed-income
    management, 89–91, 92–93, 106,
    110, 142
  12b-1, 76, 77
  value-added, 17
Fidelity Growth and Income mutual fund,
  256
Fiduciaries
  audits, 298, 302–303, 304–305, 310,
    326–327
  core-satellite approach's importance for,
    6–7, 10
  liability, 306, 329
  managers and, 41, 44–47, 293
  risk and, 37–41, 44, 47, 48, 82
  roles/responsibilities of, 3–4, 5, 17–18, 21,
    44, 83–84, 189, 303, 319
Financial Analysts Journal, 270–271, 272
Financial Risk Management, 273–274
Financials sector, 226, 236, 247
Findlay, Gary, 310
Fitch Ratings, 20, 95
Fixed-income management, 88–89, 169, 184
  core, 87–112
  fees and transaction costs with, 89–91,
    92–93, 106, 110, 142
  indices and, 87–90, 92–99, 101–110

inflation-indexed bonds and, 169, 184,
  189–190
risks and, 87–92, 94–95, 97–110
Floating-rate obligations, 118
Foreign countries
  bonds issued by, 119
  laws regarding investment in, 298
Foreign currencies, 91, 145–167, 292–293
  returns and risks with, 150–166
Foreign income, 39
Foreign stocks, 71
Forward contracts, hedging with, 150,
  165–167
Forward differential, 150–153
Foundations, 51, 93, 300, 318–319
401k plans, 332, 333
The Frank Russell Company, 69–70, 71
Fung, William, 279, 282
Futures, 80, 216

Gains, losses and, 31, 150–155, 158, 160,
  167–1. *See also* Capital gains
Gas, natural, 199–201, 214–215, 221–5
General Electric, 19
Government regulation, 297–300
Greenwich Associates, 324
Growth style, value *v.*, 16–17, 288–289

Hammond, P. Brett, 172
Hard assets, 170, 199–222
  risks and returns of, 201–220
Harding, David, 258
Harvey, Campbell, 290–291
Health care sector, 226, 236
Hedge funds, 36, 138, 309
  bank loans and, 117
  fees for, 142, 266
  illiquidity and, 258, 266–270, 284
  indices relationship with S&P 500,
    267–269
  returns and risks for, 253–286, 293
  spreads for, 282–283
Hedging
  foreign currency fluctuations and, 145,
    150–167

Hedging (*continued*)
  against inflation, 40, 169–171, 173, 175,
    181, 190, 192, 200, 207
High-yield bonds, 36, 115–144
  asset characteristics and returns for,
    125–130
  bank loans and, 117–118, 126, 132
  corporate bonds *v.*, 130–133
  defaults for, 115–117, 119–122, 124–125,
    126, 276
  fixed-income management with, 88, 91,
    95, 98
  illiquidity of, 267
  management of, 137–141, 143
  market history for, 119–123
  ratings for, 115–116, 121–125, 127–128,
    130–133
  returns and pricing for, 5, 125–130
  risks for, 116, 126–130
Holdings-based analysis, 45–47
Homeowner's insurance like risk factor
    model, 38
Hospital administrators as fiduciaries, 51
Hsieh, David, 279, 282

Ibbotson Associates, 7, 35, 196–8
Illiquidity, 33, 36, 65
  risk measurement and, 258, 265–270, 284,
    288, 290
Incomes, 39, 55. *See also* Fixed-income
    management
  capital gains and, 214–216
  inflation and, 169, 172, 176, 194–195
Indices, 64, 82, 121. *See also specific*
    indices
  asset classes and, 12–13
  benchmarks and, 13, 18–20, 52, 57–73,
    82–84, 88–99, 102, 104, 106–107,
    110, 325
  broad markets, 4–5, 12–13, 21, 52, 64–73,
    83, 207
  changes in, 53, 82
  with dividends, 68, 70
  fees and, 12, 82
  fixed-income management and, 87–90,
    92–99, 101–110

foreign currency, 146–149, 153–154,
    158–161, 164
growth/value, 16
reconstitution/rebalancing of, 66, 67–68,
    69, 70, 80
returns measurement against, 46
rules for, 65
turnover and transaction costs, 67, 79
Industrials sector, 236
Inflation, 39, 299
  breakeven, 175–176, 178–180
  endowments and, 40
  hard assets and, 199–200, 202–207, 213,
    219
  hedging against, 40, 169–171, 173, 175,
    181, 190, 192, 200, 207
  -indexed bonds, 169–197
  interest rates and, 202, 204–205
  premium, 175, 177–178, 181, 192–194,
    196–6
  -protected securities, 91, 97
In-kind contributions, 332–333
Institutional Investor, 290
Insurance companies, 117, 118, 287, 293
  high-yield/distressed debt and, 135,
    137–138, 140
Interest
  carried, 142
  compound, Manhattan Island sale and, 7
Interest rates, 38–39. *See also* Forward
    differential
  bonds and, 47–48, 88–91, 95, 100–101,
    126
  forward, 216, 221–6
  inflation and, 202, 204–205
  nominal, 174, 196–3
  pension funds and, 40
International banks, 288
International equity, 35–36
International stocks, 59, 202, 203–208, 211,
    218–220
Investment Company Act of 1940, 80
Investment policy statement (IPS), 314–315,
    321, 325, 326
Investment-grade bonds (U.S. credit), 93,
    115
  CDOs and, 123, 124

distressed debt and, 135, 143
downgrade of, 121–122
returns for, 126–129
Investors, 37, 38, 66
asset classes and, 11
assumptions about returns, 23–25, 31
and inflation-indexed bonds, 171, 173,
180–181
institutional, 51, 83, 116–117, 135, 138,
140, 150, 171, 224, 297–338
IPS. *See* Investment policy statement
Israel, and inflation-indexed bonds, 170

Japanese yen (JPY), 146, 148–150
Journal of Alternative Investments, 261, 264
Journal of Political Economy, 263
Journal of Portfolio Management, 255, 265,
267, 272, 279, 285, 291
Junk bonds, 116, 133

Kat, Harry, 263, 264–265, 270, 278, 291
Kenmar Global Investment, 271–272, 274,
284
Koh, Francis, 272
Krishnan, Hari, 266
Kurtosis. *See* Returns

Laws
regarding best practices, 298–300,
305–306, 310–311, 322, 329, 331,
334–335
distressed debts and, 141
for investors, 37, 38
for mutual funds/ETFs, 74–75, 80
LBOs. *See* Leverage buyouts
Ledoit, Olivier, 263, 273
Lehman Brothers Indices, 13, 92–99, 102,
104, 107, 172
Leland, Hayne, 259
Leverage, 272
returns and, 254–255, 259, 261, 266, 272,
283–284
Leverage buyouts (LBOs), 108, 120
Leveraged loans, 117–118, 137
Liabilities, 54–55, 306, 329, 334
LIBOR (London InterBank Offer Rate), 118

Limited partnerships (LPs), 69, 139–140,
142, 201
Liquidity, 51, 272. *See also* Illiquidity
bonds and, 91, 96, 117, 118–119, 126,
129, 132
of core equities, 53
distressed debt and, 139–140
of ETFs, 77–78
of large/mid-companies, 62
with mutual funds, 74, 75
of satellite benchmarks, 96
of small/large companies, 19
TIPS and, 175, 177–178, 180–181, 190
Lo, Andrew, 270–271
Long Term Capital Management (LTCM),
257–258
Losses
with CDOs, 125
gains and, 31, 150–155, 158, 160, 167–1
of principal, 20, 125
probability of, 153–155, 158–162, 167–1
risk measurement and, 256, 260–261,
264–265, 273, 275, 279–280, 283,
286–288
Lottery, 263, 273
Low, Cheekiat, 291–292
LPs. *See* Limited partnerships
LTCM. *See* Long Term Capital Management
Lucas, Gerald, 191
Lux, Hal, 290

MacKinnon, Ian A., 110
Managers
active *v.* passive, 53–59, 63–64, 66, 68,
83–84, 325
currency overlay management programs,
145, 149–165
diversification among, 162
expenses/trading commissions for, 11
fiduciaries and, 41, 44–47, 293
for high-yield/distressed debt, 137–141,
143
option replication methods for, 155
performance by, 53, 57, 64, 68
selection of, 5, 298, 300, 307, 308, 312,
322–327, 330
styles and, 41–47, 258

Market capitalization, 39
    AMEX-listed companies by, 18–19, 22–3
    of large/small stocks, 42–43, 224, 226,
        228, 229
    market sizes and, 18–20
Market risk (beta risk), 52–58
Markets
    bear/bull, 8–9, 291–292
    Beta, 289
    capital, 6, 55, 316
    emerging, 59, 88, 91, 95, 119
    proxy, 52, 58, 126, 192
    sizes, 18–20
    upswings/downturns in, 53, 280
    weights, 13–14
Markowitz, Harry, 6, 29, 263–265
    on asset allocation/portfolio theory, 3, 5–6,
        23, 26, 31, 32
McGraw-Hill, Inc., 70, 71
Mean-variance analysis, 33, 182–189, 201,
    207–208, 218–220
    risk measurement and, 263–265, 275, 291
Mean-variance efficient bond benchmarks,
    99
Mean-variance optimization, 28, 35, 37,
    183–189, 207–208, 265
Merrill Lynch U.S. Broad Market Bond
    Index, 94
Metals, precious, real assets of, 200
Middle office concept, 305, 311–312
Milken, Michael, 120
Miller, Anderson & Sherrerd, 224
Mitchell, Mark, 280
Money market funds, 172
Moody's Investors Services, 20, 95, 131, 136
Mortgage Bankers Refinancing Index, 107
Mortgage bonds, 94, 95
    exposure, 107–111
    fixed-income management and, 88, 91, 94,
        95, 97, 99–100
    risks of, 88, 91, 97, 99–100, 107
MSCI EAFE (EuropeAsiaFarEast) Index,
    34–36
Mutual funds. See also Exchange traded
    funds
    bank loans and, 117
    best practices and, 297, 300, 311–313, 338

    closed-end, 22–3, 69
    diversification through, 62, 83
    fees for, 74, 77, 82, 141–142
    high-yield funds within, 138
    holdings analysis for, 45
    investing in, 65–66, 67, 71, 74–84
    laws for, 74–75, 80
    loads for, 76, 142
    as open-end investment companies, 74
    pricing for, 76–77, 78, 82
    returns-based analysis for, 46
    reward-to-variability ratio and, 254
    risks for, 279
    SEC on, 77, 311, 313
    share classes for, 75–76, 77

Naik, Narayan, 275, 279
NASDAQ, 18–19, 22–3, 69, 77
National Conference of Commissioners on
    Uniform State Laws, 299
Natural gas, 199–201, 214–215, 221n5
NBER articles, 288
Nelken, Izzy, 266
Net asset value (NAV), 78, 79
New York Stock Exchange (NYSE), 18–19,
    22–3, 69, 76

Oberhofer, George, 269
Oil, 38, 199–201, 214–215, 221–5
144a securities, 117, 118
Operational reviews, 298, 302–304, 310,
    323, 326–327, 336–13
Overlay management programs, currency,
    145, 149–165

Pension Benefit Guaranty Corporation
    (PBGC), 317
Pension plans, 4, 55
    best practices regarding, 297–302, 305,
        310, 312, 314, 317–318, 320, 323,
        326, 328, 332–335, 336–8
    bonds v. stocks in, 8
    inflation-indexed bonds for, 169, 171, 172
    interest rates and, 40
Pensions and Investments, 326
Performance, 51, 66. See also specific
    investments

best practices regarding, 301, 302–303, 307–308, 309, 316, 317, 325–326, 334
by managers, 53, 57, 64, 68
relative, 93, 101, 107
Portfolios, 3, 5–6, 21, 75
efficient, 28–30, 33, 35–37
forecasting, 55
individual assets *v.*, 30
international fixed-income, 149
measurement, 63–64
rebalancing, 20, 107
Pound sterling (STG), 146, 148–149, 164
Price/book value, 223, 247, 288–289
Price/earnings (P/E) ratios, 223–248
Price/net asset value, 223, 247
Pricing. *See also* Consumer price index
of asset classes, 4–5
for bank loans, 118
of distressed debt, 135
for energy, 201, 214–217
fluctuations and capitalization rankings, 67
inflation and, 169–171, 173–175, 176, 180–181, 191, 194, 196–5
intraday, 77–78
for mutual funds, 76–77, 78, 82
of oil, 38
and returns for high-yield bonds, 5, 125–130
of shares, 71
stale, 270
transparency, 129, 135, 143
Prime rate funds, 117
Principal
interest and, 20, 95, 126
loss of, 20, 125
for Treasury bonds, 170–171, 173, 176–177, 181
Private equity, 5, 15, 36
Private placement loans, 118–119
Probability. *See also* Bell-shaped curves
callable securities and, 101
of loss with foreign currency, 153–155, 158–162, 167–1
Producer Price Index, 215
Proxy, 64, 66, 136
for bond market, 126

for expected inflation, 192
for stock market, 52, 58
voting, 300, 312, 315, 322, 331
Prudent Practices (Foundation for Fiduciary Studies), 300, 314, 316
Public funds, 328–330
Publicly traded notes/bonds, 116–117
Pulvino, Todd, 280

Quantitative approach, 5–6, 10, 21, 23–49, 31–36
Queck, Timothy, 197

Railroad stocks, 63
Ratings. *See* Credit ratings
Real assets, 200
Real estate, 170, 200, 247
best practices and, 300, 309, 323, 331, 332–333
Real options theory, 266
Rebalancing, 20, 107, 267
best practices regarding, 307, 315, 317–318, 321–322
and reconstitution of indices, 66, 67–68, 69, 70, 80
Recession, 38, 120
Reider, Robert, 292
REITs, 22–3
Relative-value bond funds, 288
Religious finance committees, fiduciaries, 4
Retail sector, 237
Retirement plans, 51
best practices for, 298, 299, 300, 302, 304, 310, 312, 317, 323, 326, 327, 328–330
inflation-indexed bonds for, 172–173
Returns. *See also specific investments*
assumptions regarding, 23–25, 31
-based analysis, 46–47
bell-shaped curve for, 23–24, 36
currency fluctuations and, 98, 145–167, 167–1
data errors and, 46–47
excess, 103, 105–106, 108–109
kurtosis and, 264–265, 273, 276–278
liabilities and, 54–55
measuring against indices, 46

Returns (*continued*)
  risks and, 10, 15, 21, 40, 41–43, 51–55,
    83–84, 253–293
  risks and variance, 23–37
  skewness of, 259–261, 263–265, 270, 273,
    276–278, 290–292
  for small *v.* large companies, 19–20
  -to-risk ratio, 21, 22–5
  volatility and, 23, 98, 103, 126, 129–130,
    135
  as weighted average, 25–27, 29
Risk Budgeting (Weisman/Abernathy),
    269–270, 283
Risk magazine, 266, 271, 272, 284, 292
Risk-free asset (RF), 29–30
Risks. *See also* Active risk; Credit risks;
    Duration; Standard deviations; *specific*
    investments
  asset allocations and, 33–40
  budgeting for active management, 52–57,
    63, 83–84
Risks
  changes in, 41
  containment program, 162, 165
  in core, 36–40
  event/default, 108
  factors, 37–40, 99–100
  fiduciaries and, 37–41, 44, 47, 48, 82
  matches/mismatches and, 88–91
  measuring, 7, 21, 25–48, 253–293
  penalty function for, 272
  premia strategies, 287–293
  reinvestment, 176
  returns and, 10, 15, 21, 40, 41–43, 51–55,
    83–84, 253–293
  returns and variance, 23–37
  spread-widening, 108–109
  tolerances, 29, 63, 83, 208, 271
  tracking error, 48
  transaction costs and, 58
  yield curve, 101–103
Roll, Richard, 32–33
Rosenberg, Barr, 288
Ross, Leola, 269
Russell 1000 Indices, 18, 59–62, 68, 70–73

Russell 3000 Index, 52, 58, 68–70, 69, 71,
    72–73. *See also* AMEX; NASDAQ;
    New York Stock Exchange

Sack, Brian, 172
Sales growth, 223–224
Sargent, Kevin H., 176–177
Satellite asset classes, 21, 36
  index selection and, 52
  returns and pricing for, 5
  risk measurement for, 38
  small stocks as, 223, 247
Satellite ring
  asset allocation, 4–5, 12–13, 16–17, 21
  bonds, 115–144
  direct energy in, 200, 202, 210, 213
  fixed-income management and, 87, 90, 91,
    93–94, 96–97
  measuring risks in, 253–293
  small-cap stocks in, 17, 19
Schlarbaum, Gary, 224
Securities Act of 1933, 74
Securities and Exchange Commission (SEC)
  bond registration with, 116–117, 118
  on mutual funds, 77, 311, 313
  Office of Compliance Inspections and
    Examinations, 320
Senior secured obligations, 117–118, 132
Senior unsecured obligations, 116, 136
SFR. *See* Swiss francs
Shares, 71
  buybacks, 226–227
  classes for mutual funds, 75–76, 77
Sharpe ratio
  with direct energy, 202, 204–206,
    211–213, 219
  with quantitative investments, 30, 36
  risk measurement and, 253–274, 277, 283,
    288, 293
Sharpe, William, 29, 253, 279
Shen, Pu, 176
Shiller, Robert J., 196–6
Shimko, David, 292
Siddique, Akhtar, 290–291
Signer, Andreas, 276

Singapore Economic Review, 272
Skewness. *See* Returns
Social security, 169
Soft assets, 200
Sony stock, 149
Sovereigns, 116, 119
St. Petersburg paradox, 285–287
Standard & Poor's 90, 71
Standard & Poor's 500 Index, 12–13, 52
  as benchmark, 13, 18–20, 57–59, 68,
    70–73, 82, 325
  changes to, 82
  declines of, 8–9
  foreign currency indices *v.*, 146–147, 152,
    154
  growth/value in, 16
  hedge fund indices relationship with,
    267–269
  returns for, 4, 7–9, 55, 172, 232, 259, 261
Standard & Poor's 1500 Indices, 68, 70,
  72–73
Standard & Poor's Corporation, 20, 95
Standard & Poor's Index Committee, 70
Standard & Poor's MidCap 400, 70
Standard & Poor's SmallCap 600, 70
Standard deviations, 52–53
  for capital market returns, 55
  with direct energy, 202, 204–206,
    208–212, 219
  with foreign currency management,
    153–154
  with inflation-indexed bonds, 182–189
  risk measurement with, 30–31, 35–36, 43,
    99, 253, 255, 258–263
STG. *See* Pound sterling
Stocks. *See also specific stocks*
  bank, 232
  bonds and, 5, 7–9, 10, 20–21, 126–130,
    187, 199–200, 202–212, 218–220
  employer, in pension plans, 332–335
  growth/value, 16, 41–46, 59–62, 288–289
  headquartered in other countries, 69
  inflation and, 170
  infrequently traded, 70
  interest rate affect on, 38

  international, 59, 202, 203–208, 211,
    218–220
  with negative earnings, 248
  selection *v.* currency management, 150
  style differences/drift and, 41–47
  undervalued, 12
  weights of, 13–14, 20, 67, 71
Stocks, large-cap, 224
  in core, 12, 13–15
  efficient portfolios in, 34–36
  growth/value and, 16–17, 59
  histogram of, 24, 259
  micro-cap *v.*, 14–15
  returns for, 182, 185
  small-cap *v.*, 291–292
  styles for, 59
Stocks, small-cap, 10, 11, 224
  efficient portfolios in, 34–35
  histogram of, 31–32
  illiquidity of, 36, 267
  large-cap *v.*, 291–292
  returns for, 223, 224, 226–248
  in satellite ring, 17
  styles for, 59, 289–290
  value in, 223–249
Stop-out rate, at treasury auctions, 178–179,
  196n5
Stutzer index, 273
Styles, investment
  asset-based style factors, 278–284
  broad market indices and, 52
  cycles, 61
  matrix, 41–43
  purity, 272
  rule-based, 279
  style drift and, 41–47, 325
  value *v.* growth, 16–17
  weighting between, 61
Survey of Professional Forecasters, 192
Swap rates, 130
Swiss francs (SFR), 164, 166–167

Taft-Hartley funds, 310, 318, 328, 330–332
Taxes, 55, 63, 79, 176, 299
Taylor, Richard D., 176–177

Technology sector, 226, 232, 237
Telecom sector, 120–121, 136, 230–231, 232, 238, 303
Terrien, Matthew, 172, 196–7
Timber, 15, 170, 200
TIPS. *See also* Treasury Inflation Protected Securities
Tracking error, 48
    active/passive, 53–54, 56–58, 66
    in mutual fund/ETFs, 66, 80, 82
Trading, 12, 39
    with asymmetric outcomes, 258, 261, 264, 274, 292, 293
    best practices regarding, 308–309, 312
    with distressed debt, 135–137
    ETFs/mutual funds, 79–82
Tranches, 123, 125, 143–3
Transfer agents, 77, 78
Treasury bills, 29, 35, 48, 182–189, 261–262
Treasury bonds, 126, 130, 169–197, 196–6
Treasury Inflation Protected Securities (TIPS), 170–197
Trusts, 69, 117, 138. *See also* Collateralized debt obligations
    best practices and, 297–299, 302, 305, 309–310, 312, 318, 328–332, 336–12
UMPERSA. *See* Uniform Management of Public Employee Retirement Systems Act
Uniform Management of Public Employee Retirement Systems Act (UMPERSA), 299, 313, 316, 329
Uniform Prudent Investor Act (UPIA), 299, 313, 316
Unions, 302, 310, 318, 328, 330–331
United Kingdom, 170
United States (U.S.)
    Department of Labor, 300, 314, 331, 333, 334
    energy producing companies, 215, 221–5
    large companies in, 4, 18–20

UPIA. *See* Uniform Prudent Investor Act
U.S. credit. *See* Investment-grade bonds
U.S. government bonds. *See also* Treasury bills; Treasury bonds
    in core, 12, 13–15
    efficient portfolios in, 34–35
    Lehman, 94, 95
    returns for, 55, 196–9
    risks of, 20, 99–100
    U.S. stocks *v.*, 7–9
USD (U.S dollar), 146–150, 156–157, 166–167
Utilities sector, 125, 226, 238

Value-at-Risk (VaR), 275–277
Values, 173, 196–2, 223. *See also* VC scores
    of cash flows, 101–102
    fixed-income management and, 87, 89, 91, 101, 110
    v. growth styles, 16–17, 288–289
    satellite ring asset allocation and, 12–13
    in small stocks, 11, 223–249
Variance, 23–37. *See also* Mean-variance
VC (Value with a Catalyst) scores, 229–238, 243–247
Venture capital, 33, 267, 331
Volatility, 27, 91, 179–180, 202. *See also* Variance
    of inflation, 175, 180, 193
    investment strategies and, 261–263, 282, 284
    returns and, 23, 98, 103, 126, 129–130, 135

Weighted average, 25–27, 29, 192
Weights, 12–15, 13–14, 20, 53, 67, 71, 97
Weisman, Andrew, 269–270, 283, 285–287
Wilshire 5000, 18, 52, 58, 65, 68–69, 72–73
WorldCom, 133, 136, 333–334
Wrase, Jeffrey M., 176

J. Clay Singleton is Professor of Finance at the Crummer Graduate School of Business at Rollins College. During his career, he has been an investment practitioner, educator, and researcher.

Before joining the Crummer faculty, he was Vice President of Ibbotson Associates, where he was responsible for the firm's consulting, training, and research activities. Ibbotson Associates is an independent asset allocation consulting firm that provides data, software, consulting, research, training, and presentation materials to the investment profession. Dr. Singleton worked with the firm's consulting clients to design asset allocation strategies and directed the firm's research efforts. He also represented the firm before practitioner audiences, introducing them to innovations in investment strategies, asset allocation, and financial practice.

In his academic career Dr. Singleton was on the faculty of the University of Nebraska–Lincoln for twelve years. At Nebraska, he was named to the Paul C. Burmeister Professorship of Investments and served as Associate Dean. He also won the University's Distinguished Teaching Award. He was subsequently named Dean of the College of Business Administration at the University of North Texas, where he served for four years. He has also taught as a visiting professor at the University of Virginia and the College of William and Mary.

Before joining Ibbotson Associates he was Senior Vice President for Curriculum and Examinations at the CFA Institute. In this capacity he was responsible for the CFA program's candidate curriculum and examinations. Dr. Singleton earned the Chartered Financial Analyst (CFA) designation in 1985.

Dr. Singleton's research in investments and finance has been widely published in both practitioner and academic journals. He has contributed articles to the *Journal of Finance, Financial Management*, and the *Journal of Portfolio Management*, among others. Dr. Singleton earned his B.A.S. in Political Science from Washington University in St. Louis in 1969 and his M.B.A and Ph.D. in Business from the University of Missouri–Columbia in 1972 and 1979, respectively.